SPECTRUM®

Phonics

Grade 1

Spectrum®

An imprint of Carson Dellosa Education
Greensboro, North Carolina

Spectrum®
An imprint of Carson Dellosa Education
P.O. Box 35665
Greensboro, NC 27425 USA

 ISBN 978-1-4838-1182-6

04-178227784

Table of Contents

Index of Skills

Phonics Grade 1

Numerals indicate the exercise pages on which these skills appear.

Name ______________________________

Consonants Review: B and C

Directions: Say the name of each picture. Circle the letter that shows the beginning sound of each picture name.

Directions: Say the name of each picture. Write the letter that shows the beginning sound of each picture name.

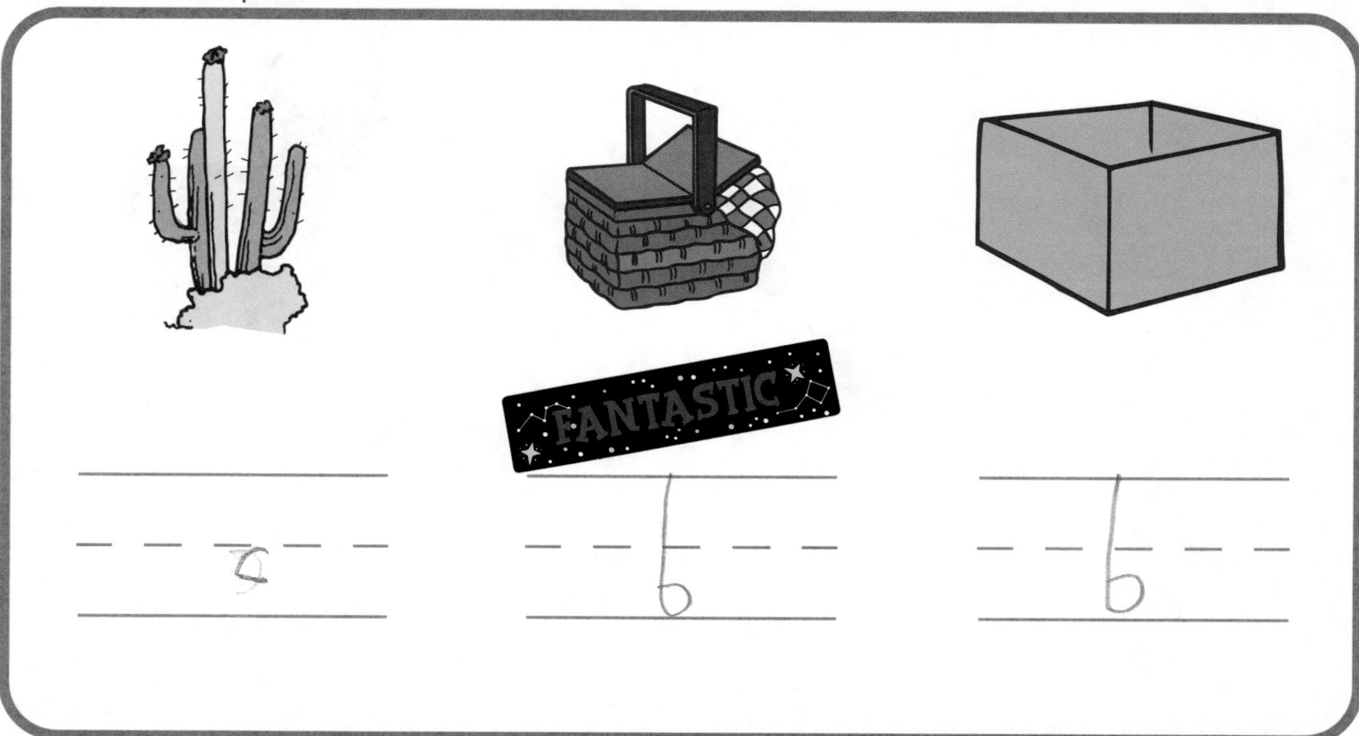

Name ______________________________

Consonants Review: D and F

Directions: Say the name of each picture. Circle the letter that shows the beginning sound of each picture name.

Directions: Say the name of each picture. Write the letter that shows the beginning sound of each picture name.

Name ______________________________

Consonants Review: G and H

Directions: Say the name of each picture. Circle the letter that shows the beginning sound of each picture name.

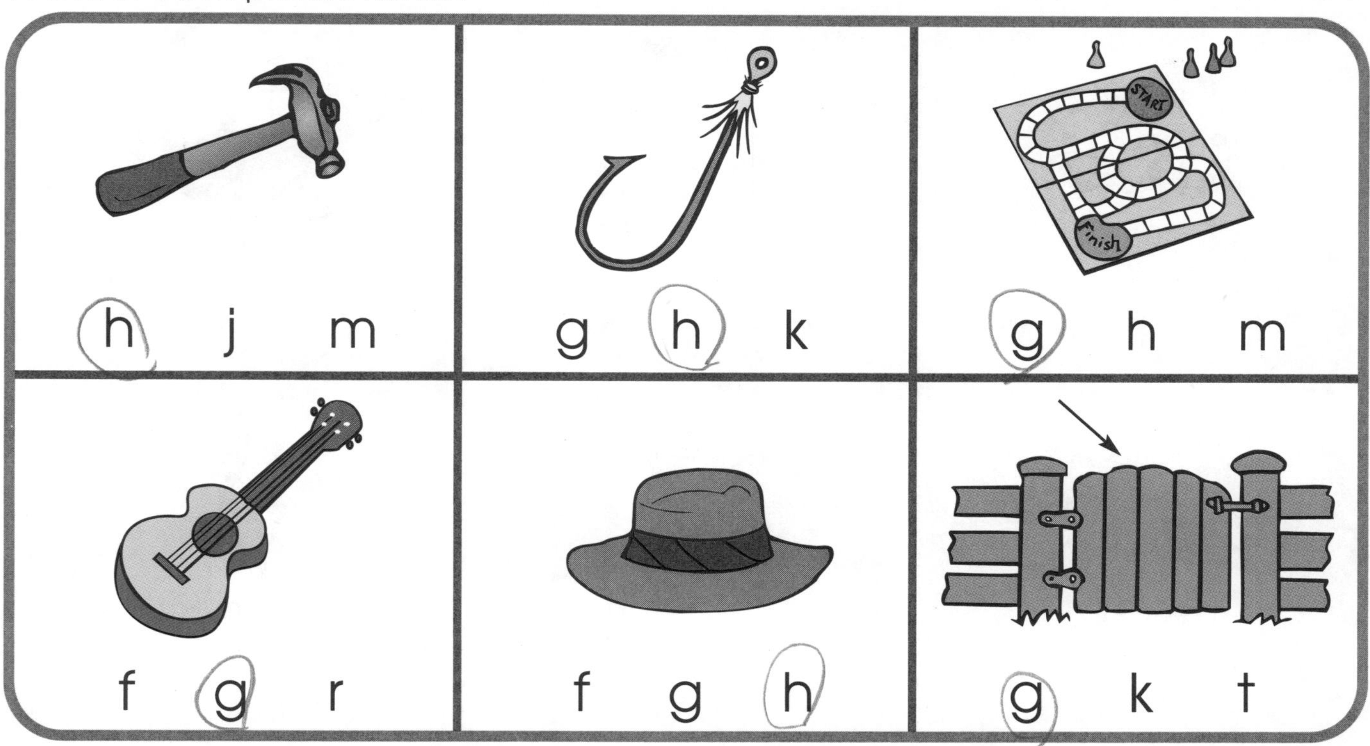

Directions: Say the name of each picture. Write the letter that shows the beginning sound of each picture name.

Name ______________________________

Consonants Review J and K

Directions: Say the name of each picture. Circle the letter that shows the beginning sound of each picture name.

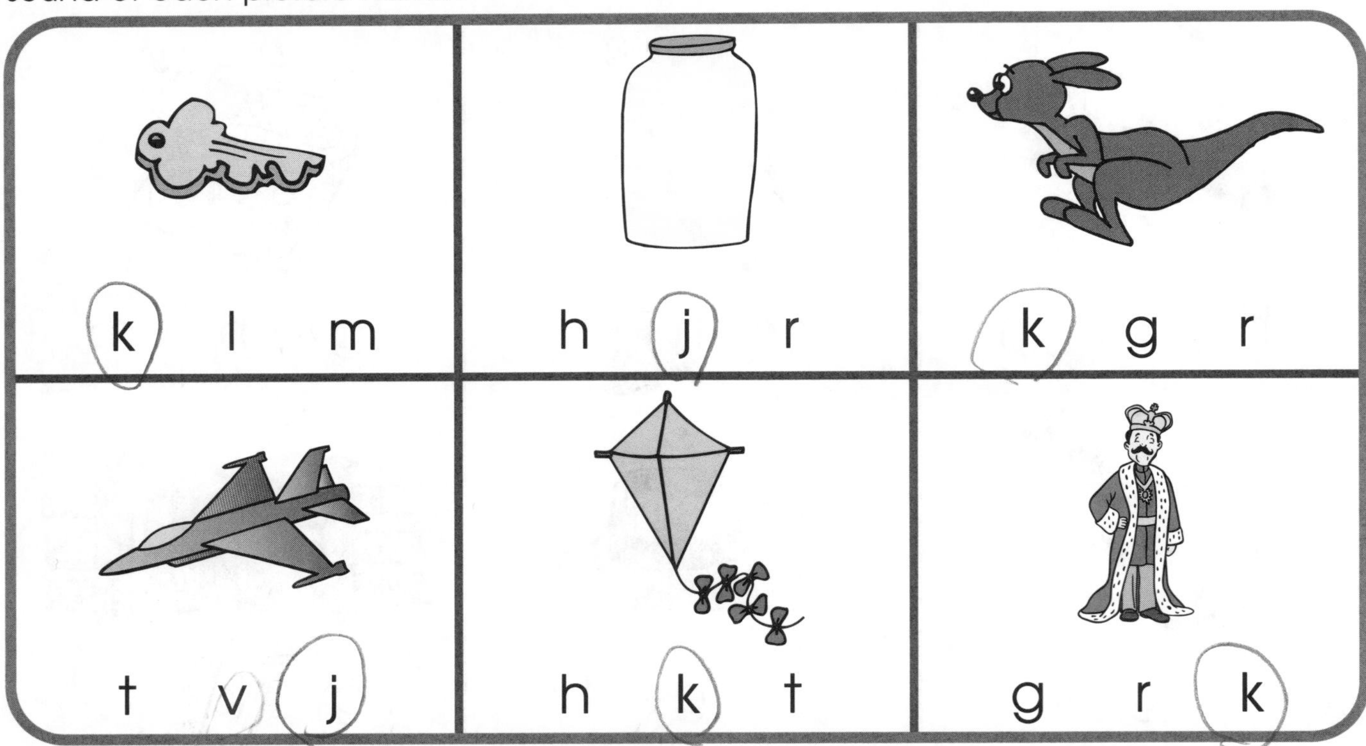

Directions: Say the name of each picture. Write the letter that shows the beginning sound of each picture name.

Name ____

Consonants Review: L and M

Directions: Say the name of each picture. Circle the letter that shows the beginning sound of each picture name.

Directions: Say the name of each picture. Write the letter that shows the beginning sound of each picture name.

Name ______________________________

Consonants Review: N and P

Directions: Say the name of each picture. Circle the letter that shows the beginning sound of each picture name.

Directions: Say the name of each picture. Write the letter that shows the beginning sound of each picture name.

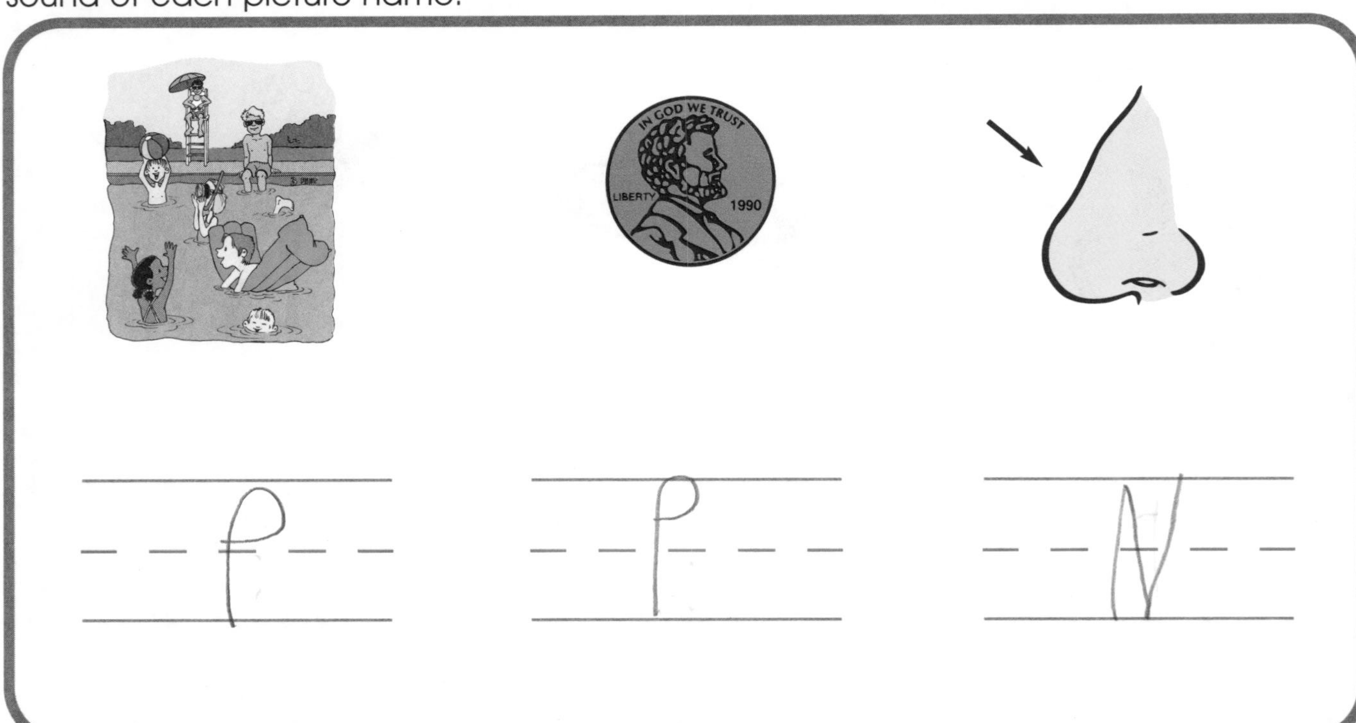

Name ___________________________

Consonants Review: Q and R

Directions: Say the name of each picture. Circle the letter that shows the beginning sound of each picture name.

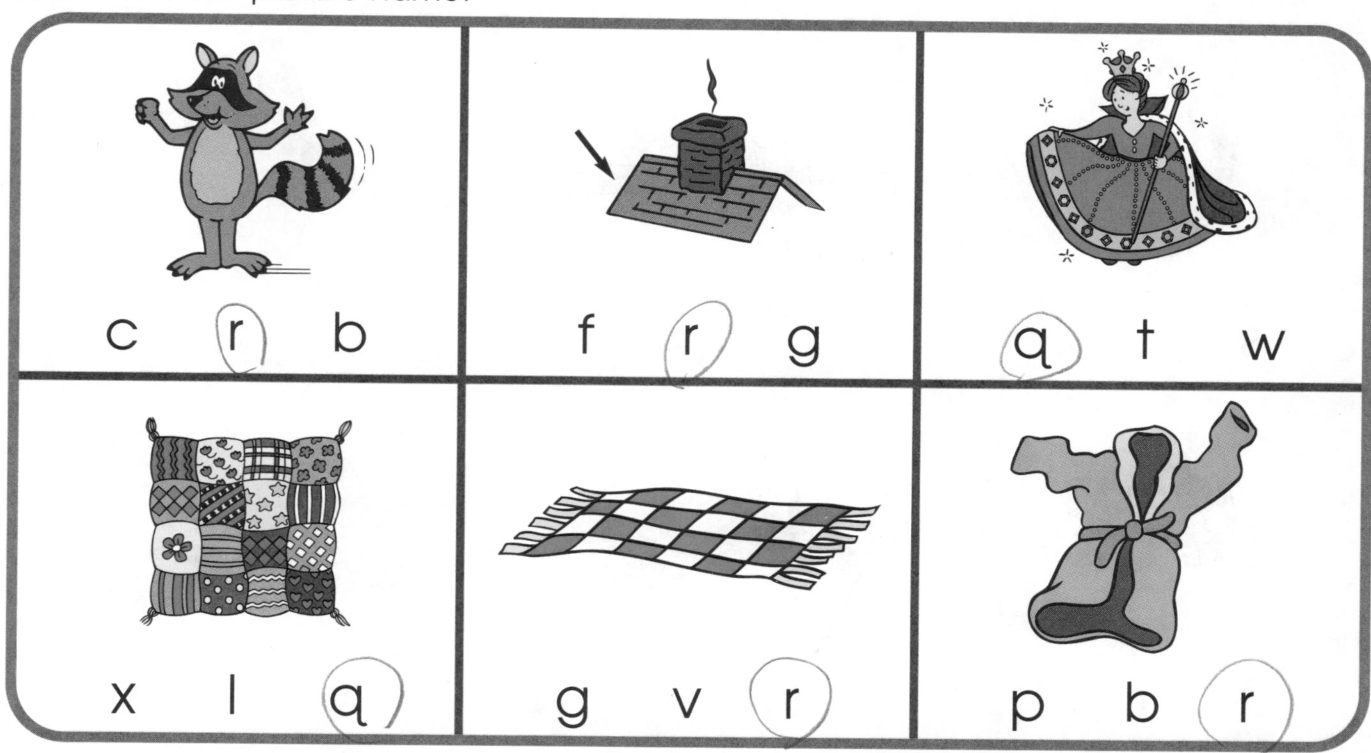

Directions: Say the name of each picture. Write the letter that shows the beginning sound of each picture name.

Name ________________________________

Consonants Review: S and T

Directions: Say the name of each picture. Circle the letter that shows the beginning sound of each picture name.

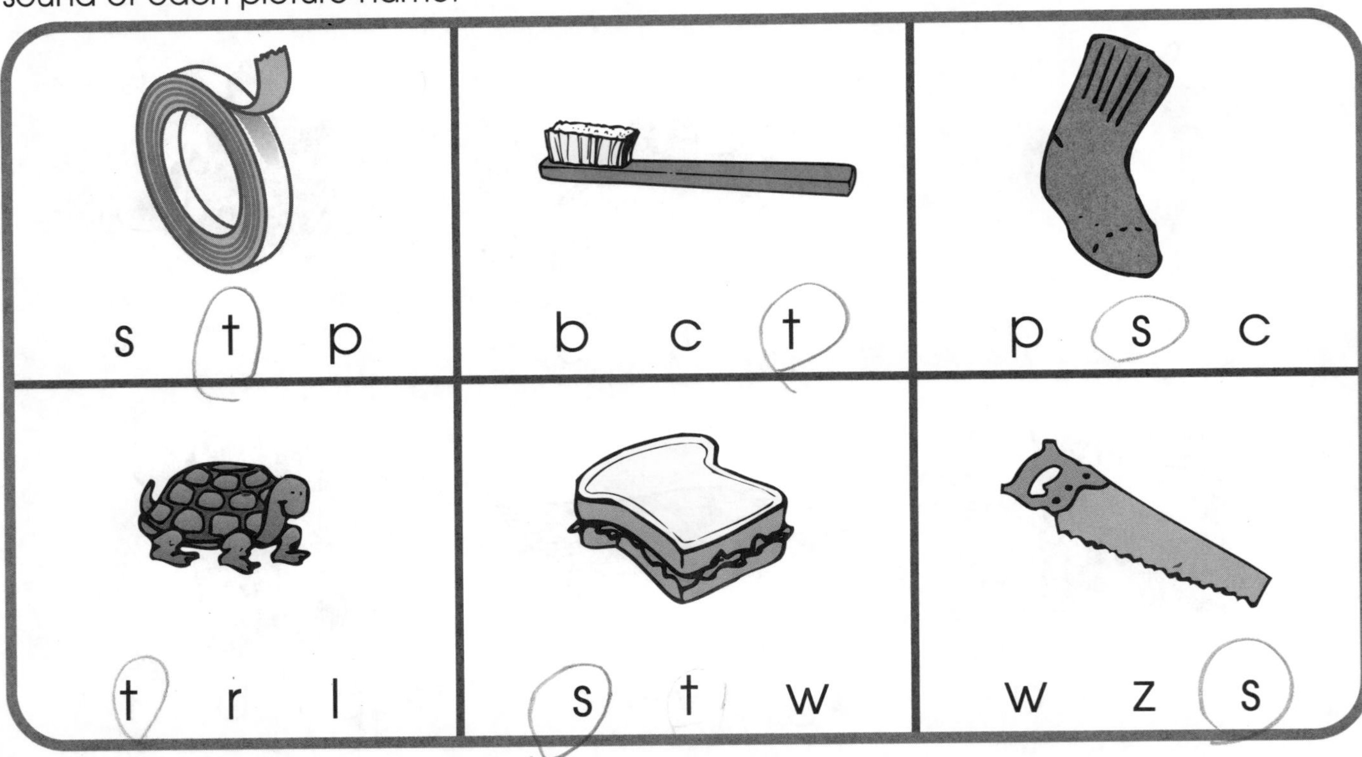

Directions: Say the name of each picture. Write the letter that shows the beginning sound of each picture name.

Name ____________________

Consonants Review: V and W

Directions: Say the name of each picture. Circle the letter that shows the beginning sound of each picture.

Directions: Say the name of each picture. Write the letter that shows the beginning sound of each picture name.

Name ______________________________

Consonants Review: Y and Z

Directions: Say the name of each picture. Circle the letter that shows the beginning sound of each picture name.

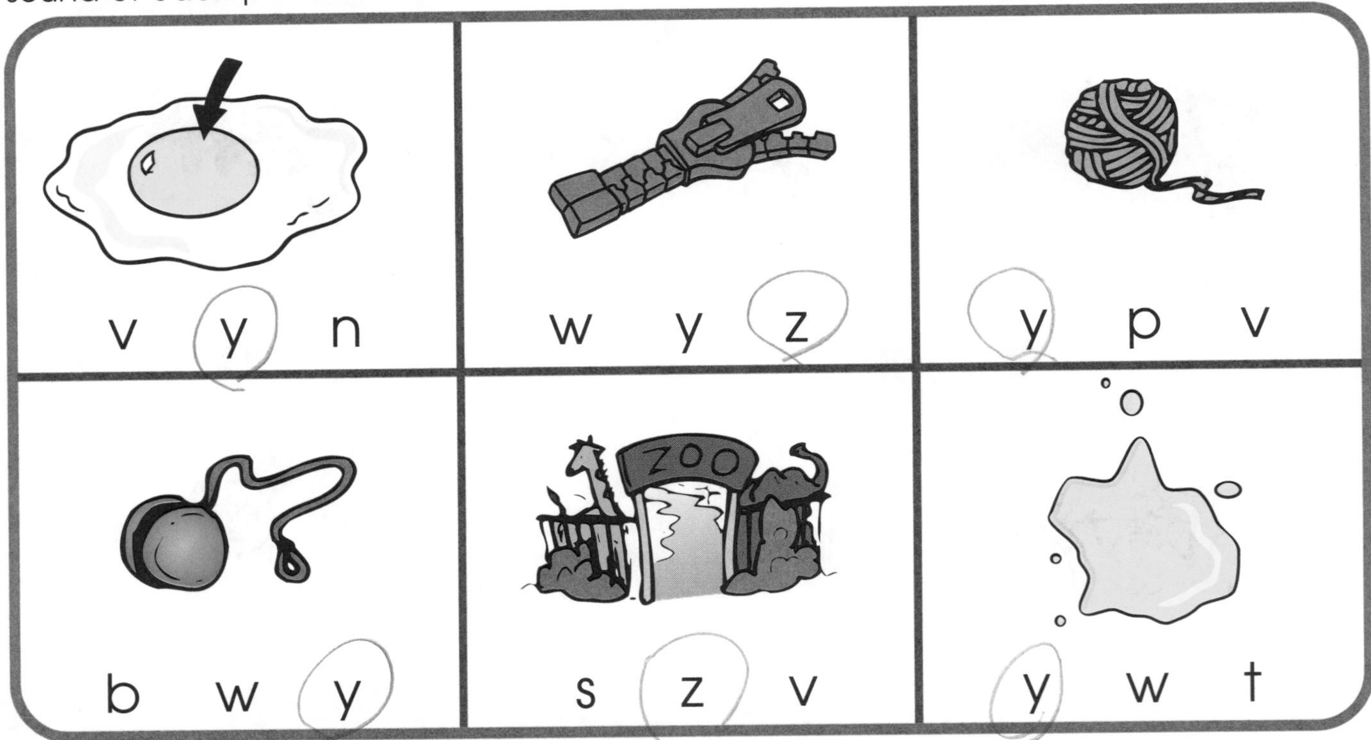

Directions: Say the name of each picture. Write the letter that shows the beginning sound of each picture.

Name ______________________________

Review: Ending Sounds

Directions: Say the name of each picture. Circle the two pictures in each row whose names end with the same sound.

Name ______________________________

Review: Ending Sounds

Directions: Say the name of each picture. Circle the pictures in each row whose names have the same ending sound as the letter at the beginning of the row.

m 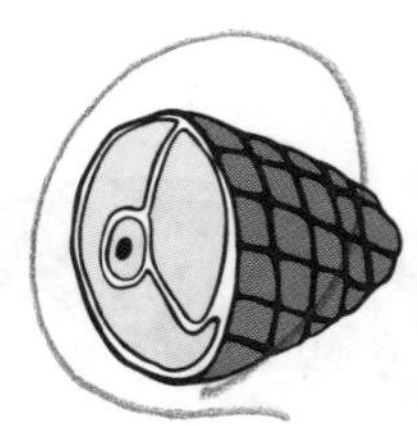  

d 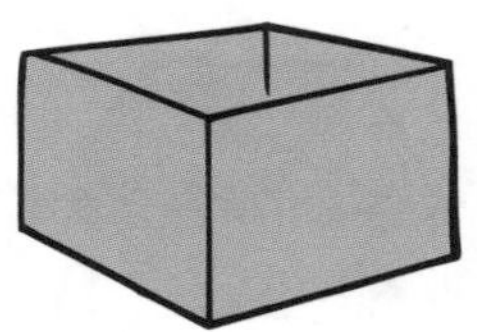 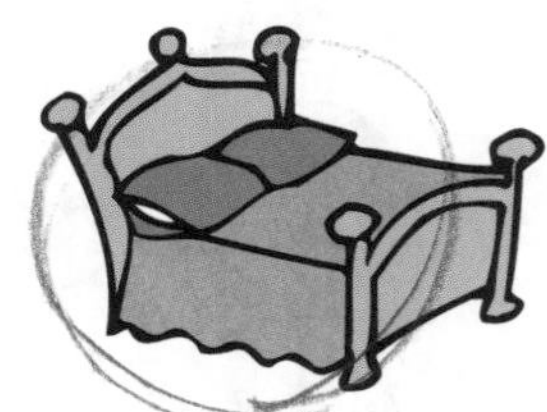 

f  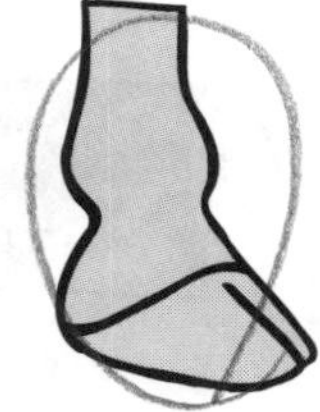 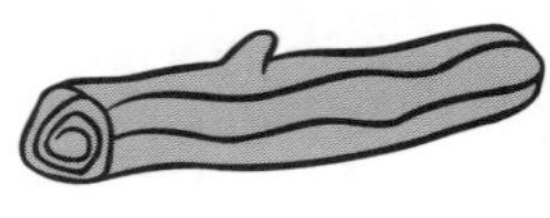

b  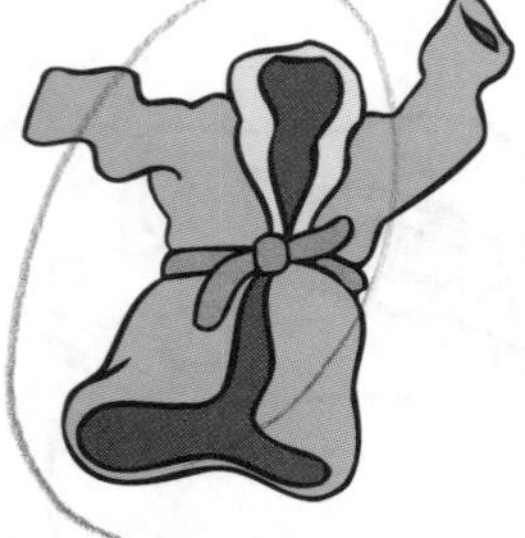 

k 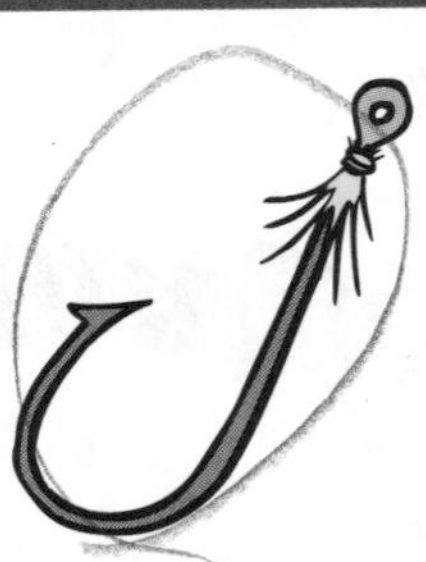  

Name ____________________

Review: Ending Sounds

Directions: Say the name of each picture. Write the letter that shows the  **ng** sound for each picture name.

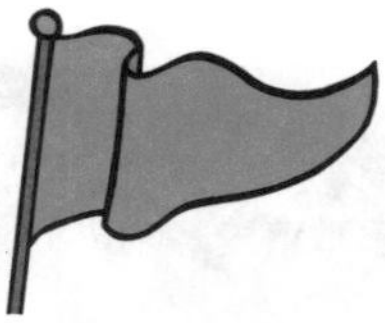

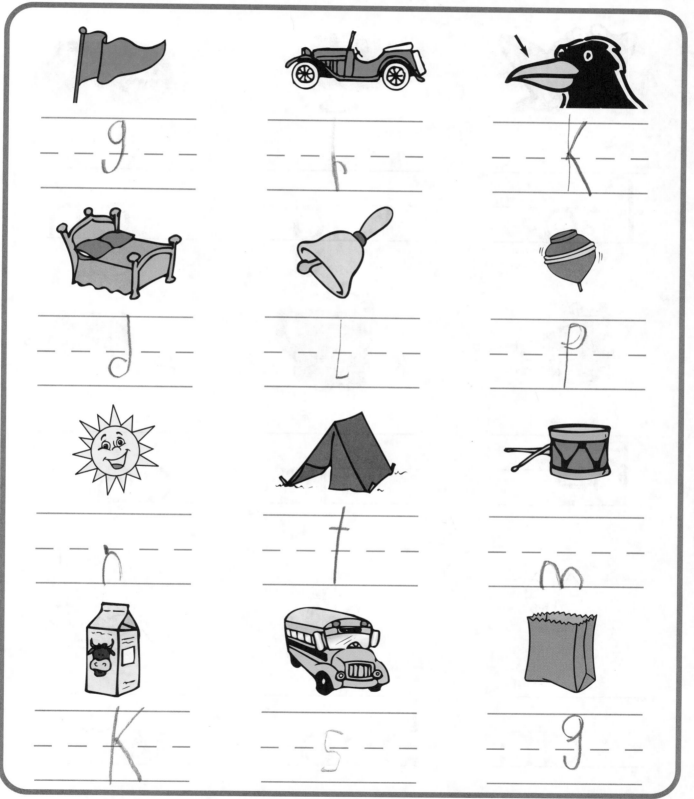

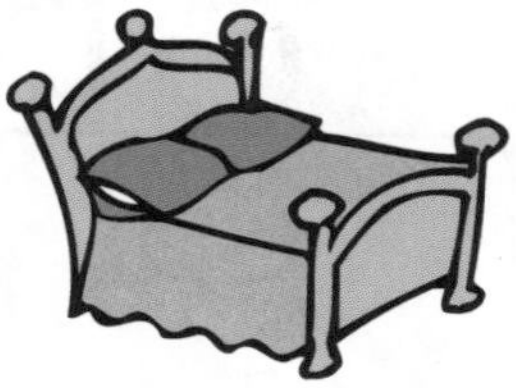

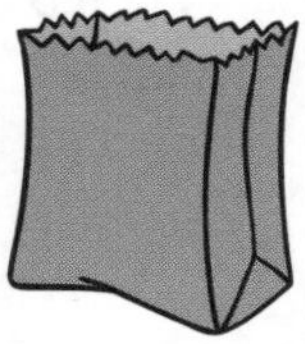

Name ____________________

Consonant Review

Directions: Say the name of each picture. Write the missing letter for each picture name.

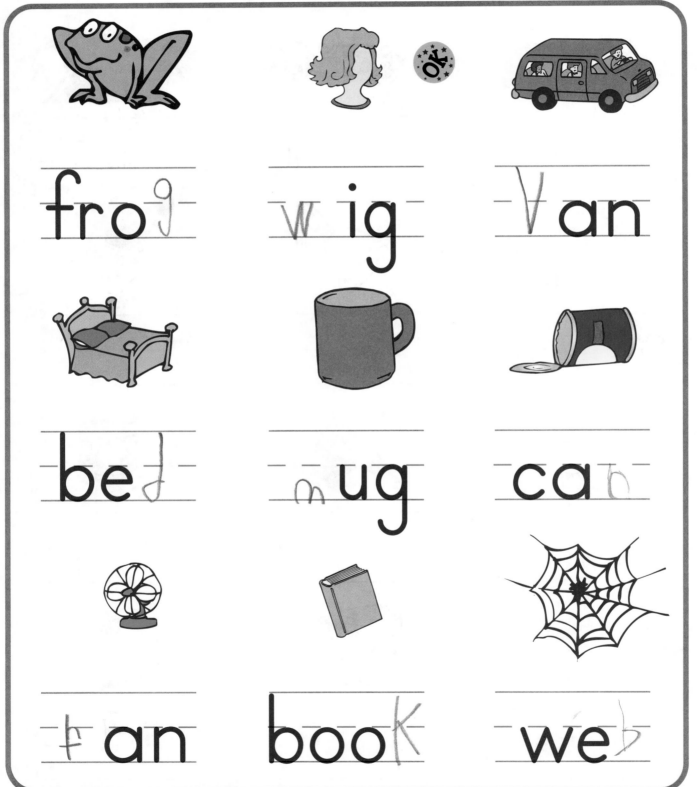

fro__

__ig

__an

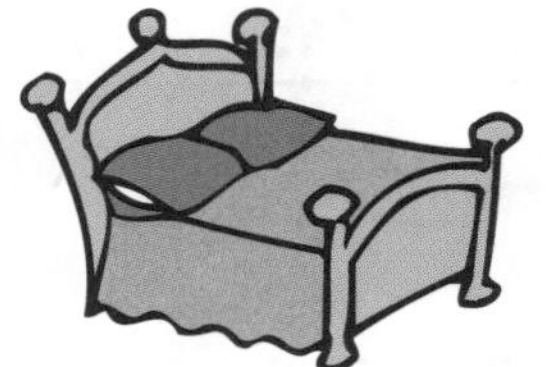

be__

__ug

ca__

__an

boo__

we__

Name ______________________________

Short a

Directions: Say the name of each picture. Draw an **X** through each picture whose name does **not** have the short **a** sound.

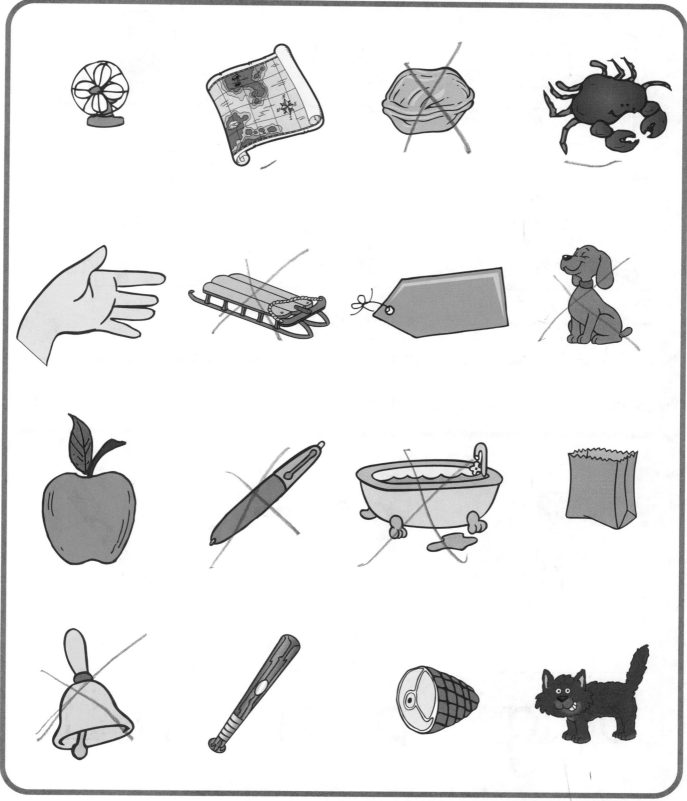

Name ________________________________

Short a

Directions: Say the name of each picture. Write the letter **a** below each picture whose name has the short **a** sound.

Directions: Say the name of each picture. Write the letter **a** to complete each word.

Name ______________________________

Short a

Directions: Say the name of each picture. Draw lines to match each picture with its name.

Name ____________________

Short a

Directions: Say the name of each picture. Write a word from the Word Box that names each picture.

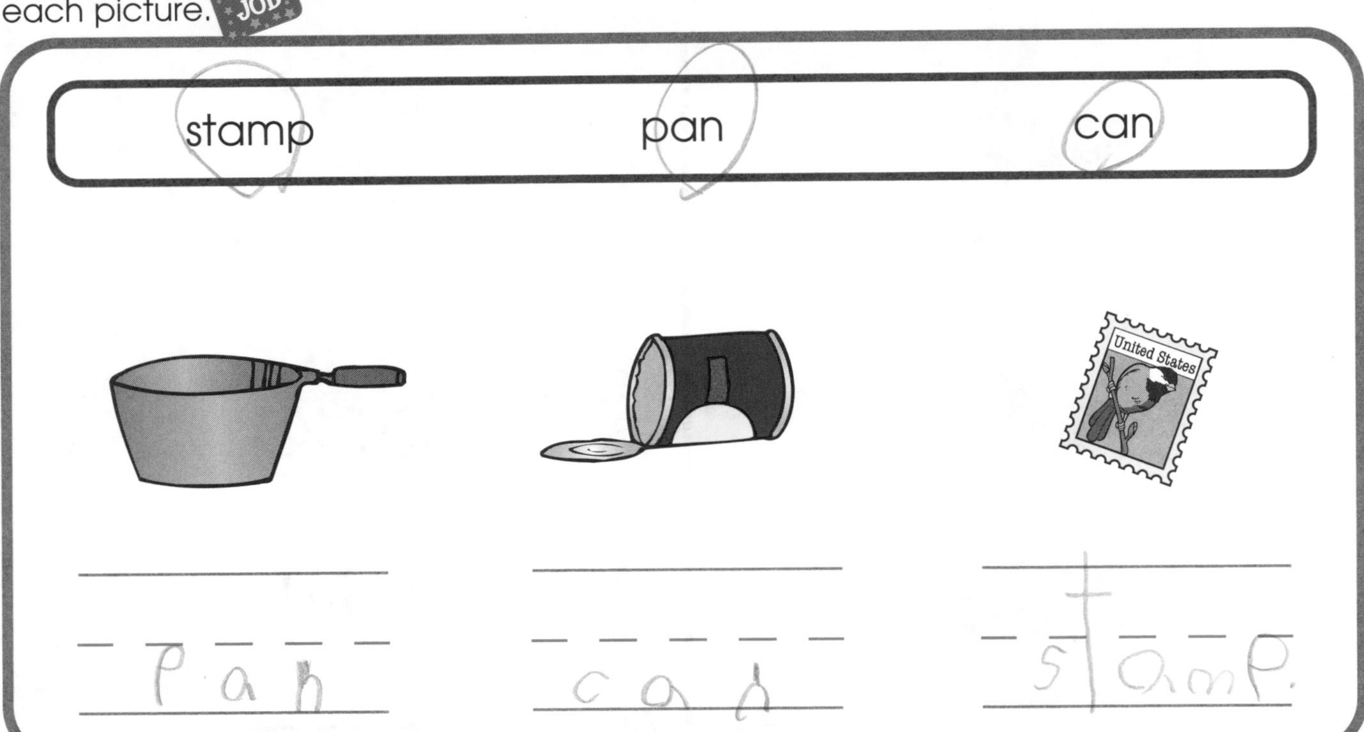

stamp pan can

pan ____ can ____ stamp ____

Directions: Write a word from the Word Box to complete each sentence.

hat sat man

1. Our dog ___sat___ on the mat.

2. That ___man___ is my dad.

3. I like my new ___hat___.

Name ______________________________

Short e

Directions: Say the name of each picture. Draw an **X** through each picture that does **not** have the short **e** sound.

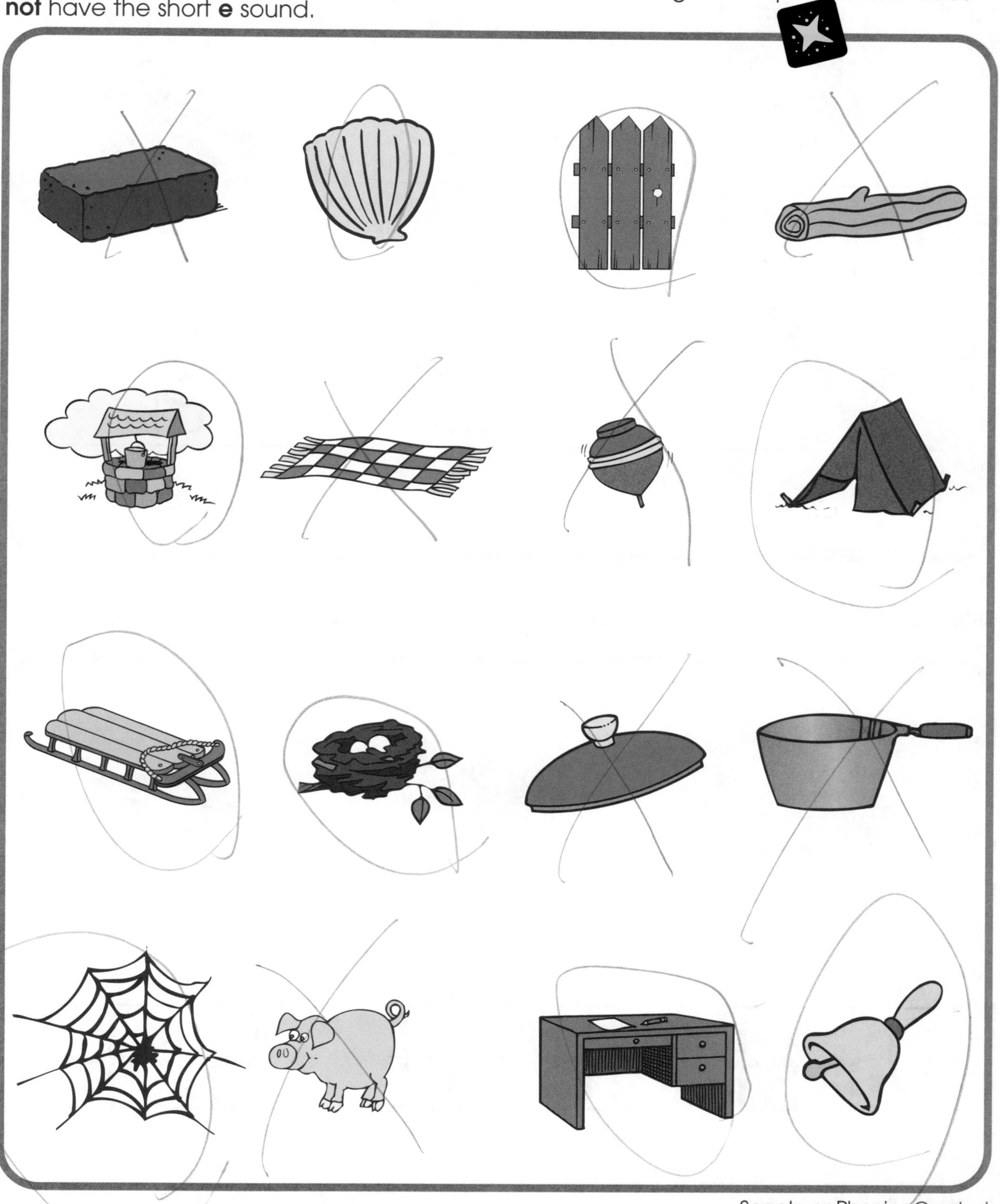

Name ______________________

Short e

Directions: Say the name of each picture. Write the letter **e** below each picture that has the short **e** sound.

Directions: Say the name of each picture. Write the letter **e** to complete each word.

Name ______________________________

Short e

Directions: Say the name of each picture. Draw lines to match each picture with its name.

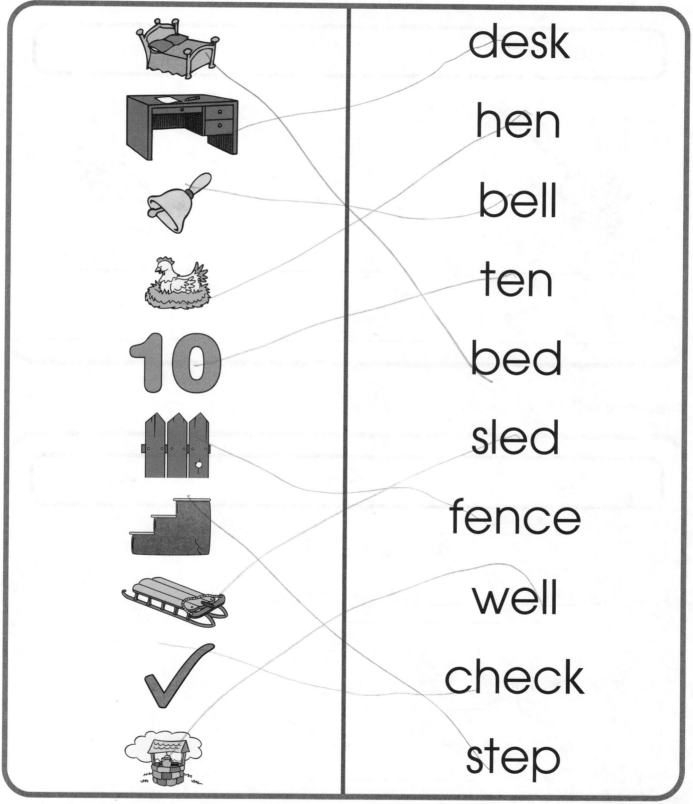

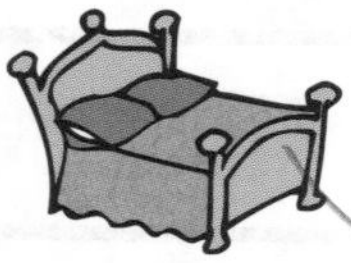

desk

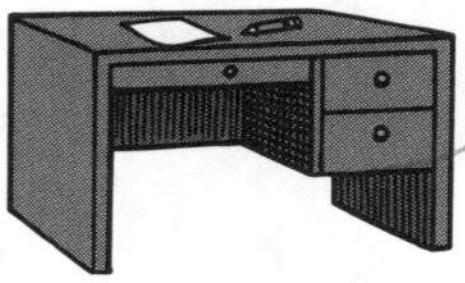

hen

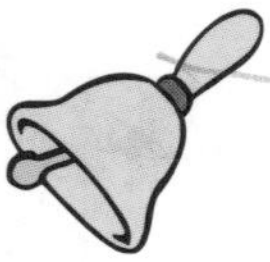

bell

ten

bed

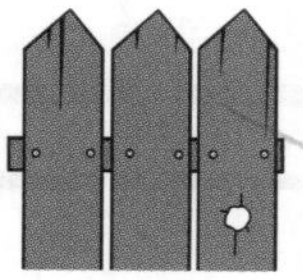

sled

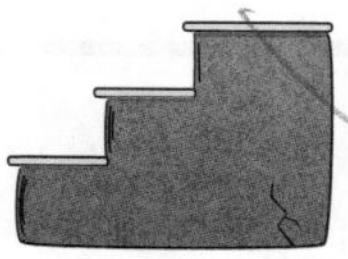

fence

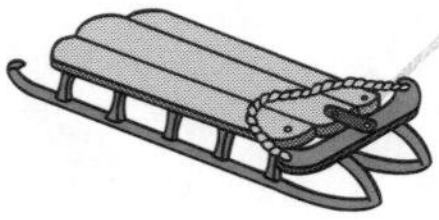

well

check

step

Name ______________________

Short e

Directions: Say the name of each picture. Write a word from the Word Box that names each picture.

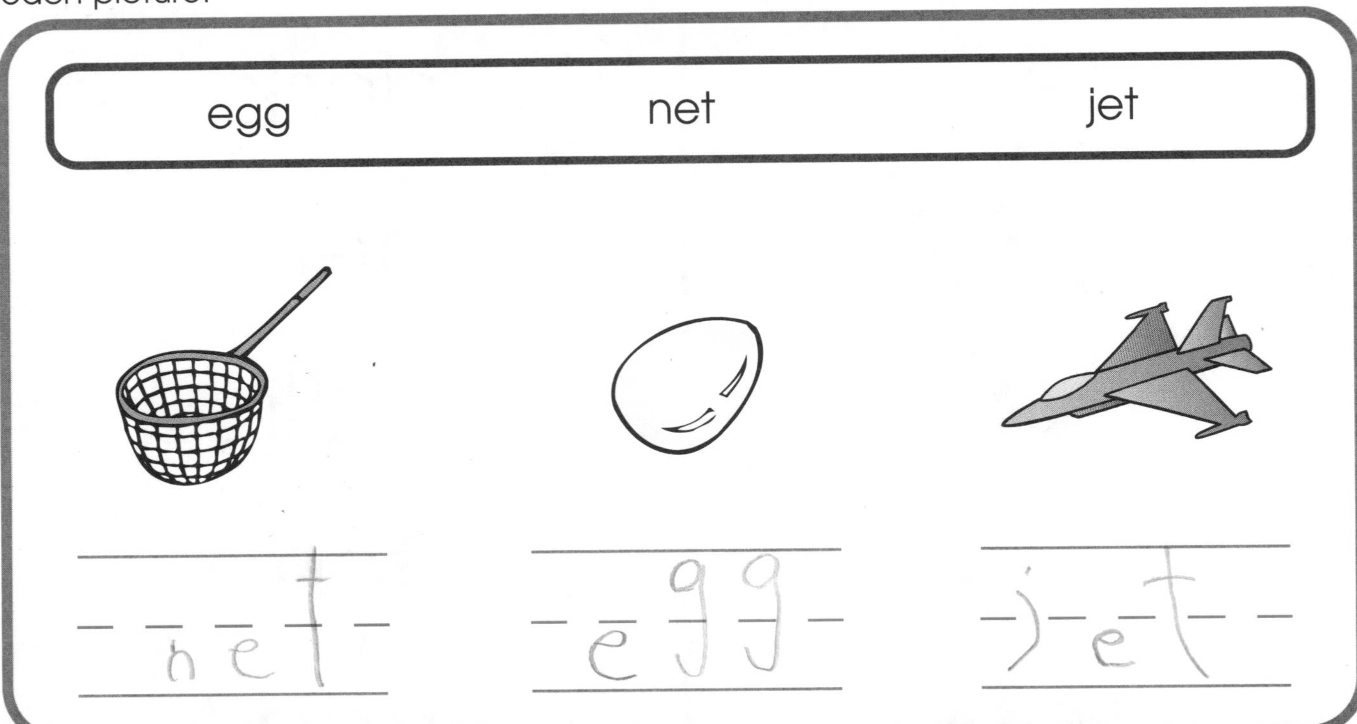

Directions: Write a word from the Word Box to complete each sentence.

bed	hen	beg

1. The hen sat on an egg.
2. It is time for bed.
3. My dog can beg.

Name ______________________________

Review: Short a and Short e

Directions: Write the letter that shows the short vowel sound for each picture n

e	a	e
e	a	a
a	a	e
a	e	a

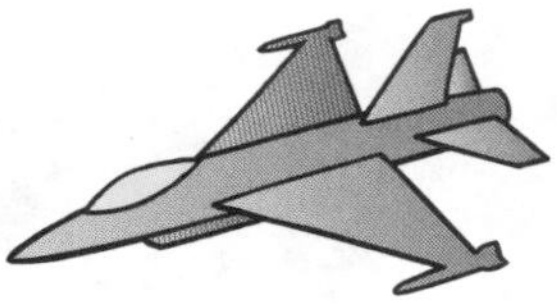

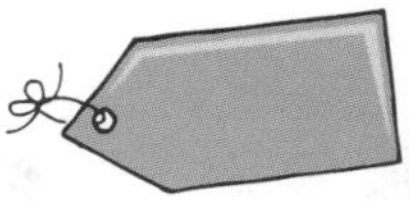

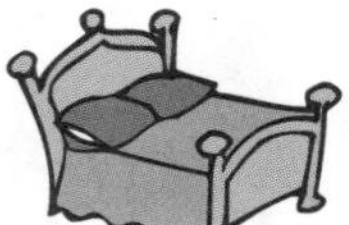

Name ______________________________

Short i

Directions: Say the name of each picture. Draw an **X** through each picture that does **not** have the short **i** sound.

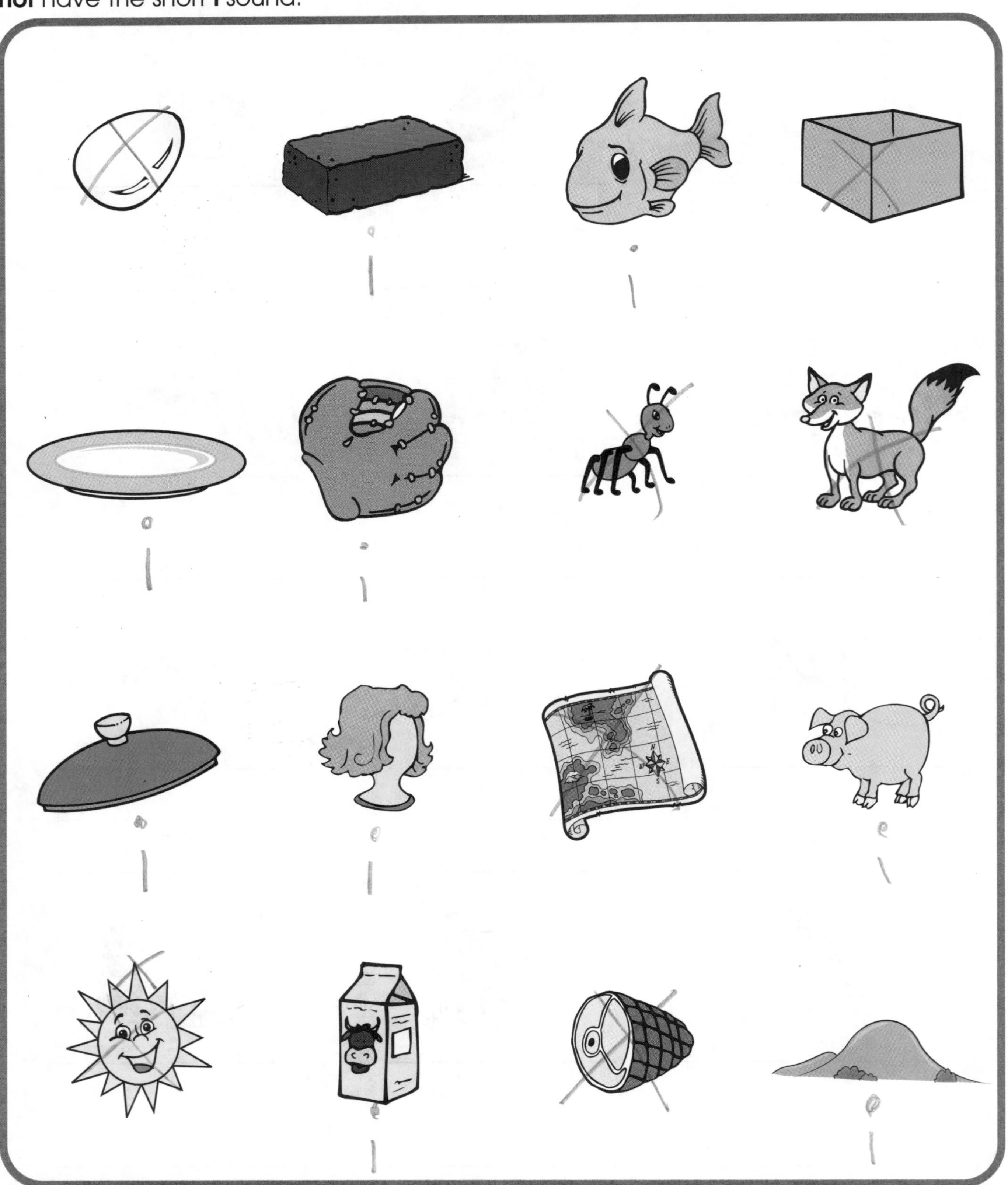

Name ________________________________

Short i

Directions: Say the name of each picture. Write the letter **i** below each picture that has the short **i** sound.

Directions: Say the name of each picture. Write the letter **i** to complete each word.

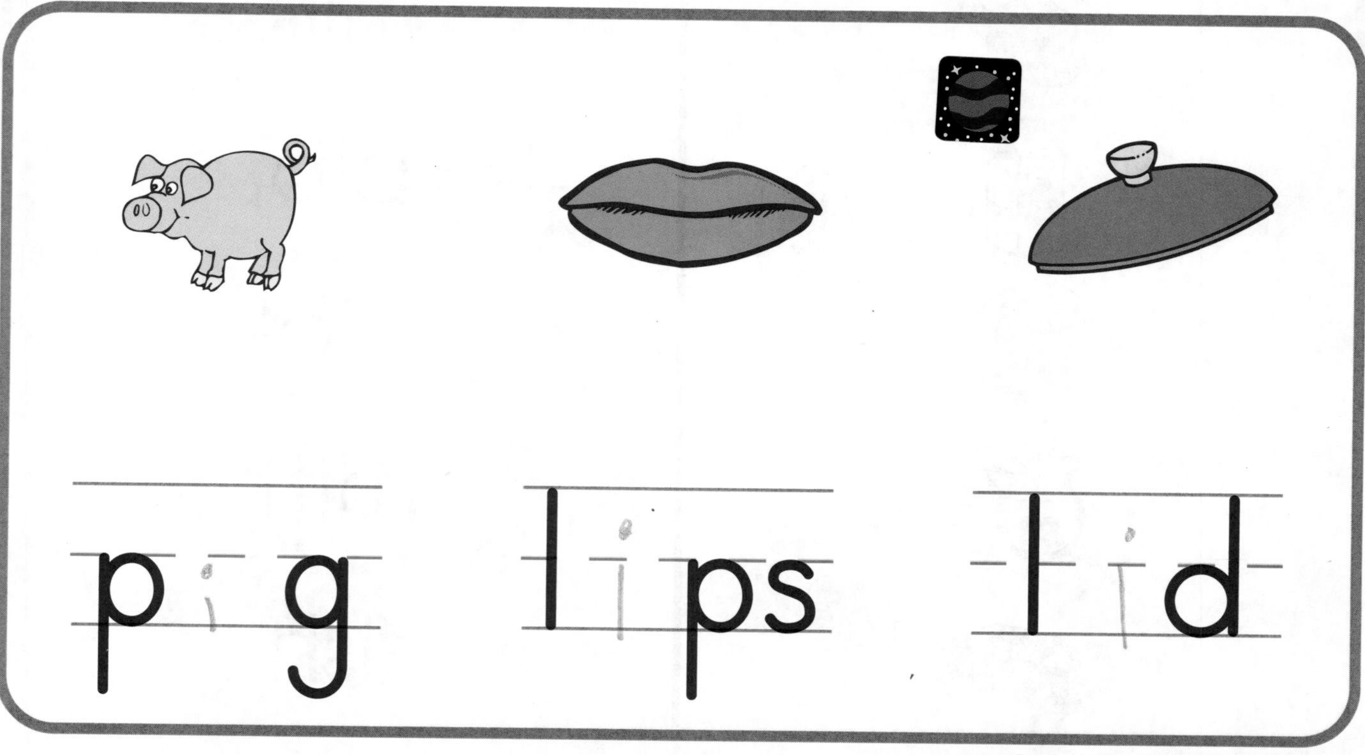

Name ______________________________

Short i

Directions: Say the name of each picture. Draw lines to match each picture with its name.

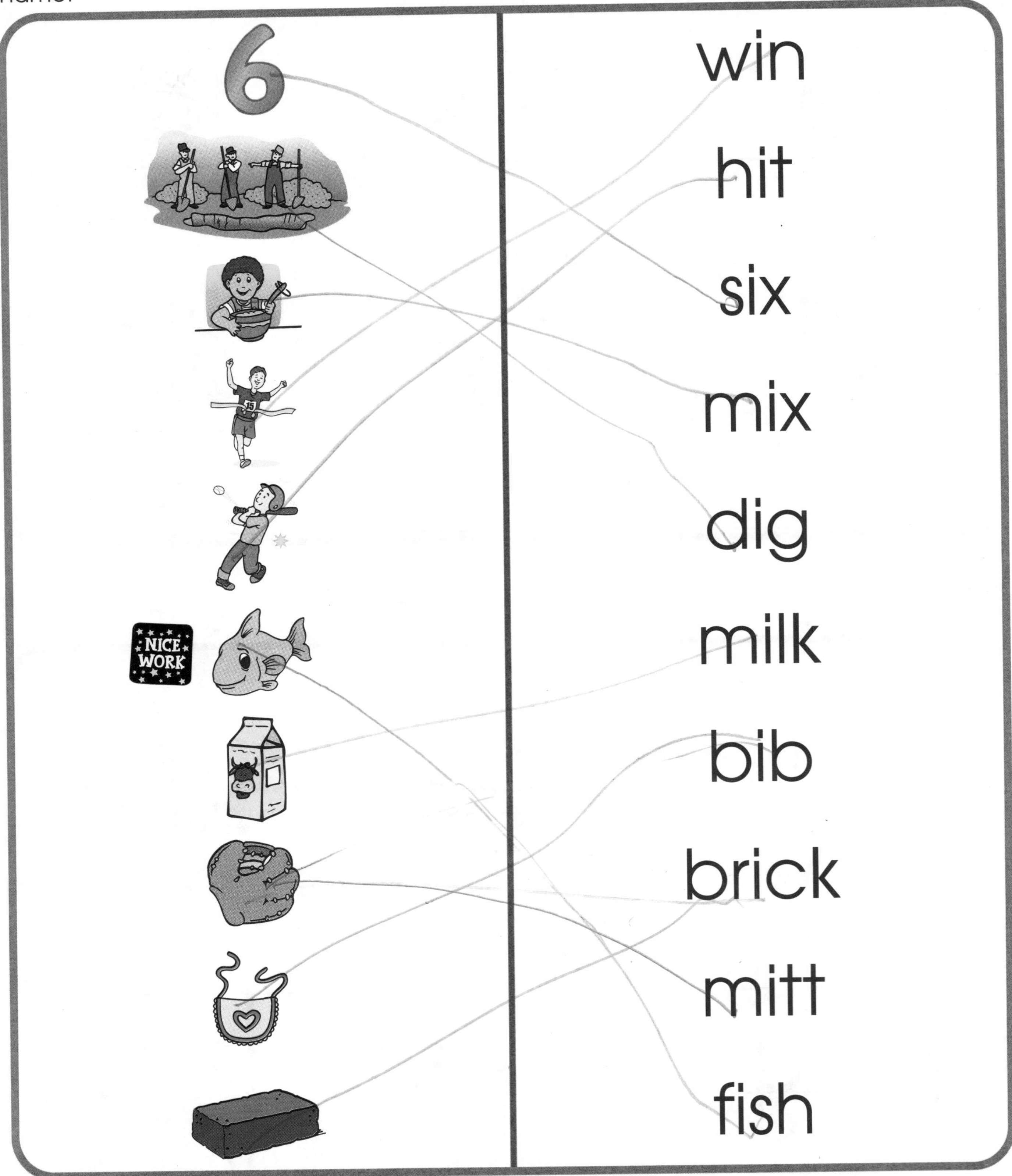

Name ______________________________

Short i

Directions: Say the name of each picture. Write a word from the Word Box that names each picture.

Directions: Write a word from the Word Box to complete each sentence.

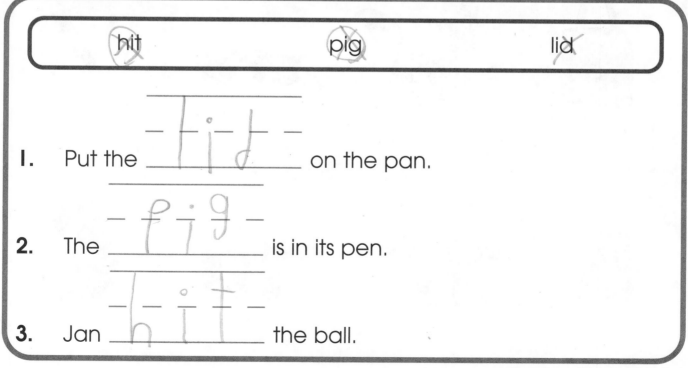

hit	pig	lid

1. Put the ____________ on the pan.

2. The ____________ is in its pen.

3. Jan ____________ the ball.

Name ______________________________

Short o

Directions: Say the name of each picture. Draw an **X** through each picture that does **not** have the short **o** sound.

Name ______________________

Short o

Directions: Say the name of each picture. Write the letter **o** below each picture that has the short **o** sound.

Directions: Say the name of each picture. Write the letter **o** to complete each word.

Name ____________________

Short o

Directions: Say the name of each picture. Draw lines to match each picture with its name.

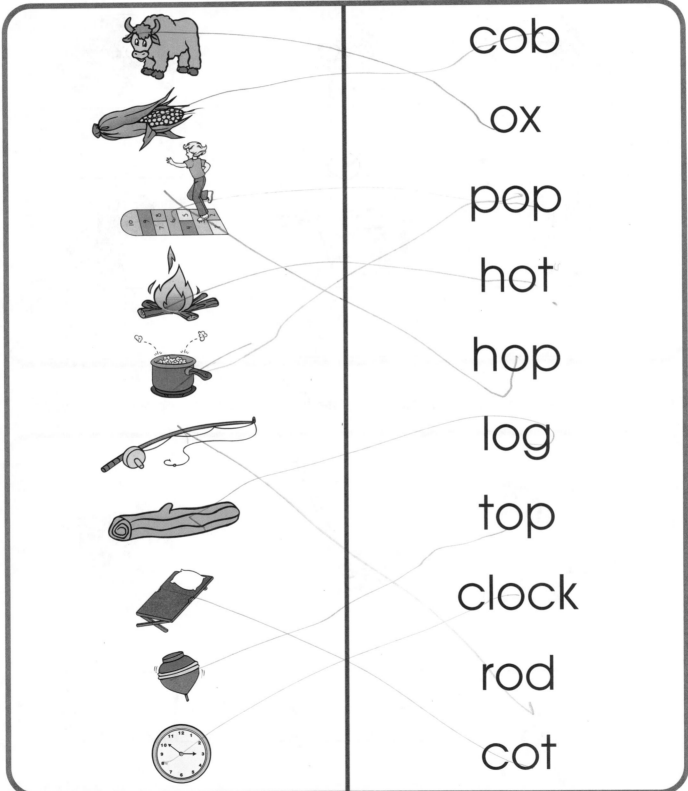

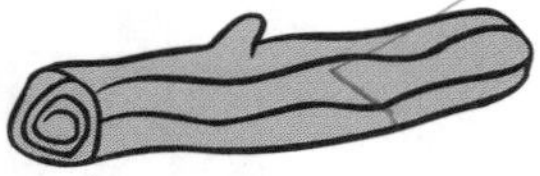

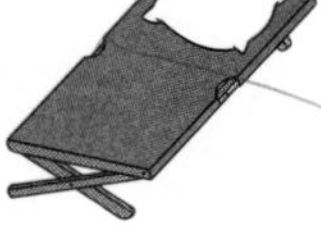

cob

ox

pop

hot

hop

log

top

clock

rod

cot

Name ____________________

Short o

Directions: Say the name of each picture. Write a word from the Word Box that names each picture.

doll	log	ox

____________ ____________ ____________

Directions: Write a word from the Word Box to complete each sentence.

fox	hop	hot

1. Watch the bunny ____________.

2. The pot is ____________.

3. See the red ____________.

Name ____________________

Review: Short i and Short o

Directions: Write the letter that shows the short vowel sound for each picture name.

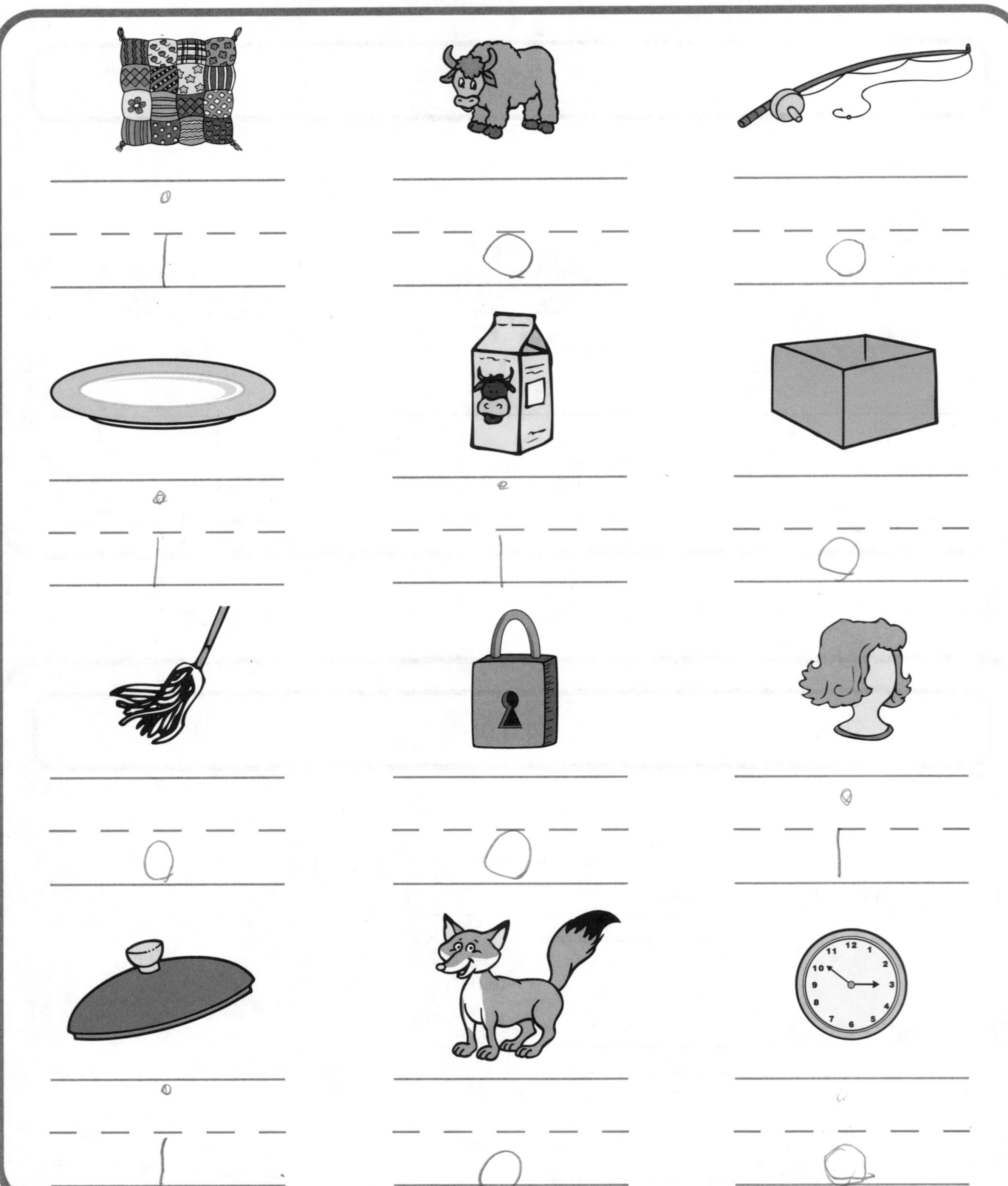

Name ____________________ 

Short u

Directions: Say the name of each picture. Draw an **X** through each picture that does **not** have the short **u** sound.

Name ______________________________

Short u

Directions: Say the name of each picture. Write the letter **u** below each picture that has the short **u** sound.

Directions: Say the name of each picture. Write the letter **u** to complete each word.

Name ______________________________

Short u

Directions: Say the name of each picture. Draw lines to match each picture with its name.

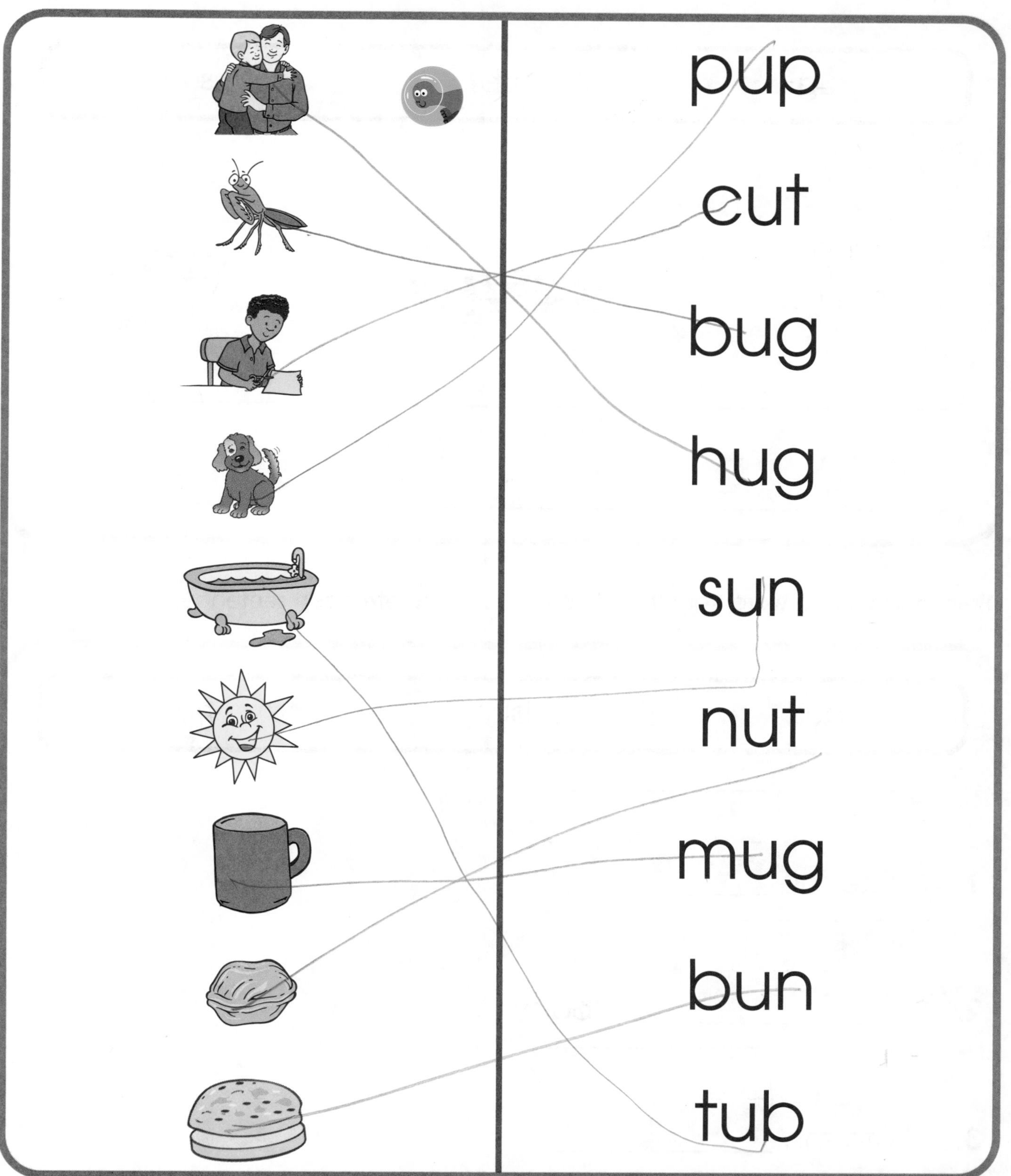

Name ______________________________

Short u

Directions: Say the name of each picture. Write a word from the Word Box that names each picture.

rug	tub	sun

sun   rug   tub

Directions: Write a word from the Word Box to complete each sentence.

bus	bun	hug

1. I ride the bus.

2. I hug the baby.

3. I ate the bun.

Name ______________________________

Review: Short Vowels

Directions: Say the name of each picture. Draw lines to match each picture with its name.

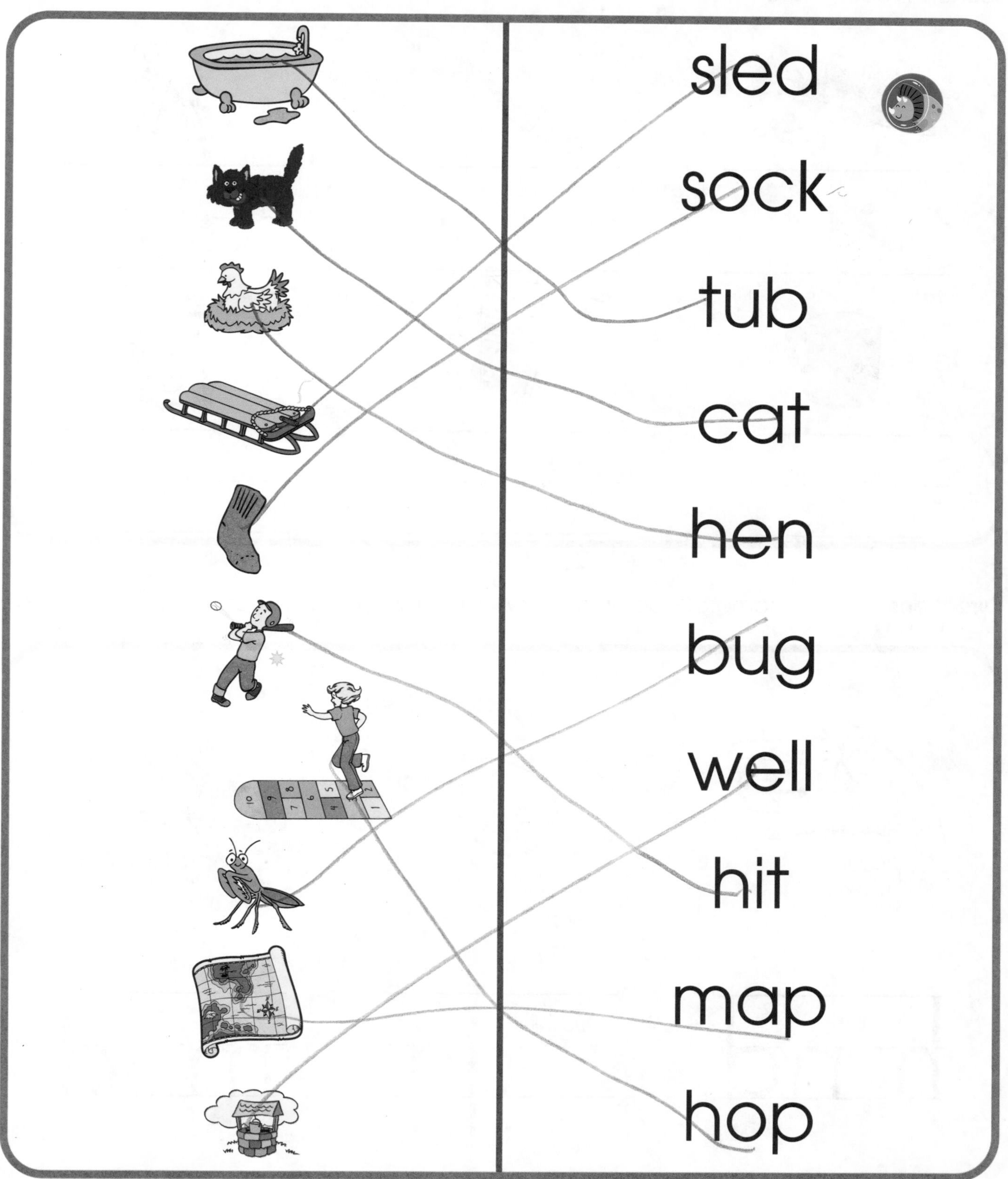

Name ______________________________

Review: Short Vowels

Directions: Say the name of each picture. Write the letter that shows the short vowel sound for each picture name.

Directions: Say the name of each picture. Write the short vowel sound that completes each word.

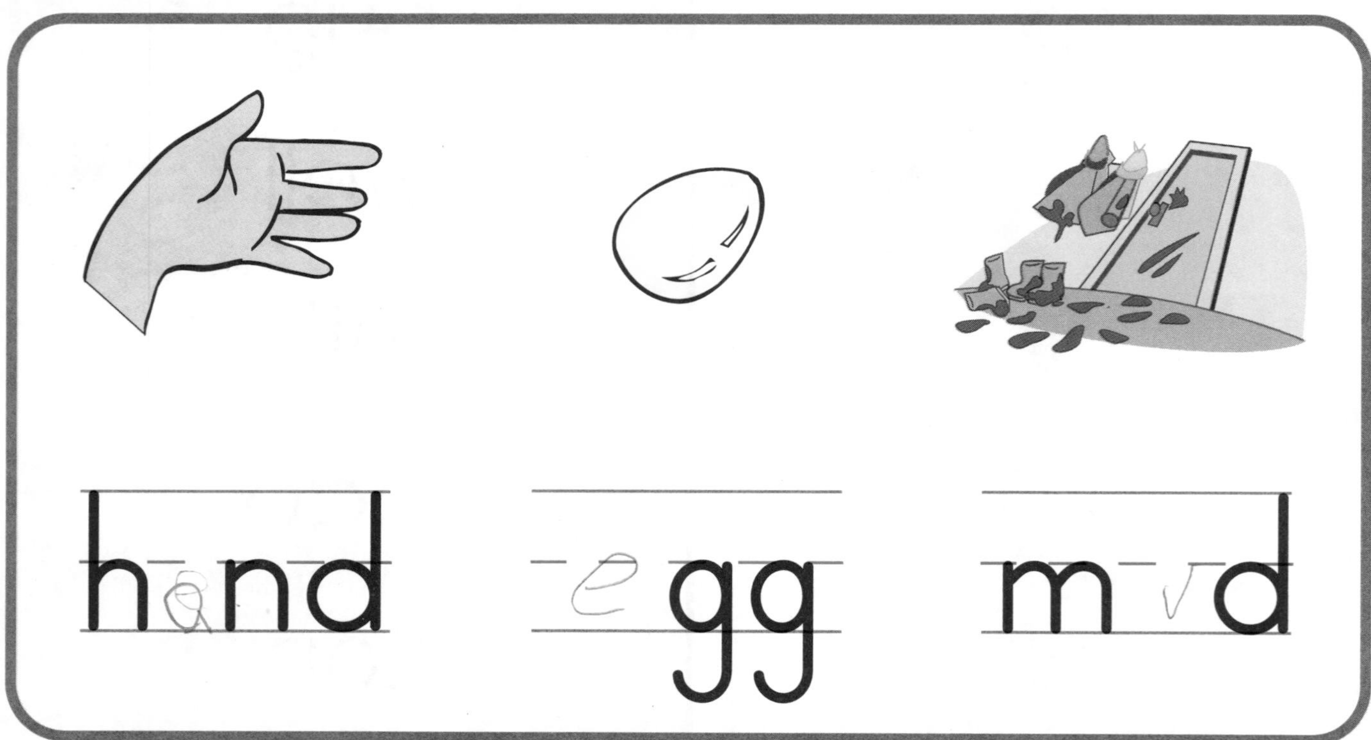

Name ______________________________

Review: Short Vowels

Directions: Say the name of each picture. Write a word from the Word Box that names each picture.

Directions: Write a word from the Word Box to complete each sentence.

fish bat sled

1. I ride a sled.
2. The fish is in the net.
3. Hit the ball with the bat.

Name

Review: Short Vowels

Directions: Draw a picture of things whose names contain the short vowel sounds of the letters below.

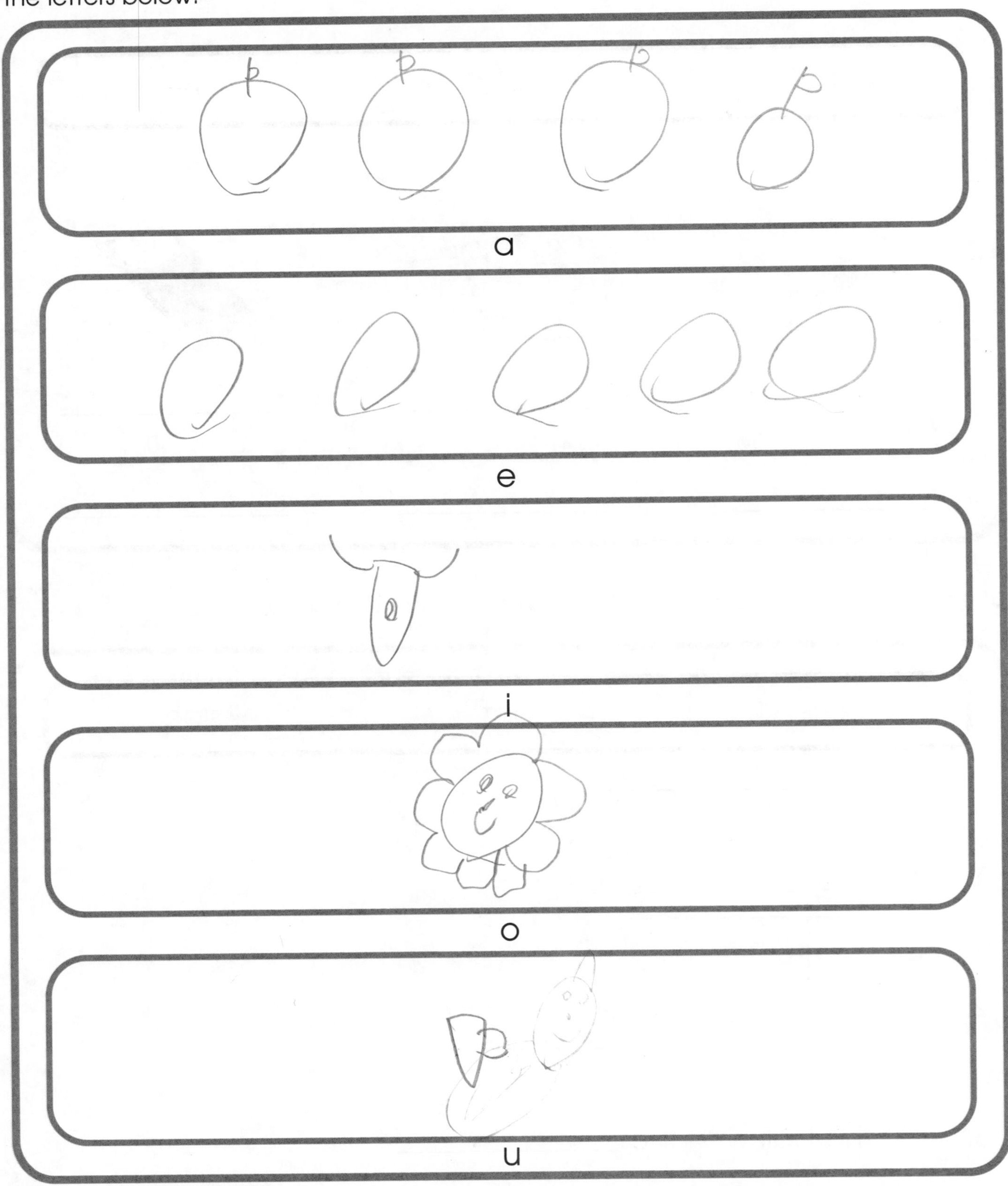

Name ________________________________

Review: Short Vowels

Directions: Write the word from the Word Box that names each picture.

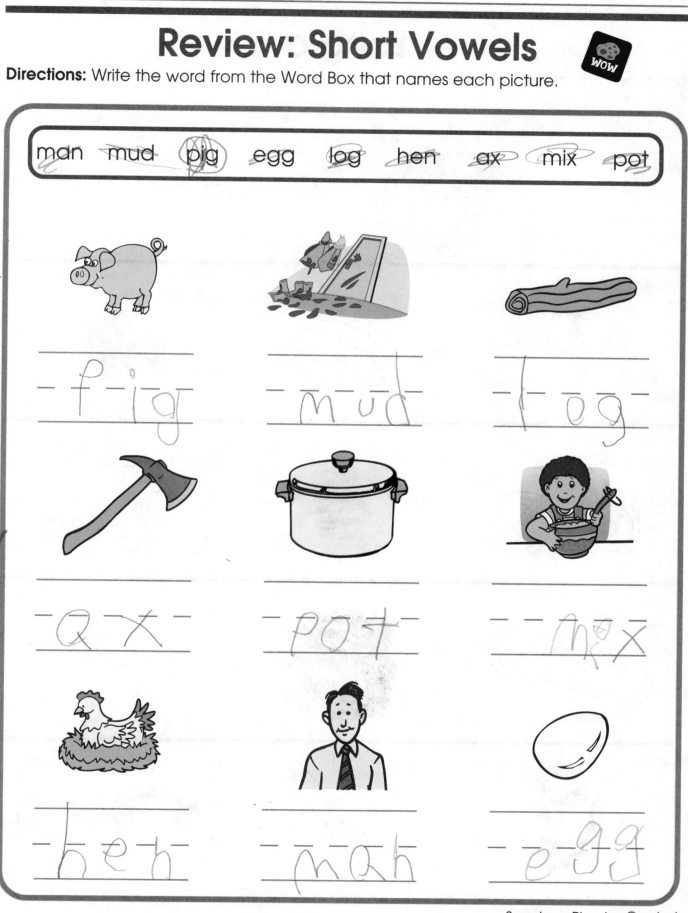

man	mud	pig	egg	log	hen	ax	mix	pot

pig ______ mud ______ log ______

ax ______ pot ______ mix ______

hen ______ man ______ egg ______

Name ____

Long a

Directions: Say the name of each picture. Color each picture whose name has the long **a** sound.

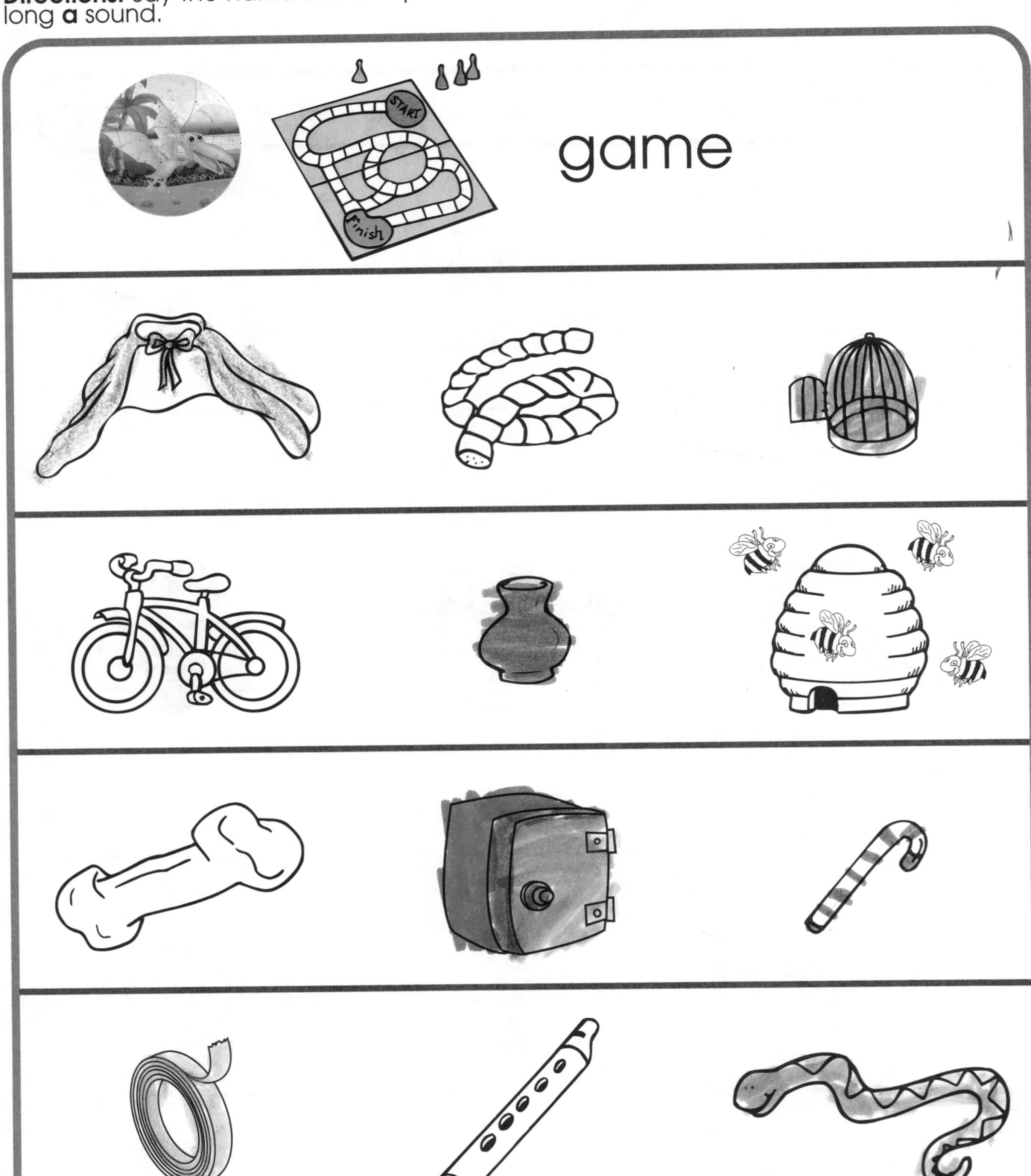

Name ______________________

Long a and Short a

Directions: Say the name of each picture. Draw lines to match each picture with its name.

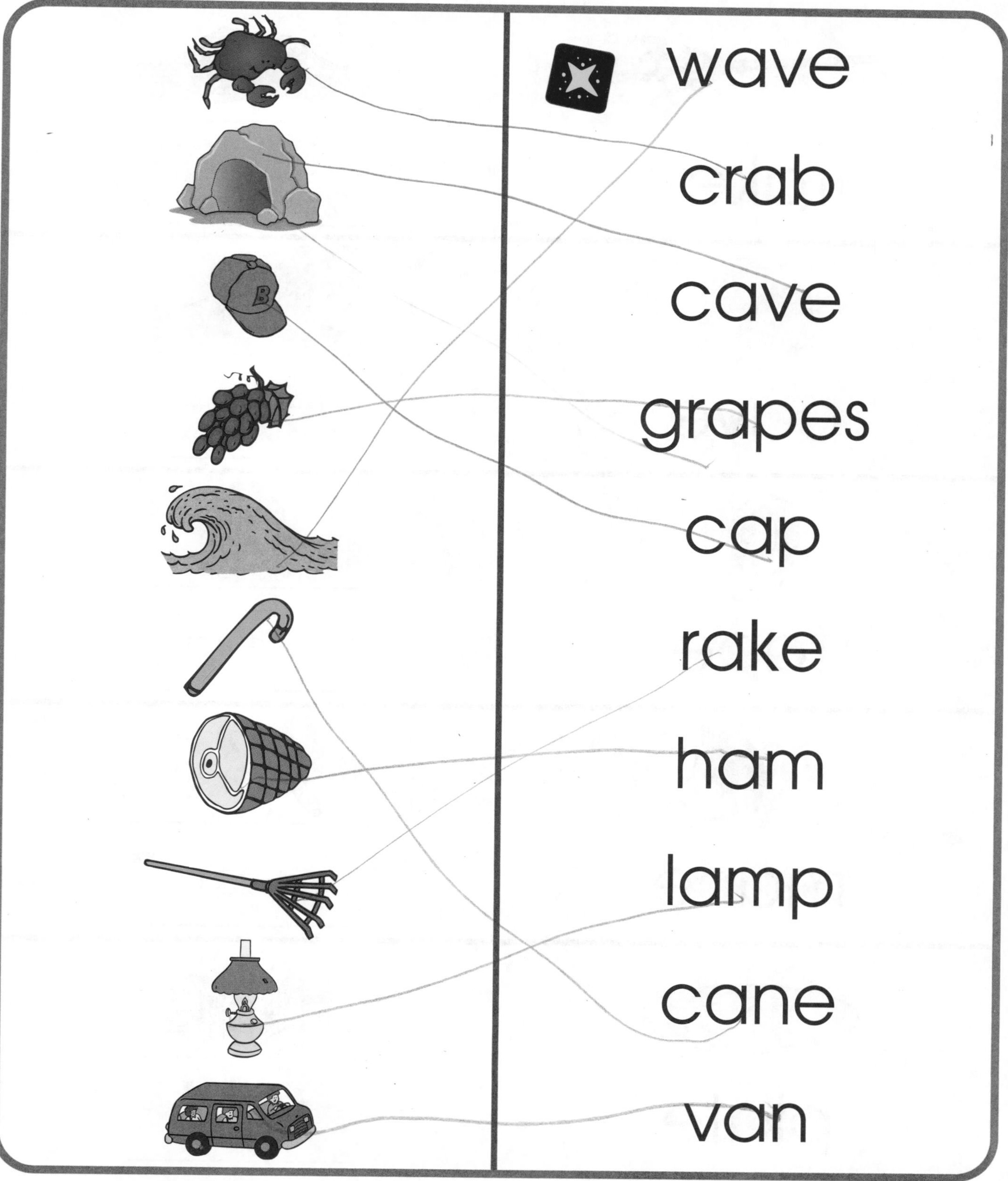

Name ______________________________

Long a

Directions: Write the word that rhymes with each long **a** word.

rake	lake
cave	Wave
tape	Ape
mane	cane
plate	gate

Name ________________________________

Long a

Directions: Write a word from the Word Box to complete each sentence.

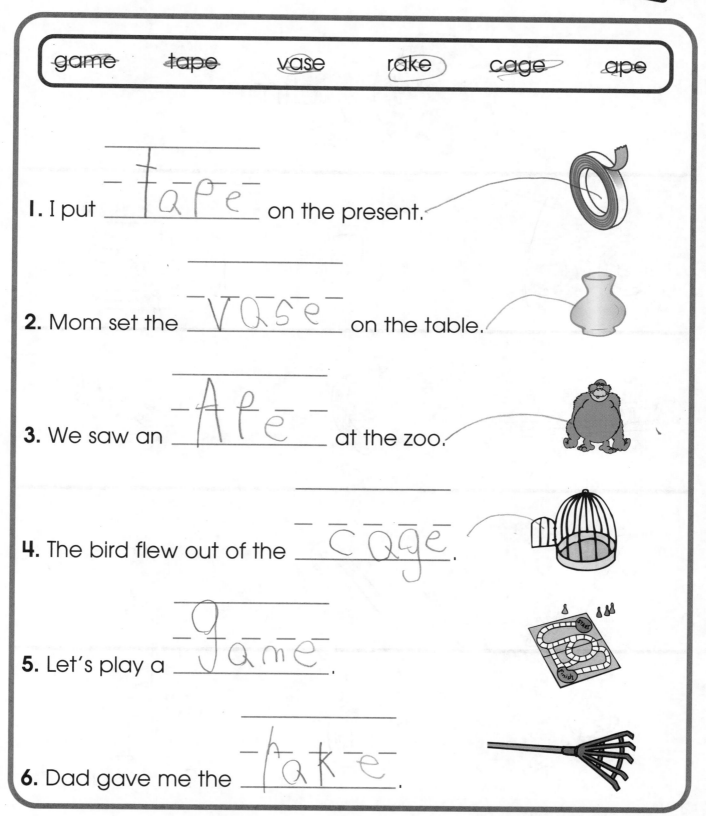

game	tape	vase	rake	cage	ape

1. I put ____________ on the present.

2. Mom set the ____________ on the table.

3. We saw an ____________ at the zoo.

4. The bird flew out of the ____________.

5. Let's play a ____________.

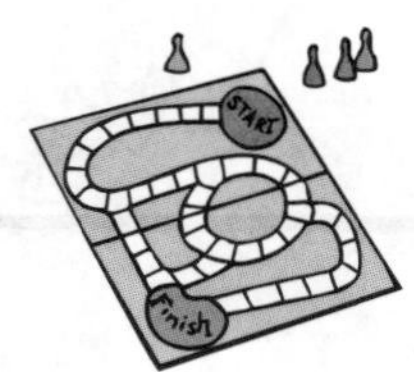

6. Dad gave me the ____________.

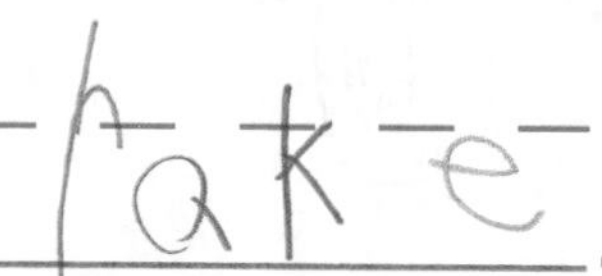

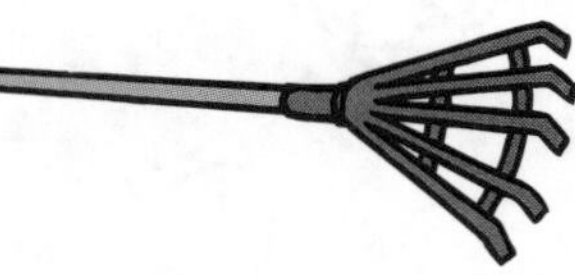

Name ______________________________

Long i

Directions: Say the name of each picture. Color each picture whose name has the long **i** sound.

dime

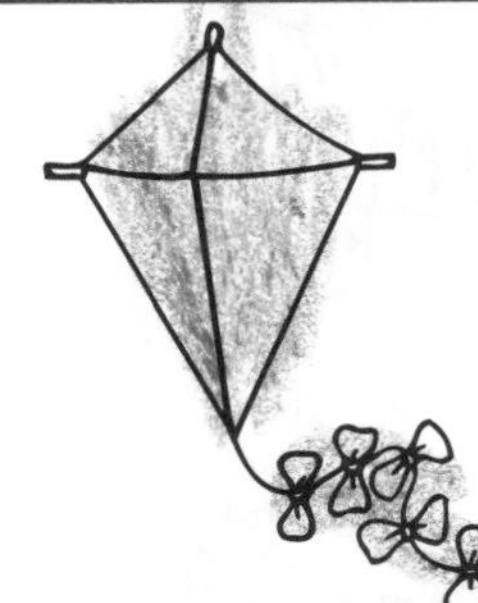

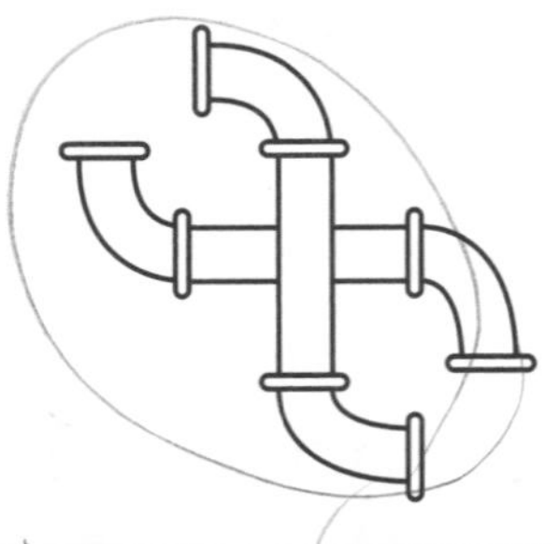

Name ___________________________

Long i and Short i

Directions: Say the name of each picture. Draw lines to match each picture with its name.

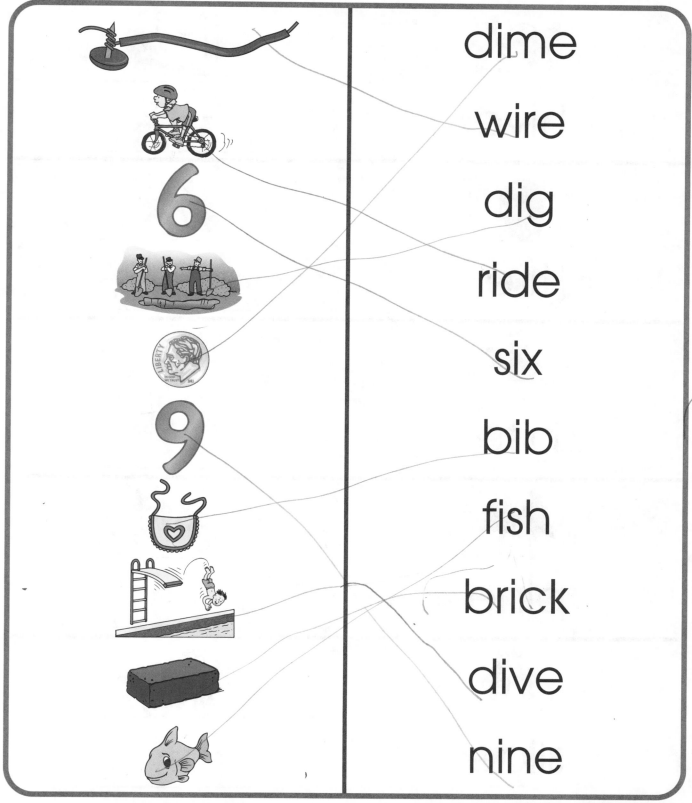

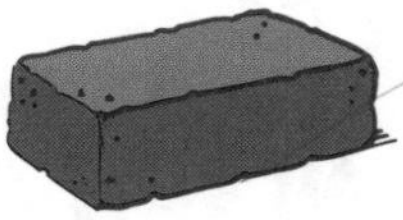

dime

wire

dig

ride

six

bib

fish

brick

dive

nine

Name ______________________

Long i 

Directions: Write the word that rhymes with each long **i** word.

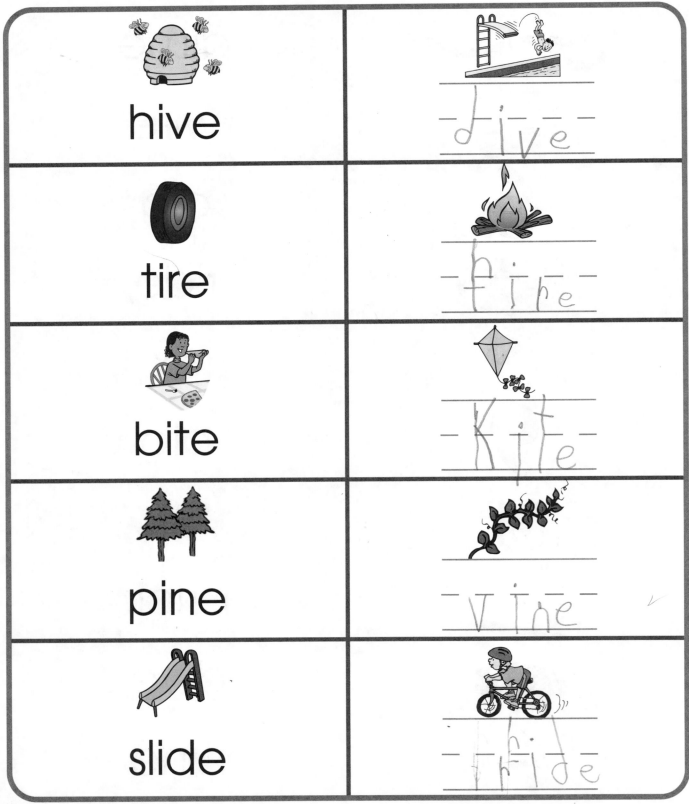

hive	dive
tire	fire
bite	kite
pine	vine
slide	ride

Name ____________________

Long i

Directions: Write a word from the Word Box to complete each sentence.

kite	nine	dive	bike	hive	bite

1. I went down the slide nine times.

2. Don't go near the bee's hive!

3. I like to ride my yellow bike.

4. Can you fly a Kite?

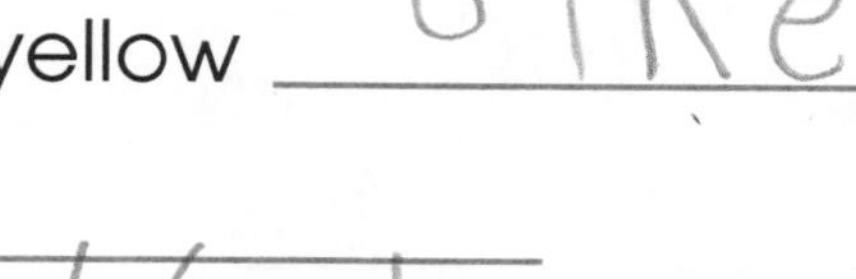

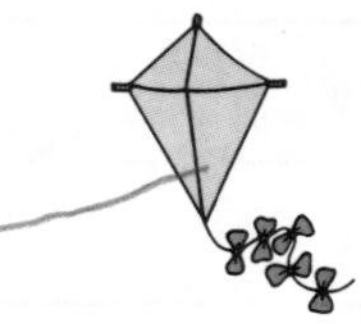

5. Take a bite of the pizza.

6. I dive into the water.

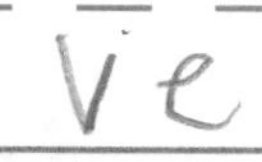

Name ___________________________

Review: Long a and Long i

Directions: Write the word from the Word Box that names each picture.

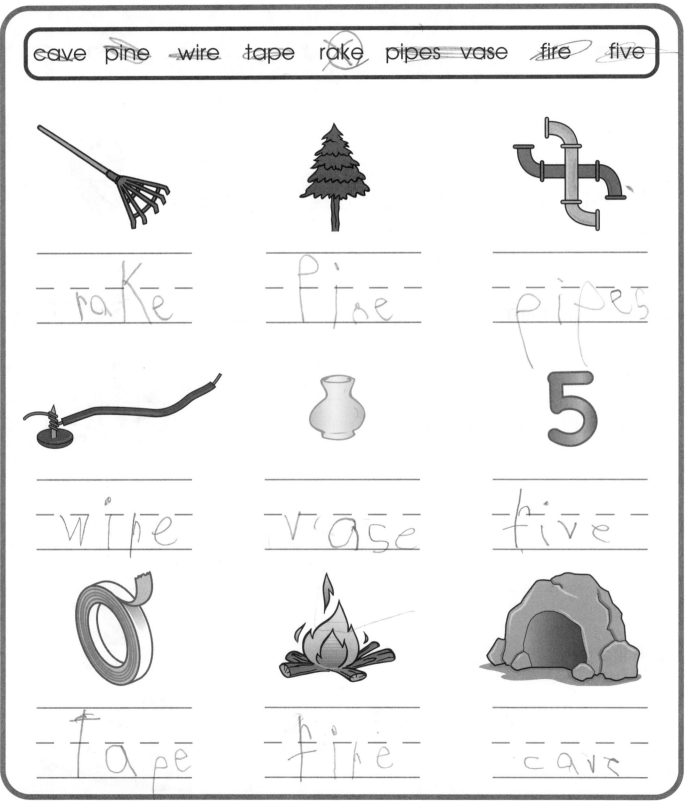

cave pine wire tape rake pipes vase fire five

rake pine pipes

wire vase five

tape fire cave

Name ___________________________

Long o

Directions: Say the name of each picture. Color each picture whose name has the long **o** sound.

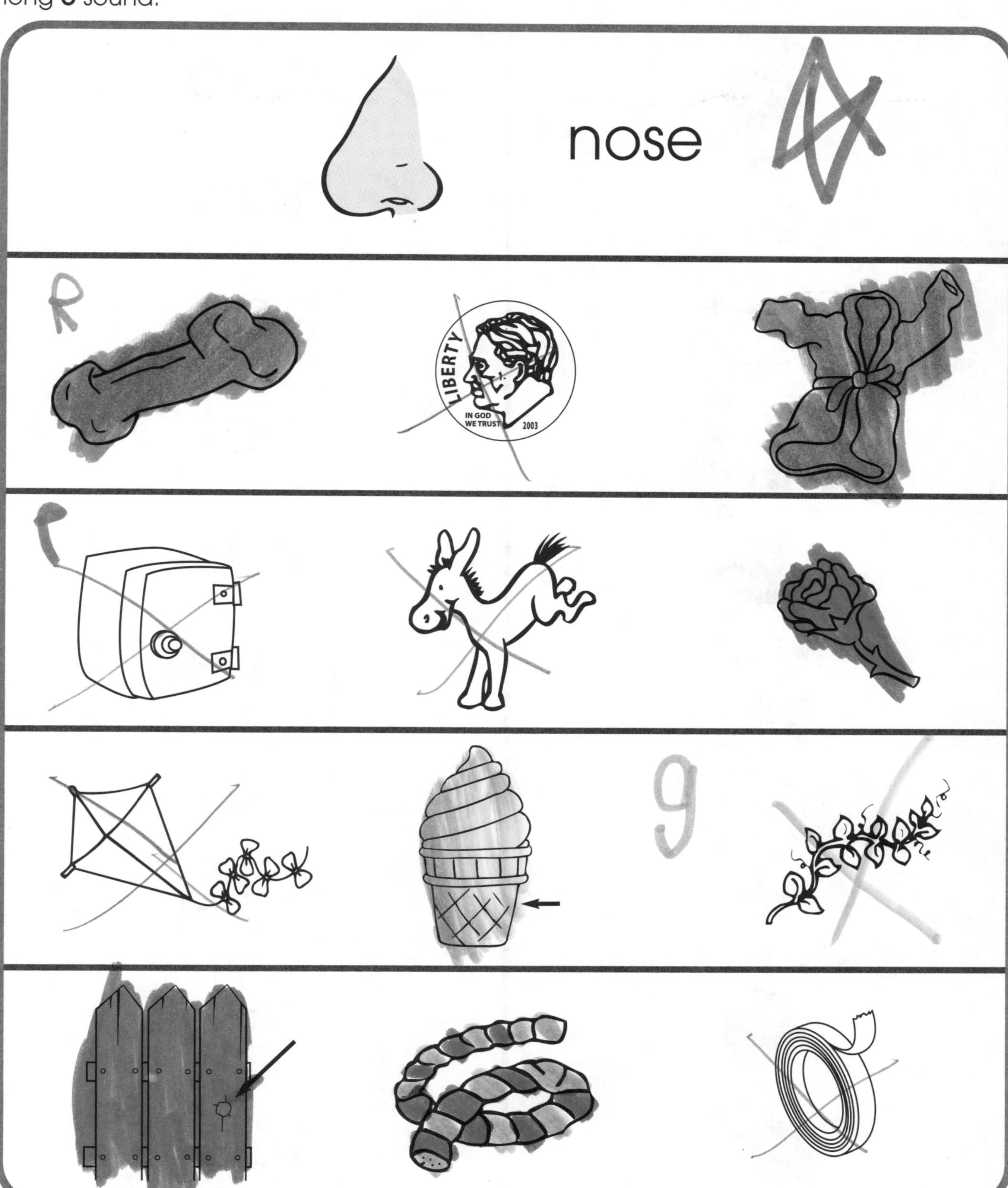

Name ______________________________

Long o and Short o

Directions: Say the name of each picture. Draw lines to match each picture with its name.

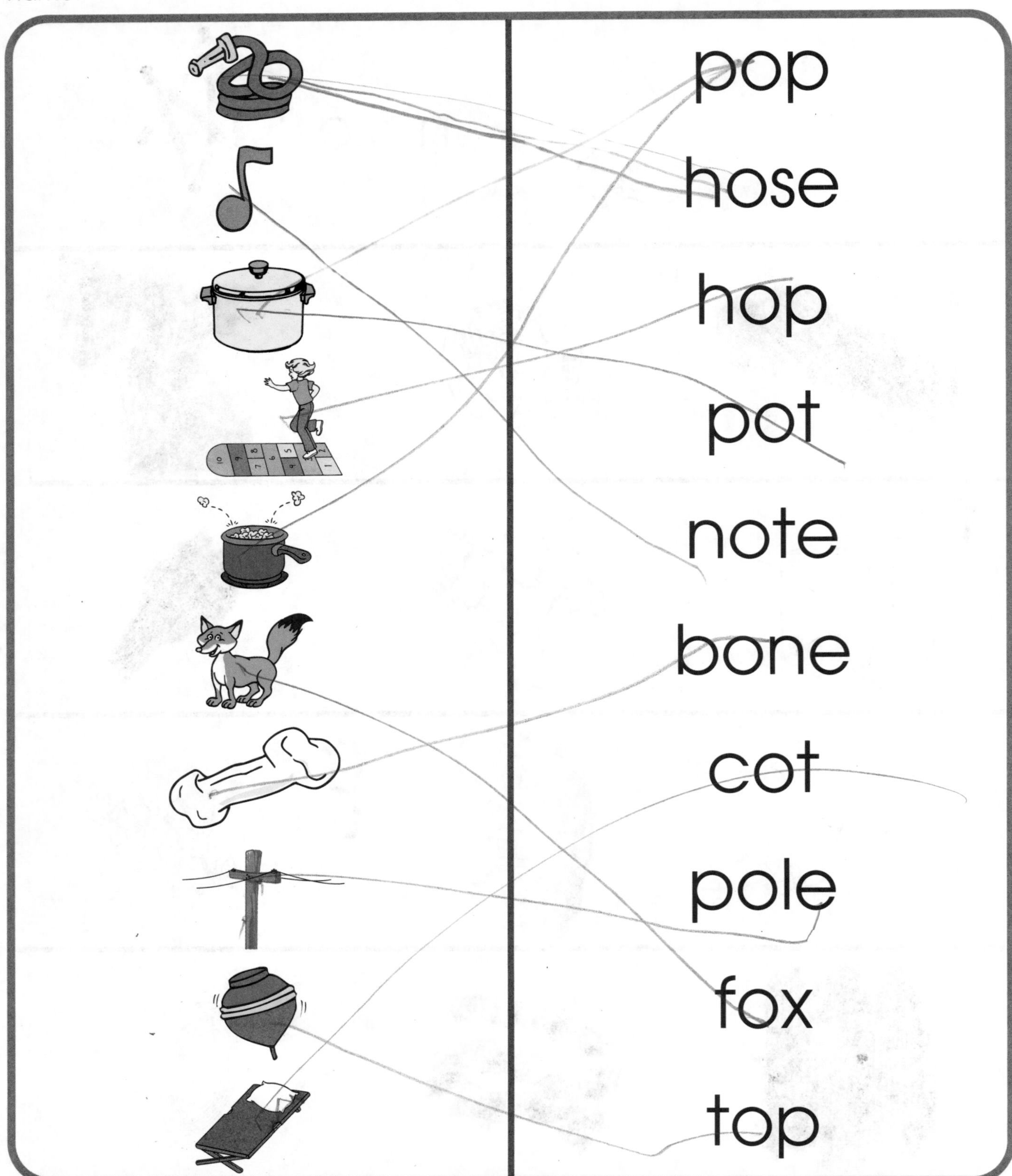

Name ______________________________

Long o

Directions: Write the word that rhymes with each long **o** word.

pole	hole
hose	rose
coat	hote
bone	cone
globe	robe

Name ______________________________

Long o

Directions: Write a word from the Word Box to complete each sentence.

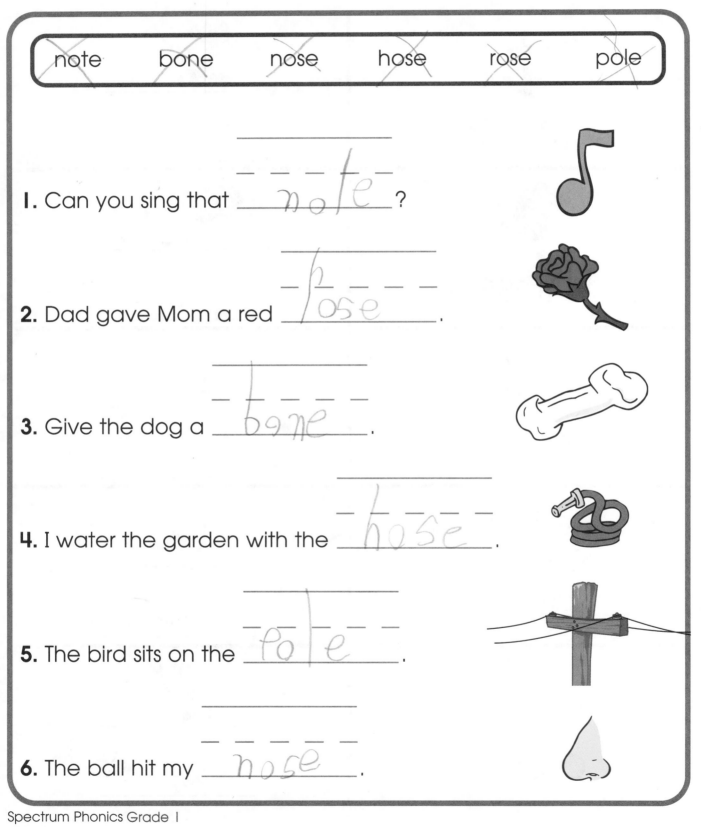

note	bone	nose	hose	rose	pole

1. Can you sing that ____________?

2. Dad gave Mom a red ____________.

3. Give the dog a ____________.

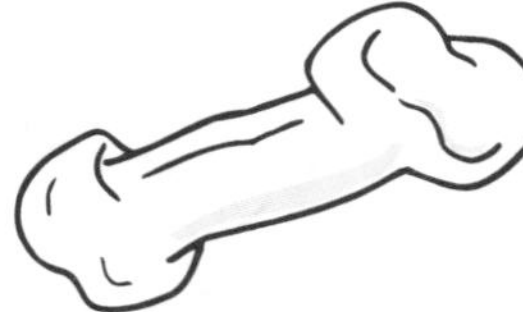

4. I water the garden with the ____________.

5. The bird sits on the ____________.

6. The ball hit my ____________.

Name ______________________________

Long u

Directions: Say the name of each picture. Color each picture whose name has the long **u** sound.

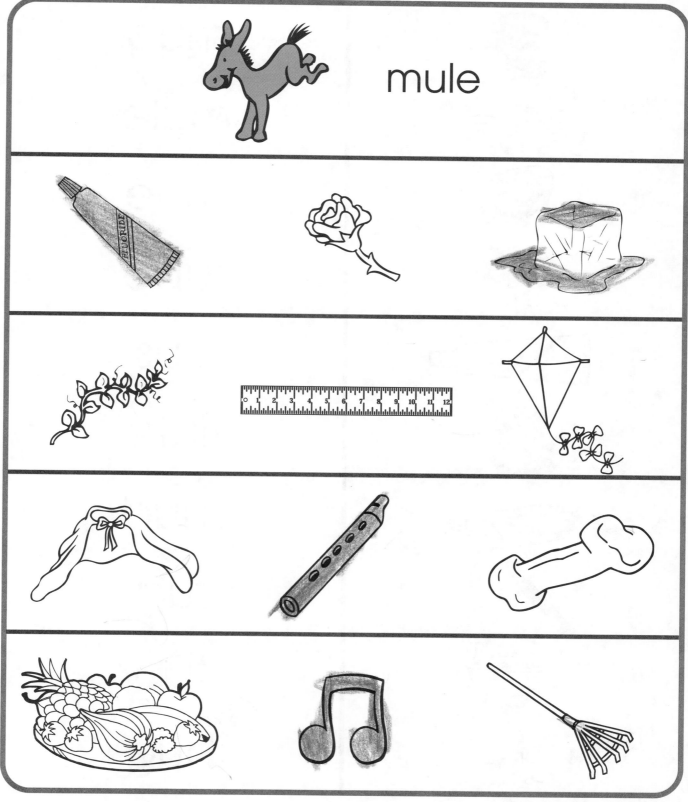

mule

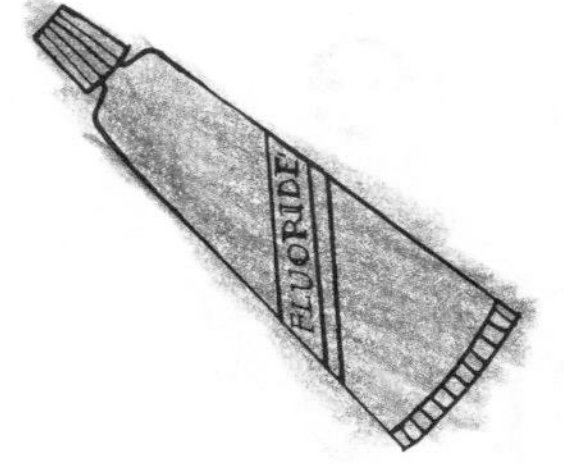

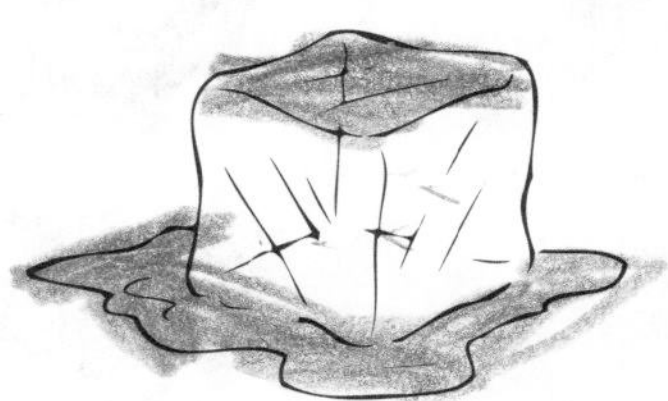

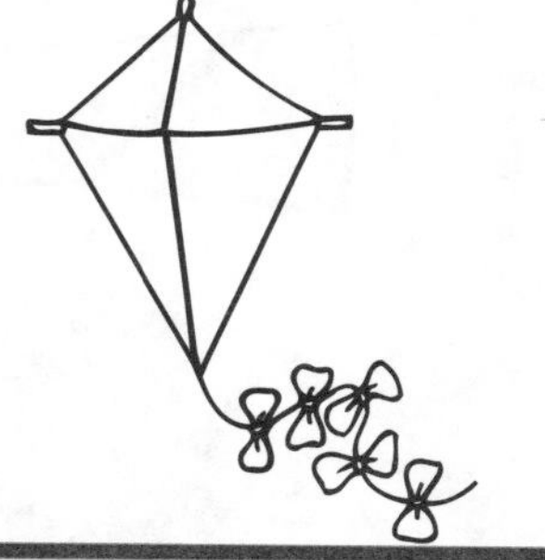

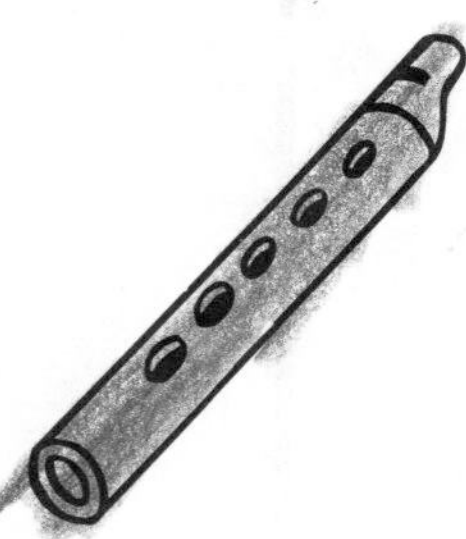

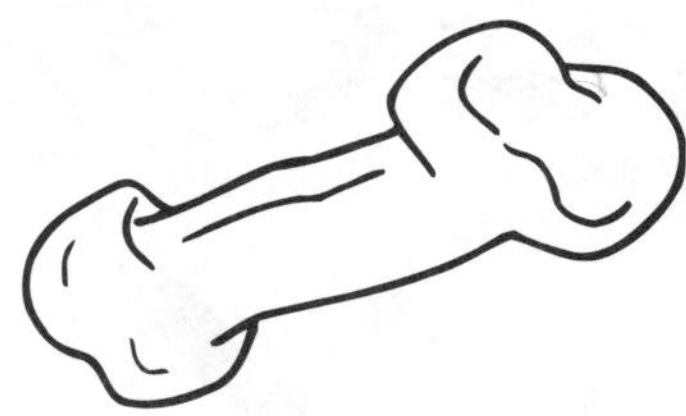

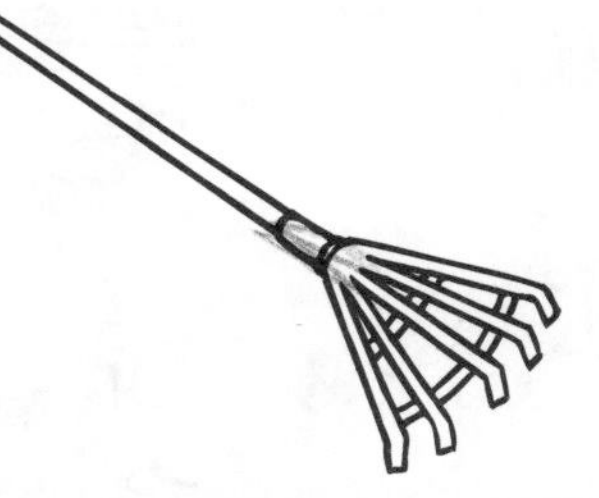

Name ______________________________

Long u and Short u

Directions: Say the name of each picture. Draw lines to match each picture with its name.

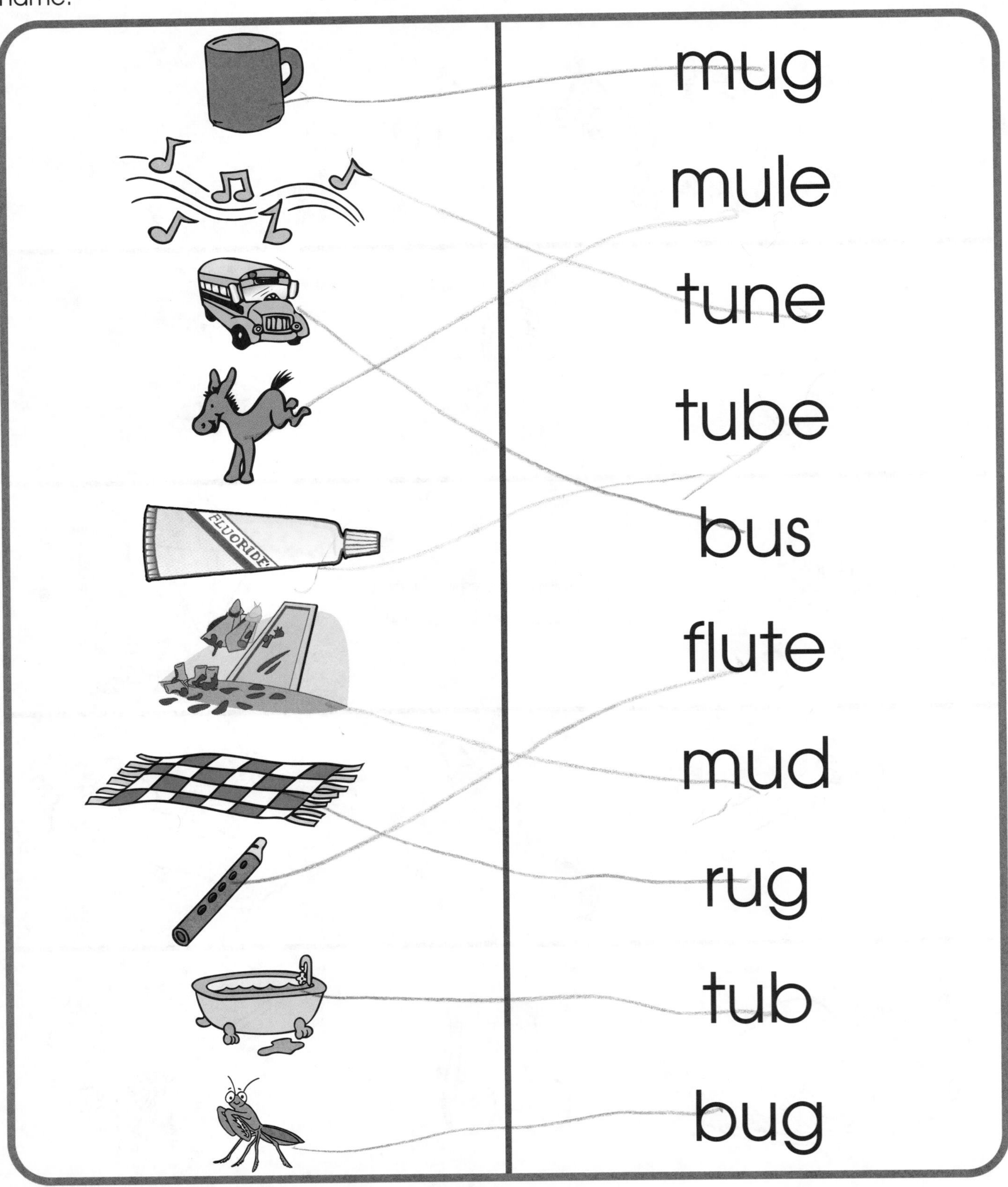

Name ______________________________

Long u

Directions: Say the name of each picture. Write a word from the Word Box that names each picture.

tube	ruler	cube	mule	tune	flute

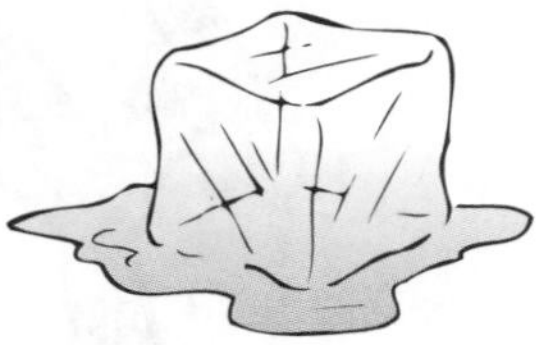

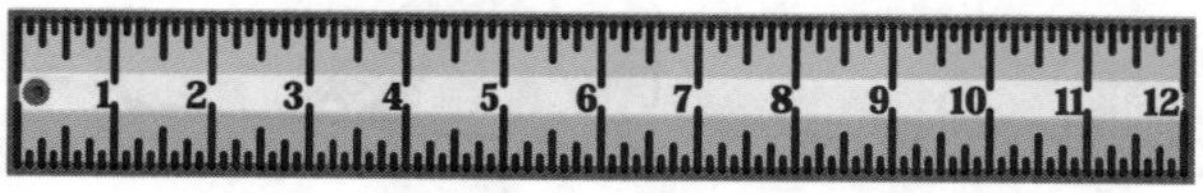

Name ______________________________

Long u

Directions: Write a word from the Word Box to complete each sentence.

ruler	mule	tube	cube	tune	flute

1. Tanya saw a ______________ at the farm.

2. Steve sings a ______________.

3. Becca plays the ______________.

4. Where is my ______________?

5. I found my ______________ of toothpaste.

6. I put a ______________ of ice in my cup.

Name ___________________________

Review: Long o and Long u

Directions: Say the name of each picture. Write the word from the Word Box that names each picture.

mule	hose	tune	cube	cone	pole	tube	robe	note

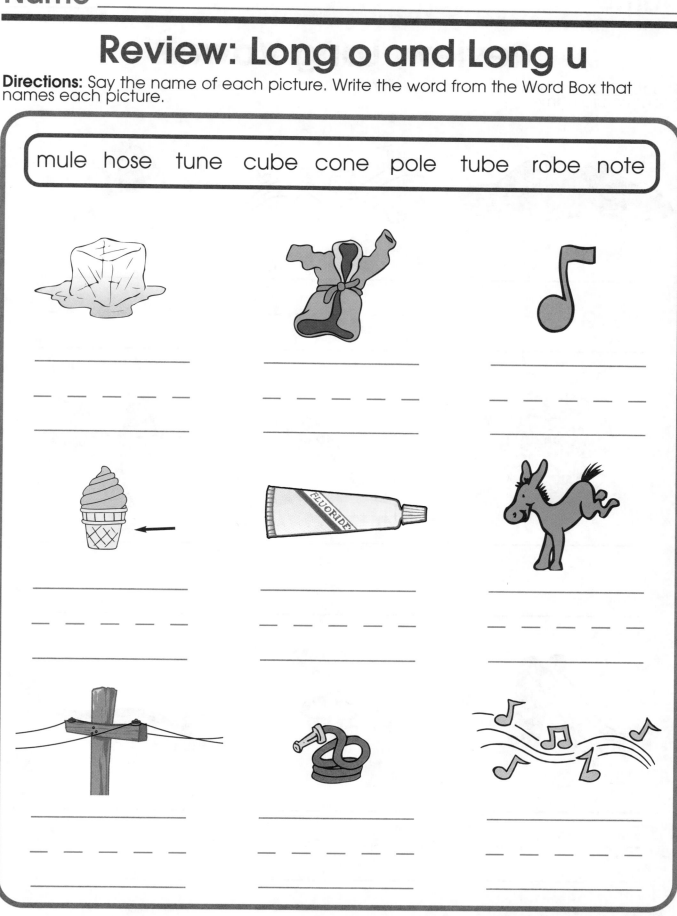

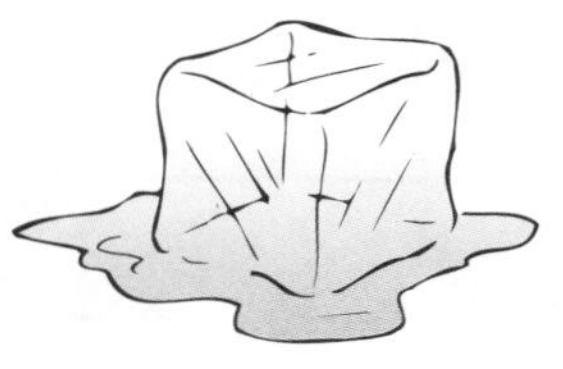

Name ___

Review: Long Vowels

Directions: Say the name of each picture. Write **a**, **i**, **o**, or **u** to show the vowel sound in each picture name.

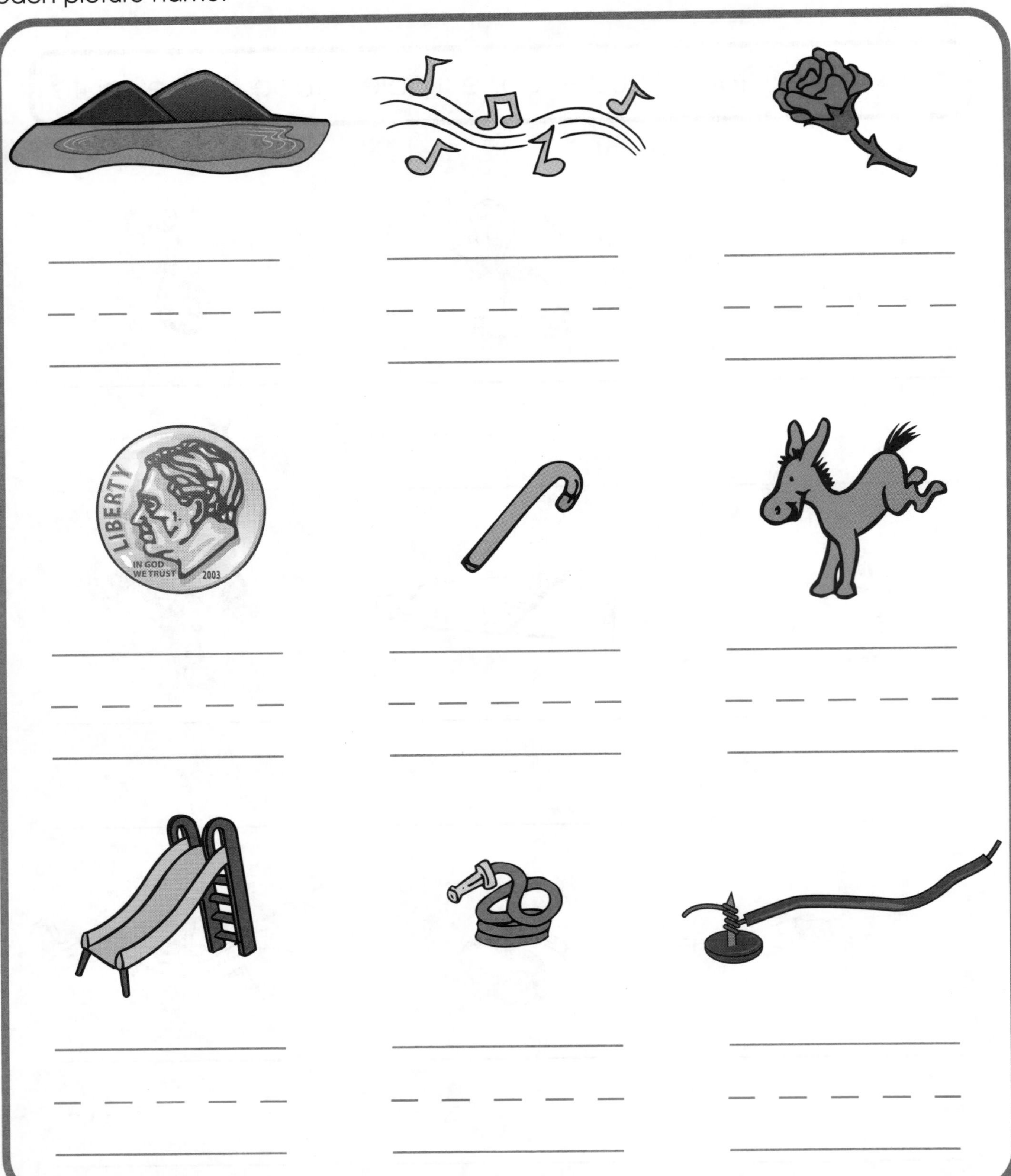

Name ______________________________

Review: Long Vowels

Directions: Say the name of each picture. Draw lines to match each picture with its name.

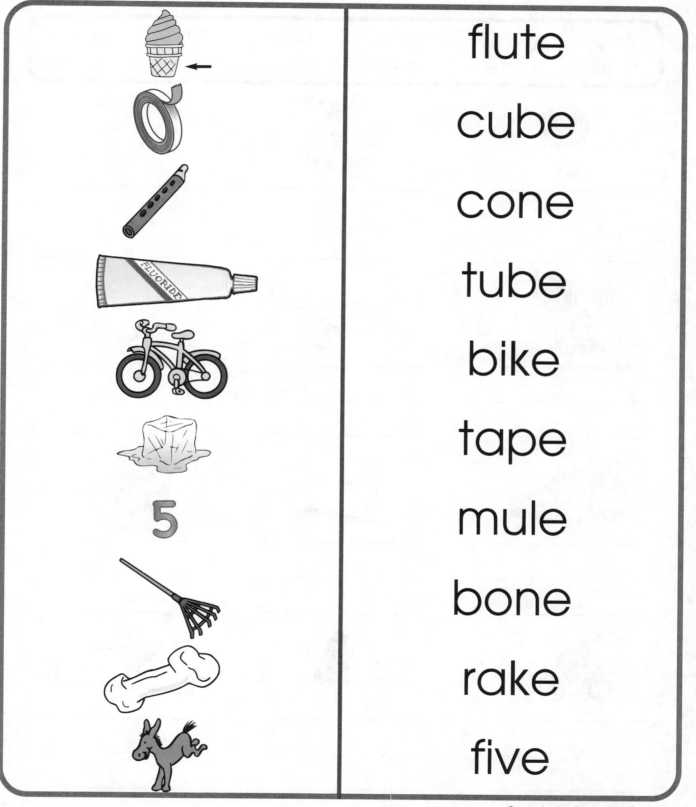

flute

cube

cone

tube

bike

tape

mule

bone

rake

five

Name ______________________________

Review: Long Vowels

Directions: Write the word from the Word Box that names each picture.

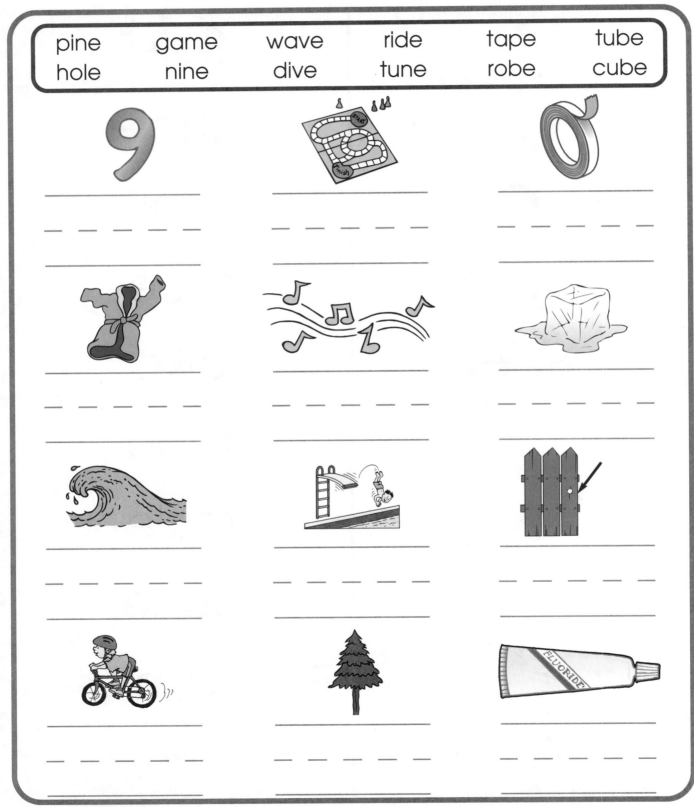

pine	game	wave	ride	tape	tube
hole	nine	dive	tune	robe	cube

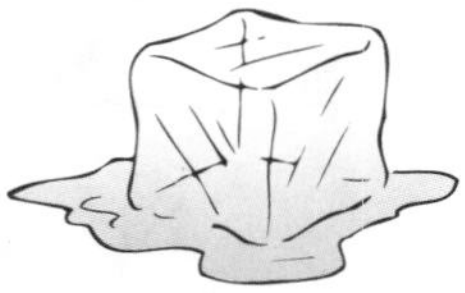

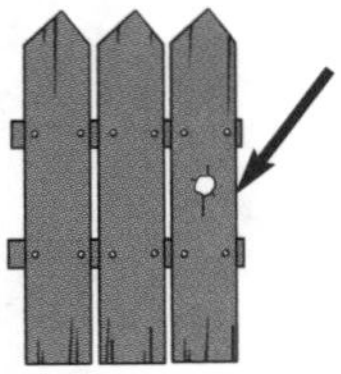

Name ______________________

Review: Long Vowels

Directions: Write a word that rhymes with each word below.

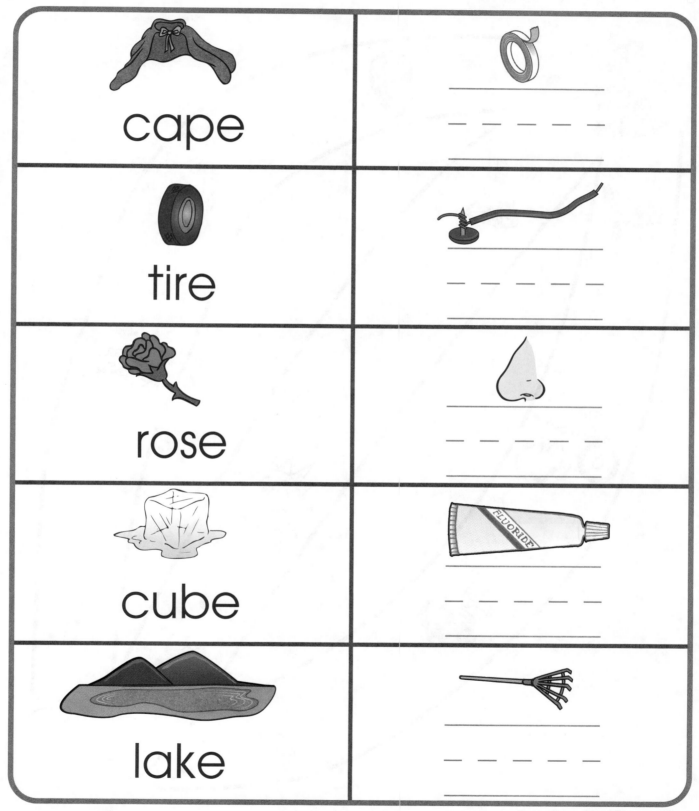

cape	______
tire	______
rose	______
cube	______
lake	______

Name ____

Review: Long Vowels

Directions: Help Fido find his bone. Draw a line along the path of pictures whose names all have long vowel sounds.

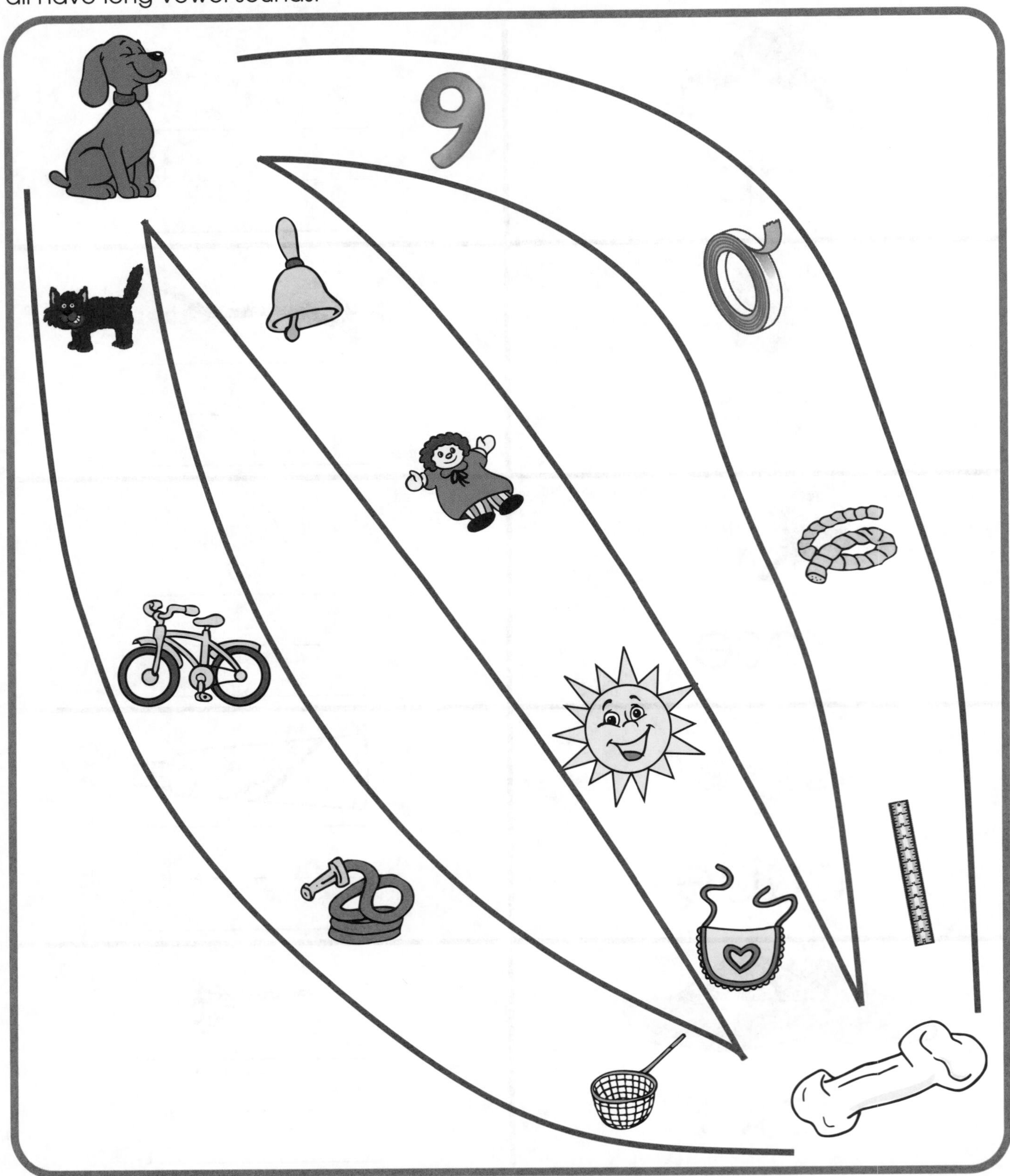

Name

Review: Long Vowels

Directions: Write a word from the Word Box to complete each sentence.

mule	bike	kite	robe	game	rose

1. The ______________ kicked its feet.

2. Nathan plays a ______________.

3. Michelle has on a ______________.

4. The ______________ is in the vase.

5. Debra rides a ______________.

6. The ______________ is in the sky.

Name ______________________________

Review: Long Vowels

Directions: Write a word from the Word Box to complete each sentence.

cape	bone	vine	tune	rope	mule

1. My brother has on a ______________.

2. My sister rides a ______________.

3. The ______________ grows on the ground.

4. Trevor plays a ______________.

5. The ______________ is in the garage.

6. The dog has a ______________.

Name ______________________________

Review: Long Vowels

Directions: Draw a picture of things whose names contain the long vowel sounds of the letters below.

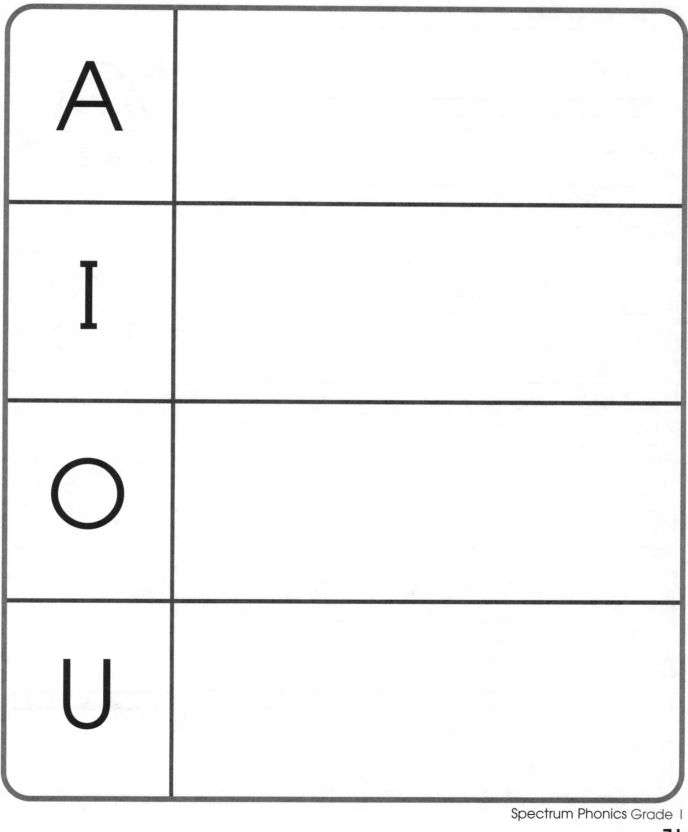

A	
I	
O	
U	

Name ______________________________

Review: Long Vowels

Directions: Write a sentence using each word that is pictured below.

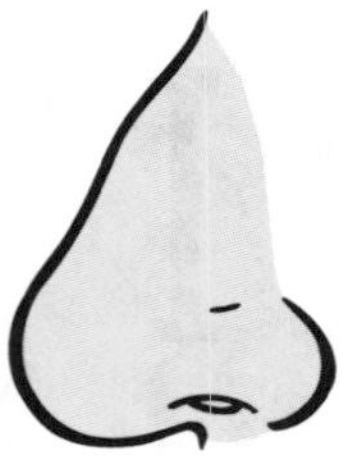

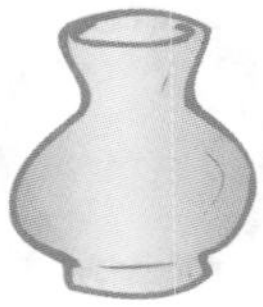

Name ____________________

Review: Short and Long Vowels

Directions: Say the name of each picture. Draw lines to match each picture with its name.

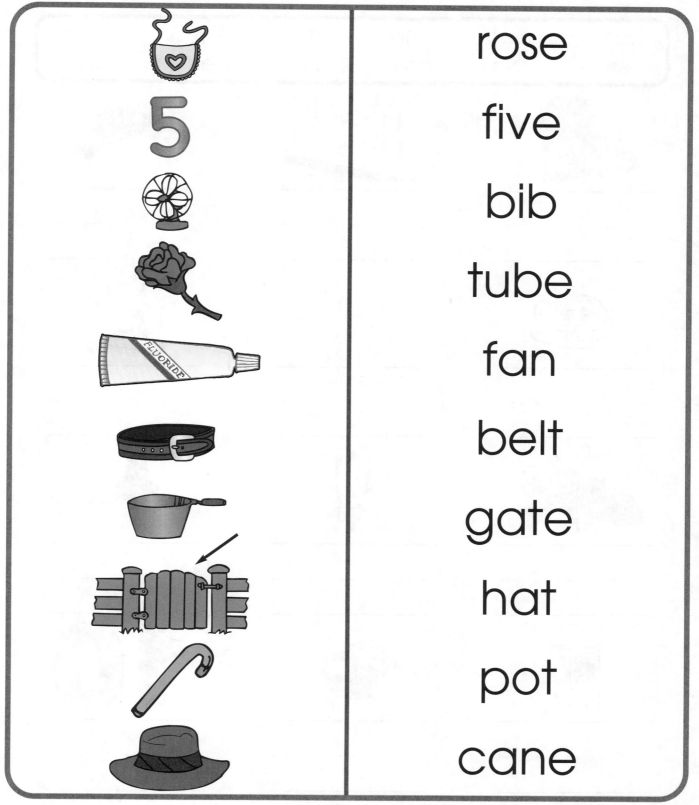

rose

five

bib

tube

fan

belt

gate

hat

pot

cane

Name ______________________________

Review: Short and Long Vowels

Directions: Say the name of each picture. Write the word from the Word Box that names each picture below.

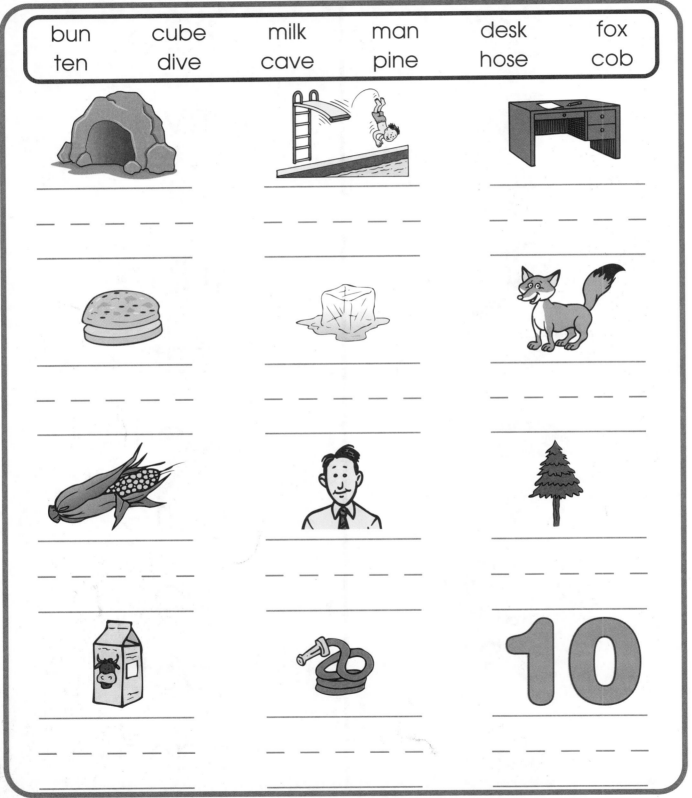

bun	cube	milk	man	desk	fox
ten	dive	cave	pine	hose	cob

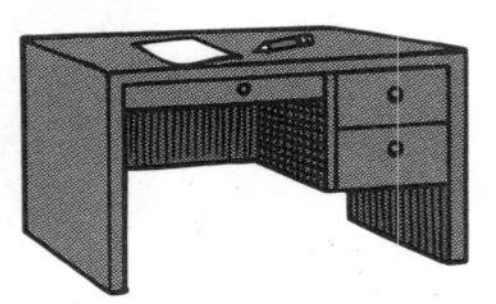

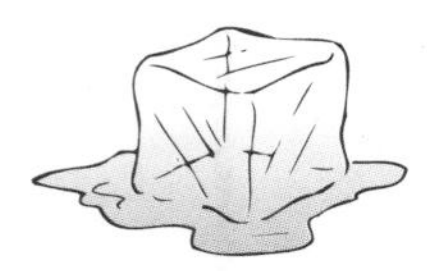

10

Name ____

Review: Short and Long Vowels

Directions: Draw a picture of what each word names below.

jet	mane	nose
hop	pen	fire
lake	bus	mule
pig	kite	bat

Name ______________________________

Review: Short and Long Vowels

Directions: Write a word from the Word Box to complete each sentence.

cub	cave	can	bike	box	hive

1. The ____________ is a baby bear.

2. The bear sleeps in a ____________.

3. Soup comes in a ____________.

4. I ride my ____________.

5. We put our toys away in the ____________.

6. The bee is in the ____________.

Name ______________________________

Review: Short and Long Vowels

Directions: Write 6 words that have a **short** vowel sound.

Directions: Write 6 words that have a **long** vowel sound.

Directions: Write a sentence using two words from your lists above. Choose one word that has a **short** vowel sound and one word that has a **long** vowel sound.

Name ______________________________

Review: Short and Long Vowels

Directions: Write a word from the Word Box to complete each sentence.

cane	kite	tape	tub	rug	cap

1. Grandpa uses a ____________.

2. Dad has the ____________.

3. Take a bath in the ____________.

4. The cat sleeps on the ____________.

5. Please wear your ____________ outside.

6. My cousins fly a ____________.

Name ___________________________

Review: Short and Long Vowels

Directions: Make a new word by adding the letter **e** to each word below.

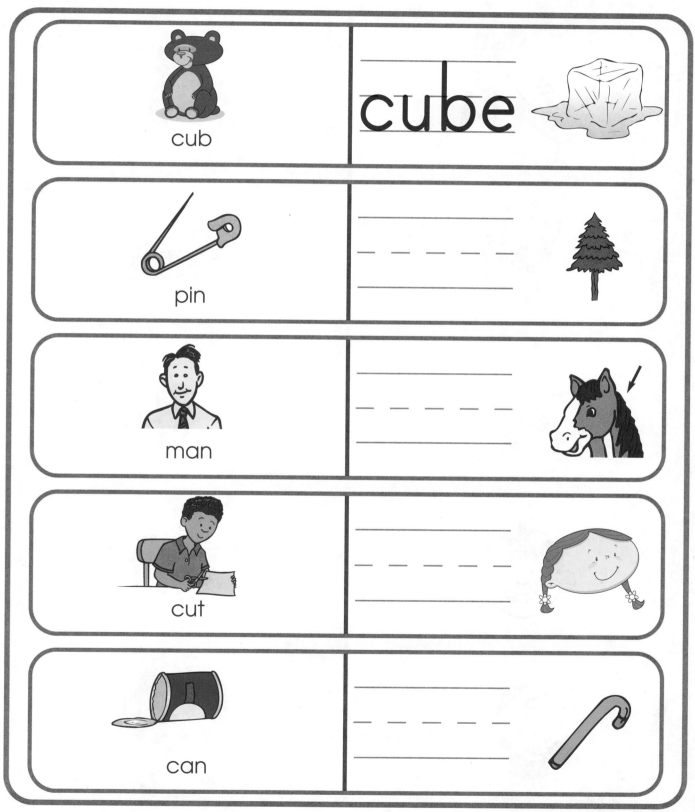

cub	cube
pin	
man	
cut	
can	

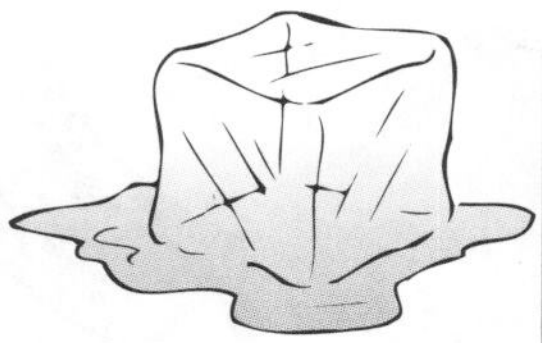

Name ______________________________

Consonant Blends With S

Directions: Say the name of each picture. Draw lines to match the pictures that have the same beginning blend.

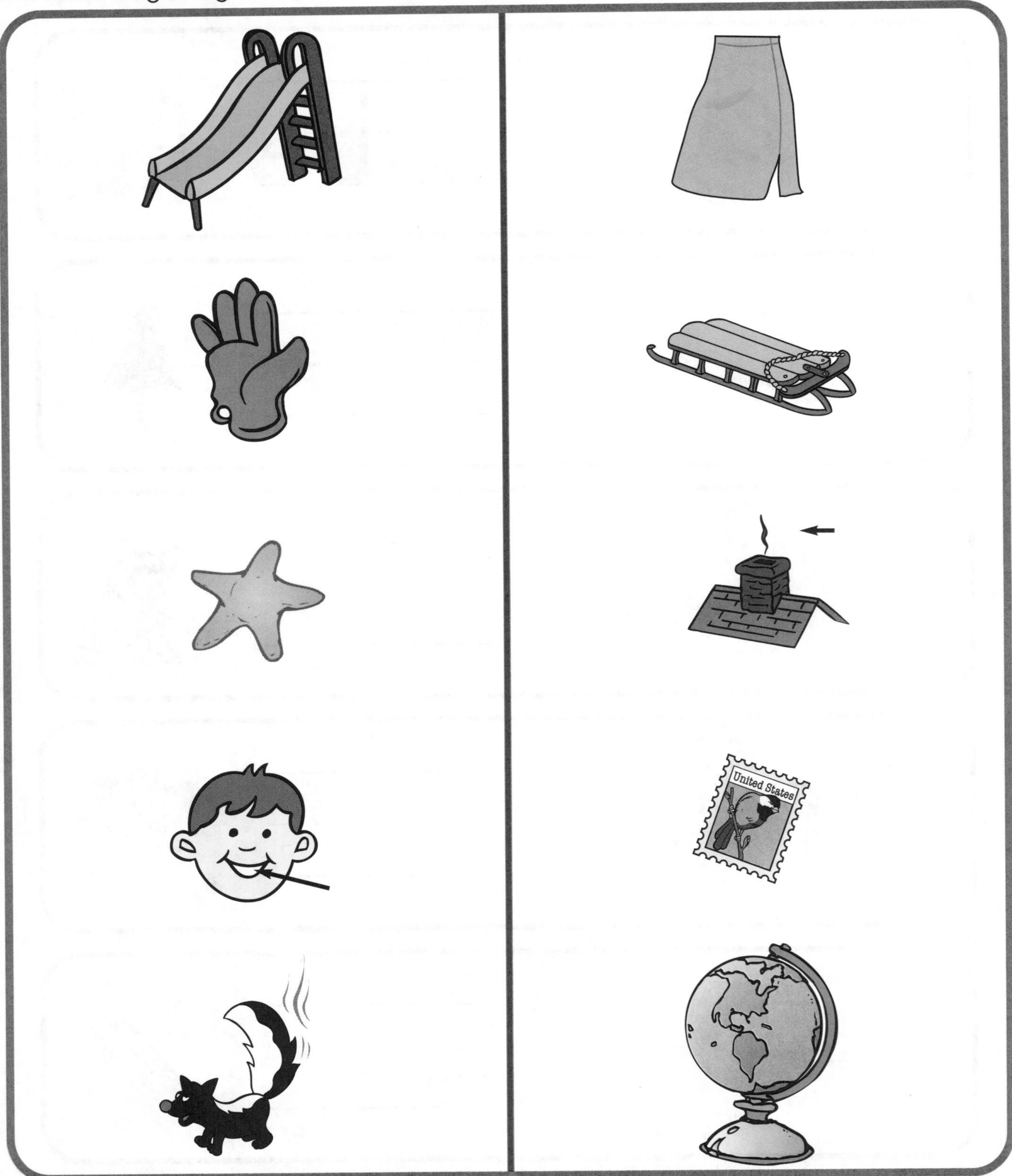

Name ___________________________

Consonant Blends With S

Directions: Say the name of each picture. Circle the pictures in each row that have the same beginning blend.

Name ________________________________

Consonant Blends With S

Directions: Say the name of each picture. Write the **s** blend that completes each word.

sk sl sm sp

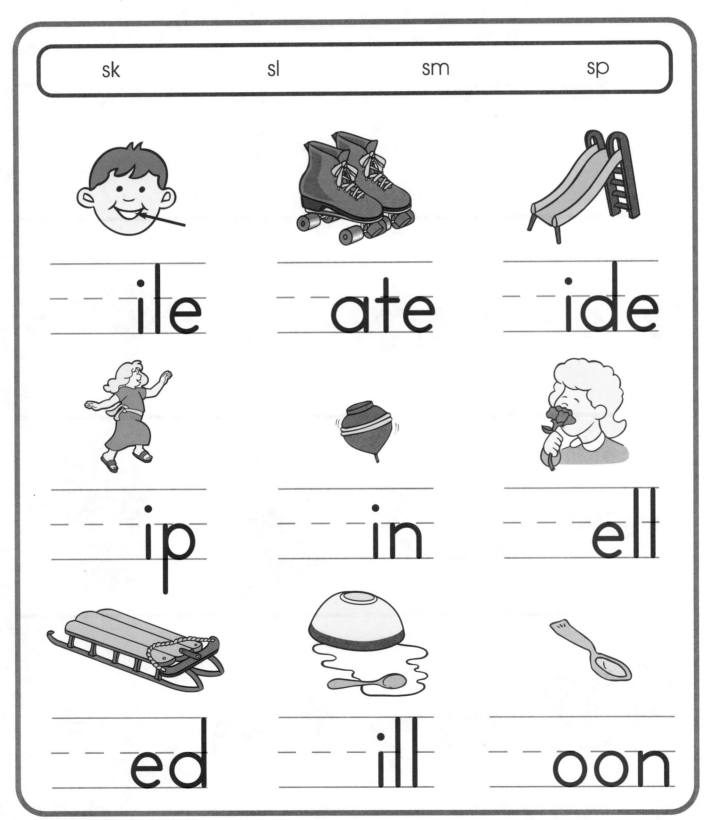

____ile ____ate ____ide

____ip ____in ____ell

____ed ____ill ____oon

Name ______________________________

Consonant Blends With S

Directions: Say the name of each picture. Write the **s** blend that completes each word.

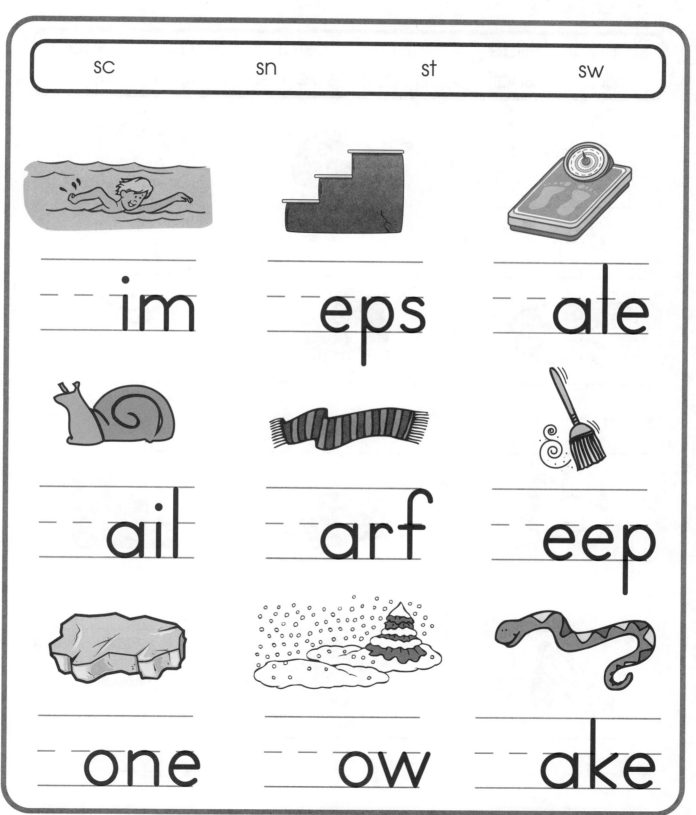

sc	sn	st	sw

____im ____eps ____ale

____ail ____arf ____eep

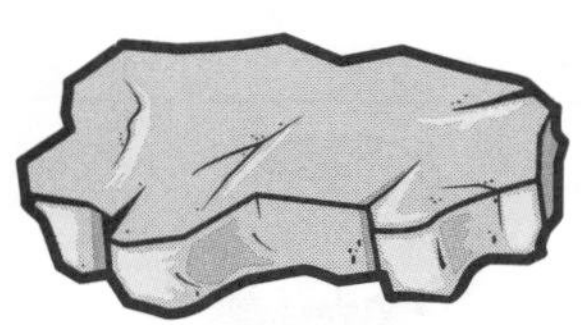

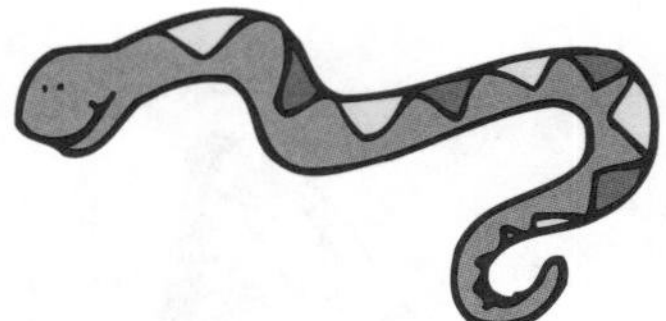

____one ____ow ____ake

Name ______________________________

Review: Consonant Blends With S

Directions: Say the name of each picture. Write the word from the Word Box that names each picture.

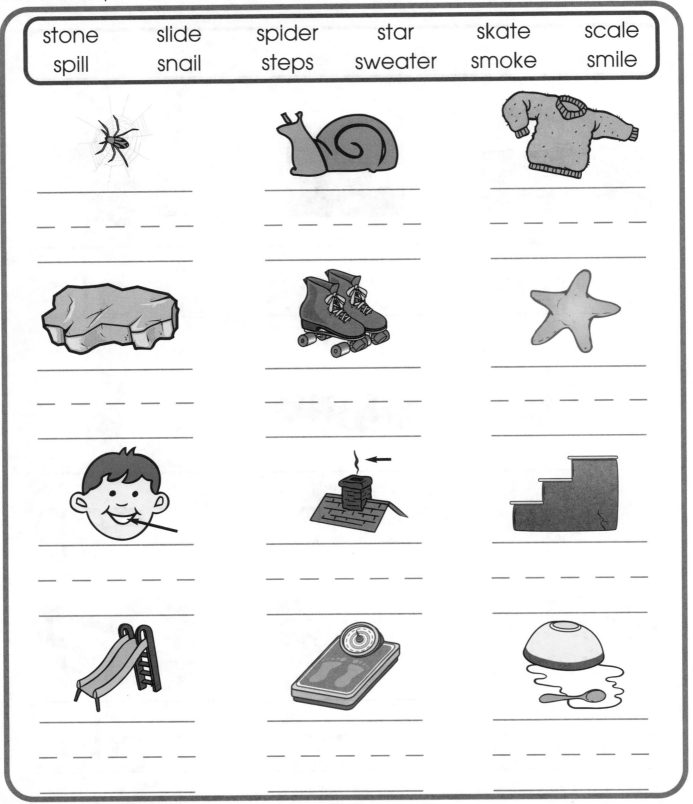

stone	slide	spider	star	skate	scale
spill	snail	steps	sweater	smoke	smile

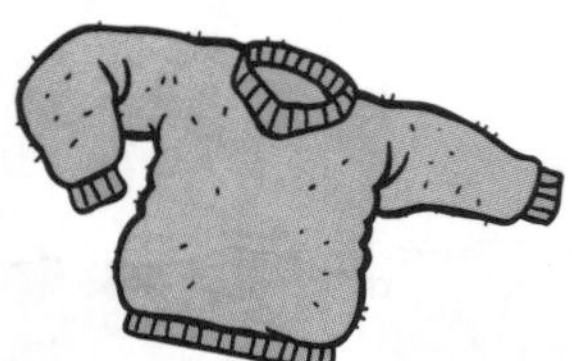

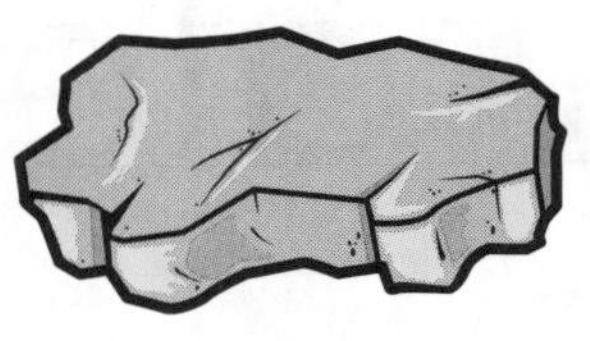

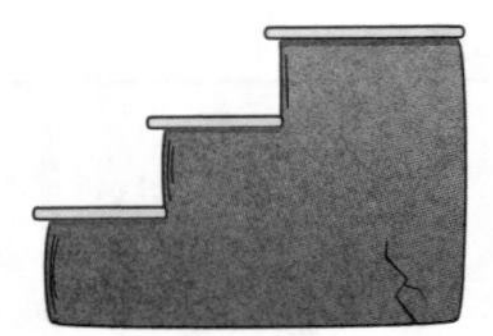

Name ______________________________

Consonant Blends With L

Directions: Say the name of each picture. Draw lines to match the pictures whose names have the same beginning blend.

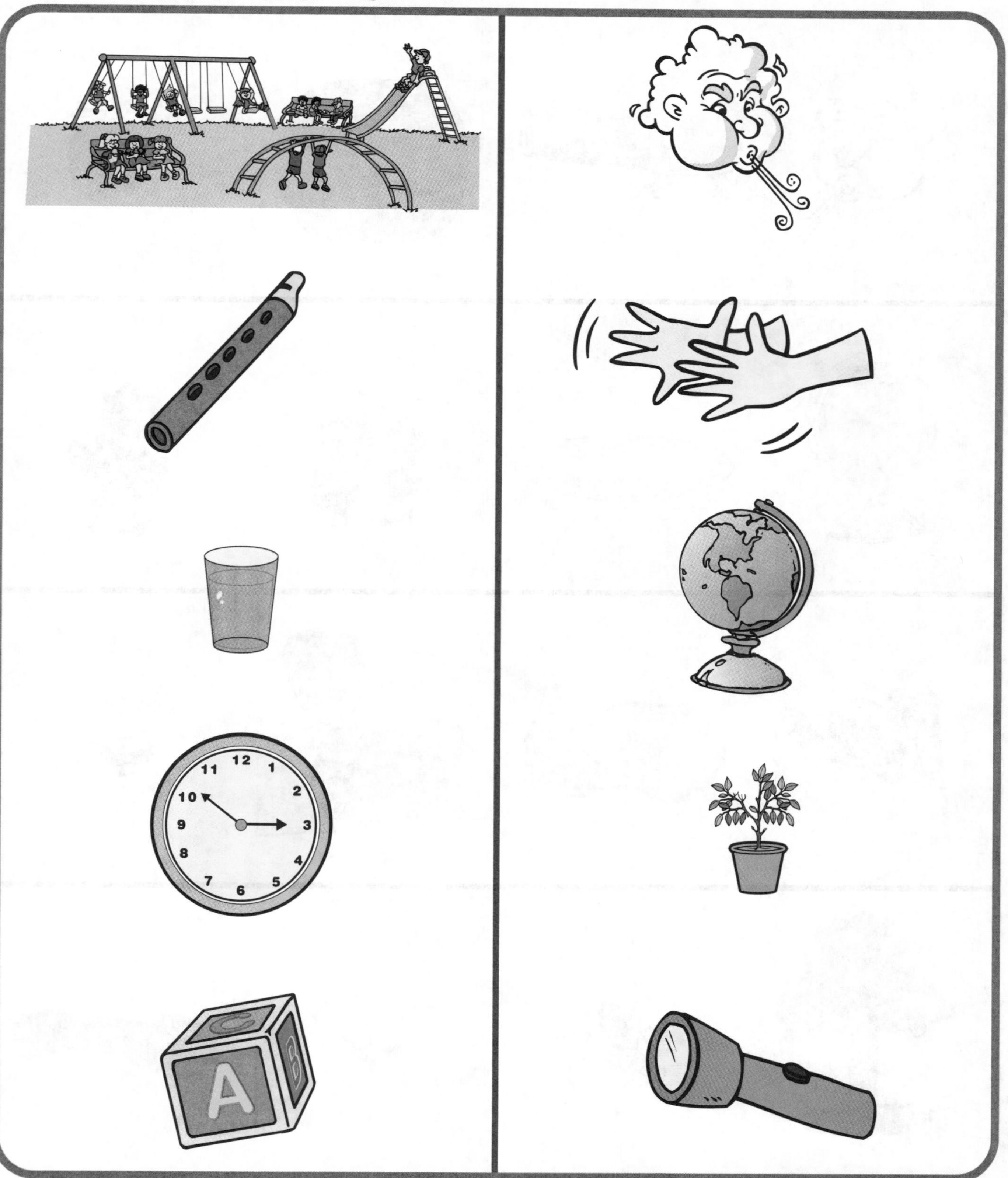

Name ____________________

Consonant Blends With L

Directions: Say the name of each picture. Circle the pictures in each row whose names have the same beginning blend.

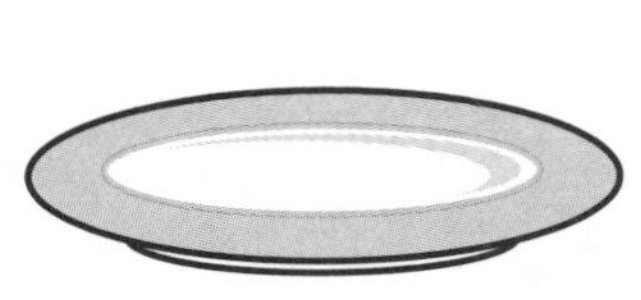

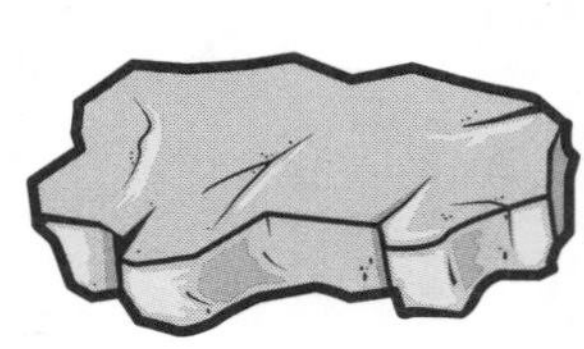

Name ______________________________

Consonant Blends With L

Directions: Say the name of each picture. Write the **l** blend that completes each word.

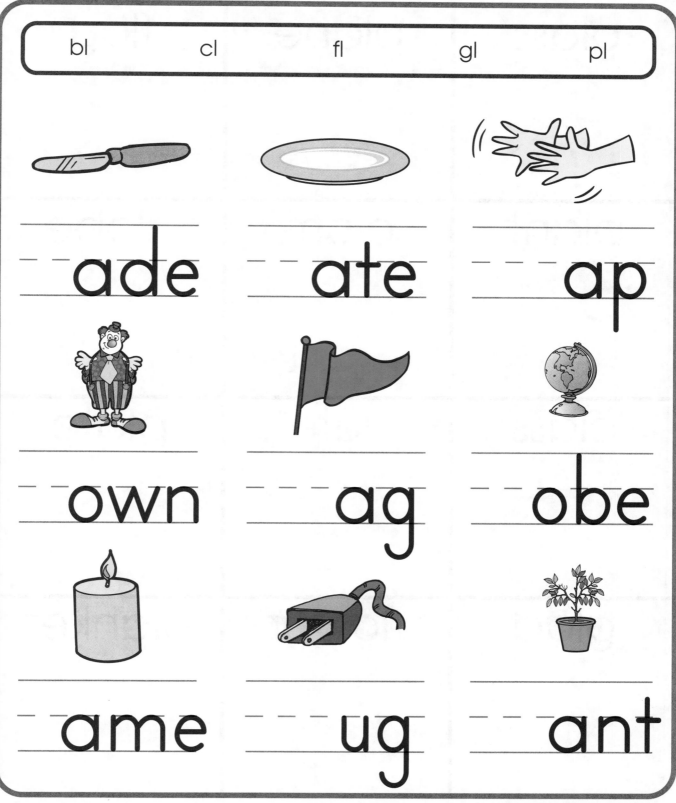

bl cl fl gl pl

____ade ____ate ____ap

____own ____ag ____obe

____ame ____ug ____ant

Name ________________________________

Consonant Blends With L

Directions: Draw a picture of what each word names below.

glass	plane	flag
plant	clam	globe
class	flute	plate
glad	flower	blanket

Name ____________________

Review: Consonant Blends With L

Directions: Say the name of each picture. Write the word from the Word Box that names each picture.

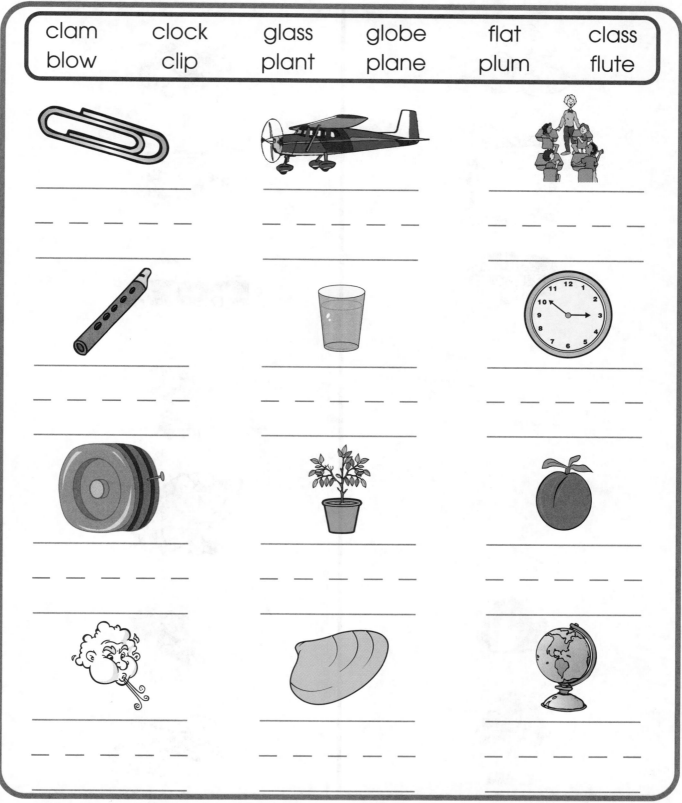

clam	clock	glass	globe	flat	class
blow	clip	plant	plane	plum	flute

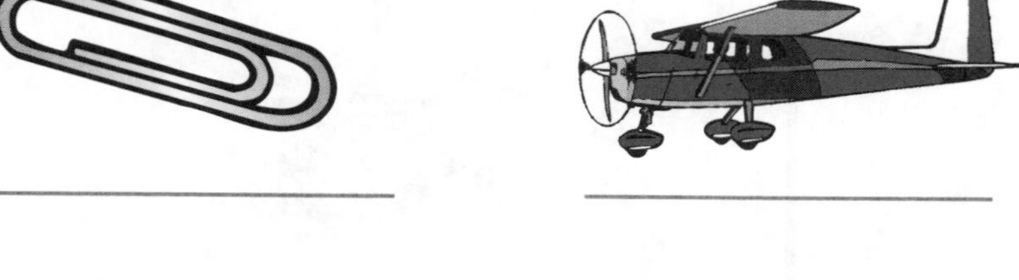

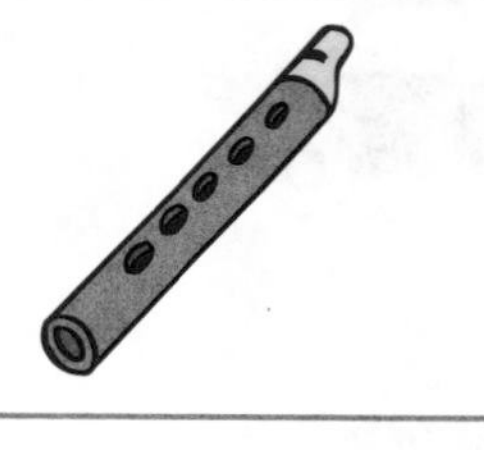

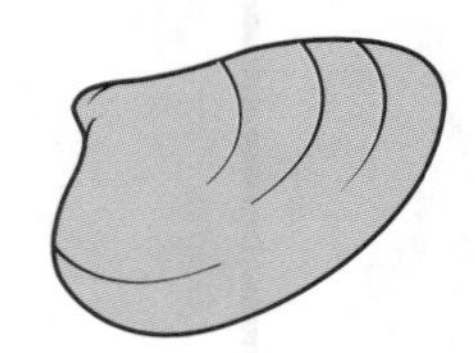

Name ___________________________________

Consonant Blends With R

Directions: Say the name of each picture. Draw lines to match the pictures whose names have the same beginning blend.

Name ___________________________________

Consonant Blends With R

Directions: Say the name of each picture. Circle the pictures in each row whose names have the same beginning blend.

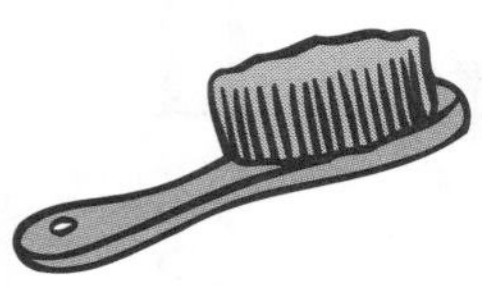

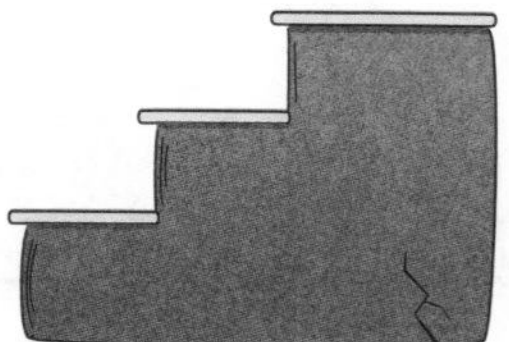

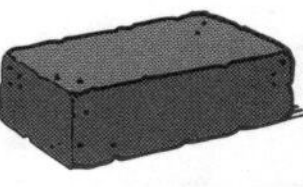

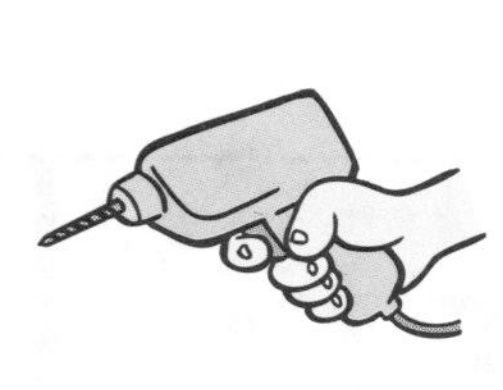

Name ______________________________

Consonant Blends With R

Directions: Say the name of each picture. Write the **r** blend that completes each word.

br cr dr fr

___og  ___ab  ___ill

___ide  ___uit  ___ame

___ip  ___own  ___ead

Name ______________________________

Consonant Blends With R

Directions: Say the name of each picture. Write the **r** blend that completes each word.

gr pr tr

____ill ____apes ____ize

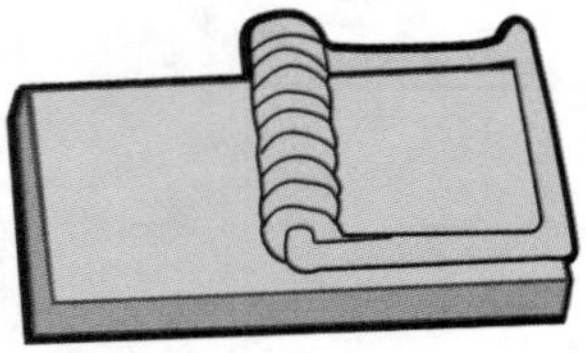

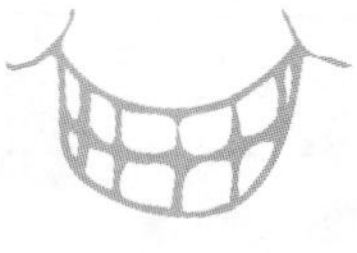

____ip ____ap ____in

____aze ____ain ____esent

Name ______________________________

Review: Consonant Blends With R

Directions: Say the name of each picture. Write the word from the Word Box that names each picture.

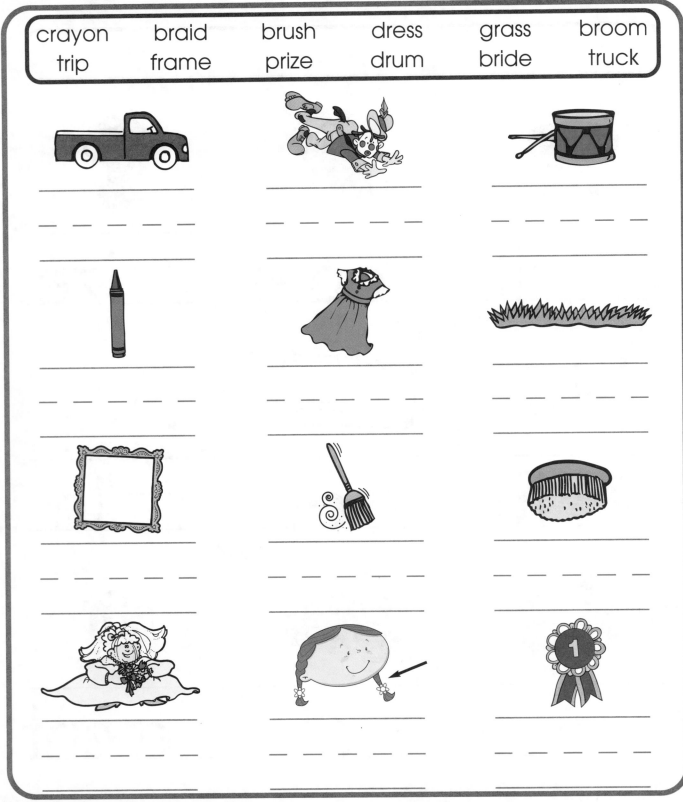

crayon	braid	brush	dress	grass	broom
trip	frame	prize	drum	bride	truck

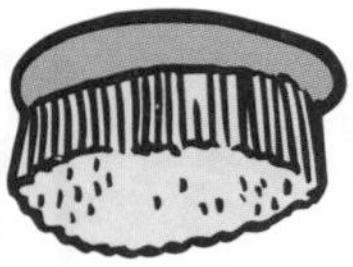

Name ____

Final Blends With S

Directions: Say the name of each picture. Circle the pictures in each row whose names have the same ending blend.

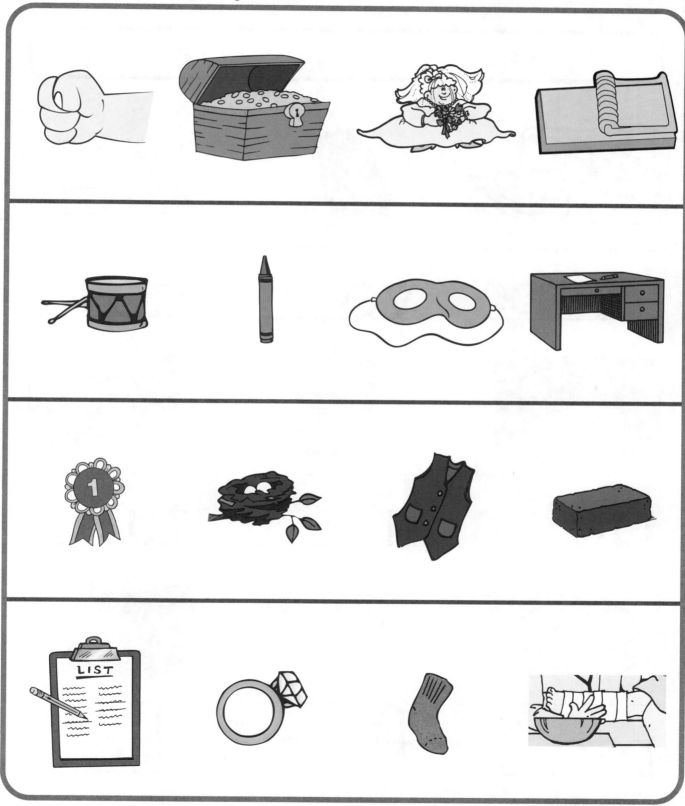

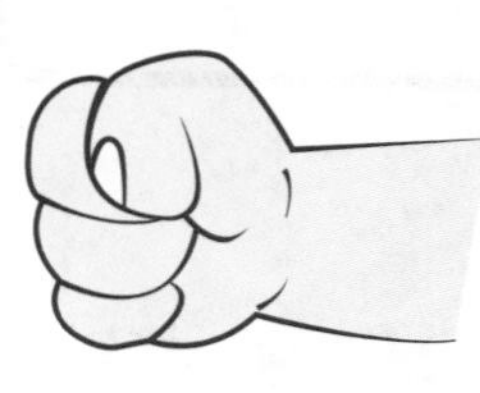

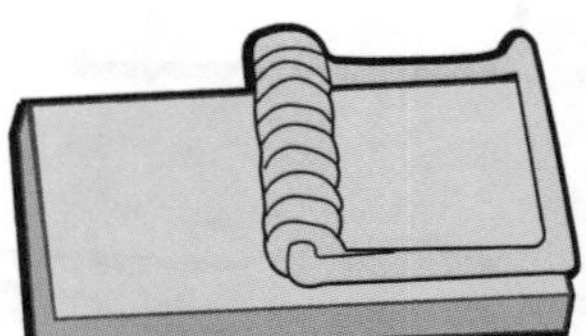

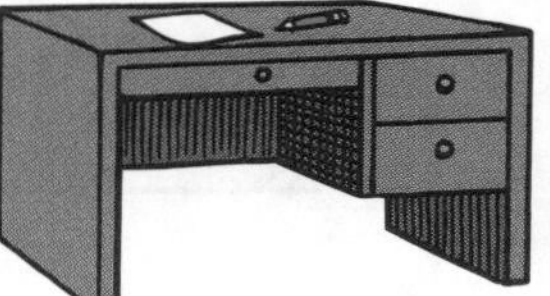

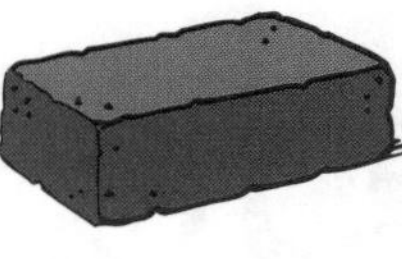

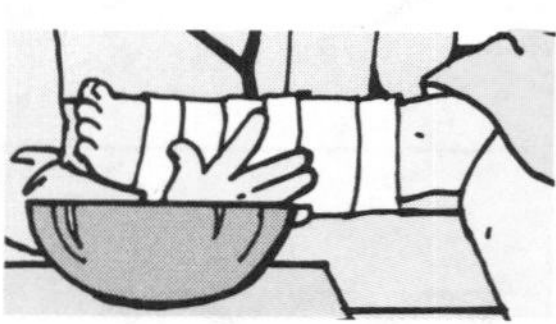

Name ______________________________

Final Blends With S

Directions: Say the name of each picture. Write the final **s** blend that completes each word.

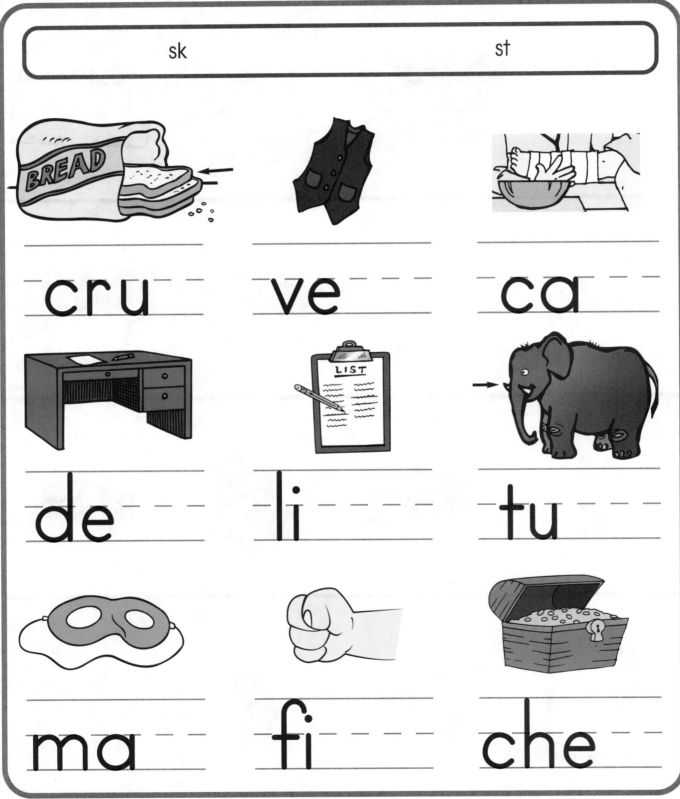

sk st

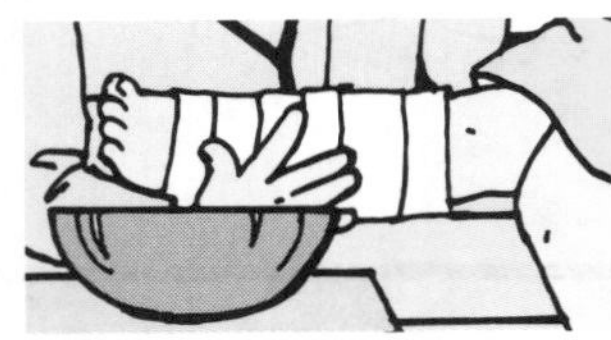

cru ____ ve ____ ca ____

de ____ li ____ tu ____

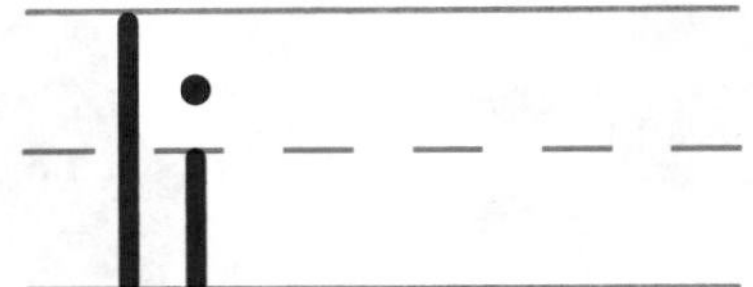

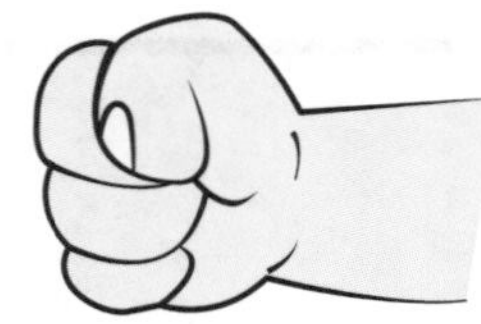

ma ____ fi ____ che ____

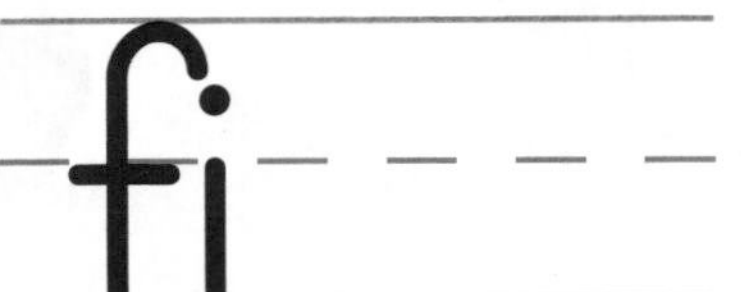

Name

Review: Final Blends With S

Directions: Say the name of each picture. Write the word from the Word Box that names each picture.

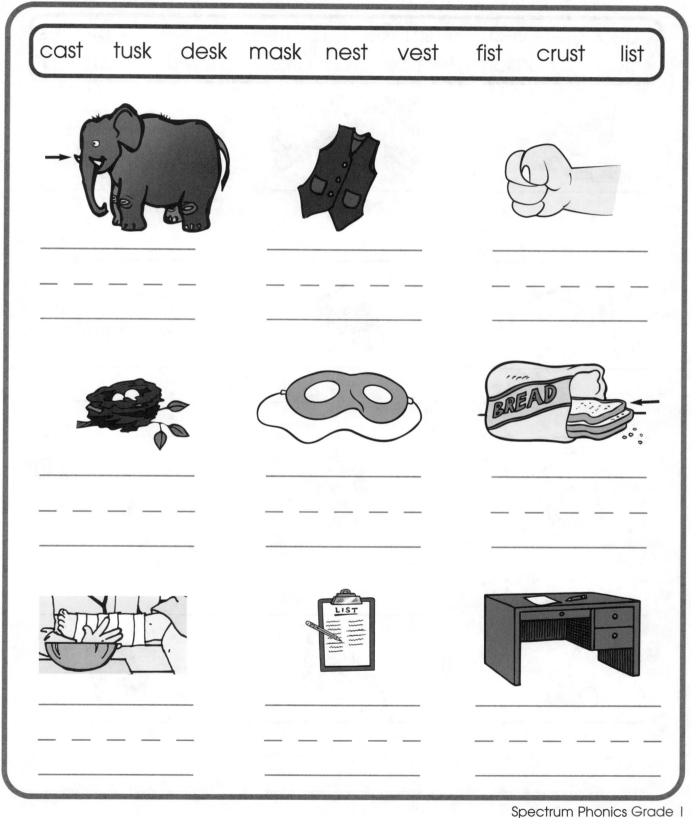

cast	tusk	desk	mask	nest	vest	fist	crust	list

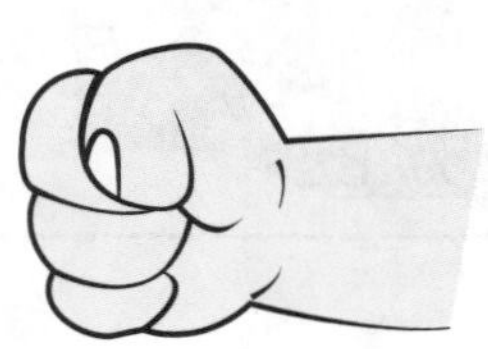

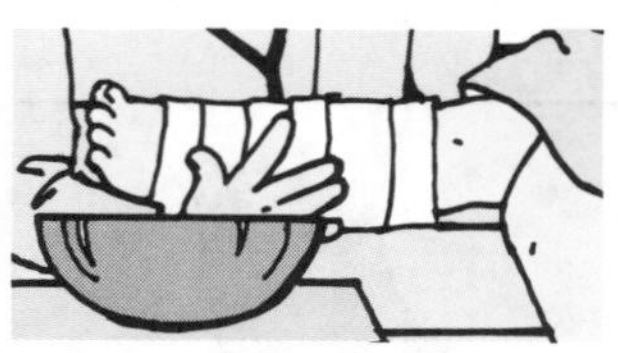

Name ______________________________

Review: Consonant Blends

Directions: Say the name of each picture. Write the word from the Word Box that names each picture.

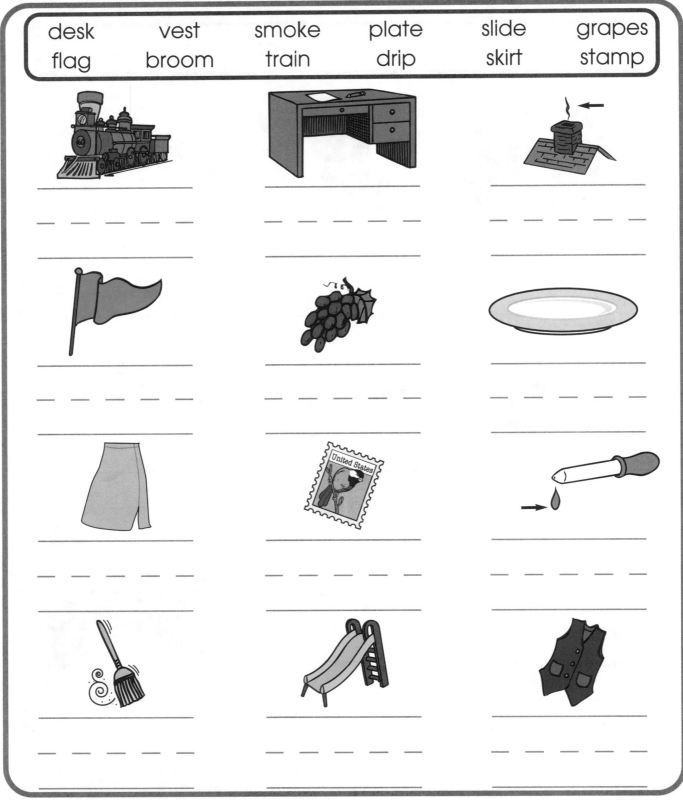

desk	vest	smoke	plate	slide	grapes
flag	broom	train	drip	skirt	stamp

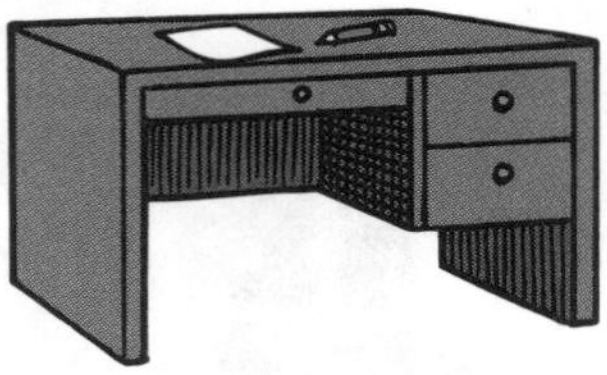

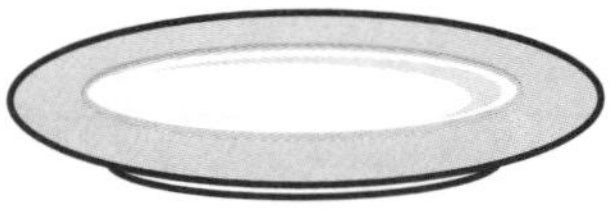

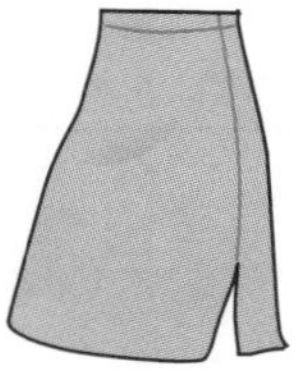

Name ______________________________

Vowel Pairs: AI and AY

The vowel pairs **ai** and **ay** make the sound of long **a**.

tr**ai**n  h**ay**

Directions: Say the name of each picture. Draw lines to match each picture with its name.

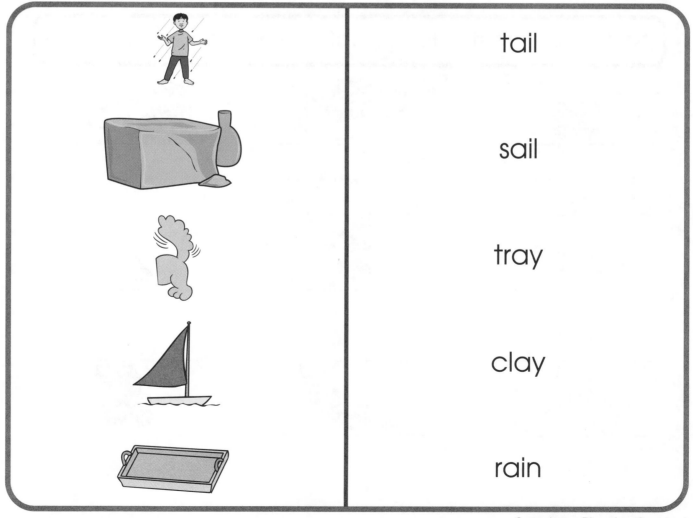

	tail
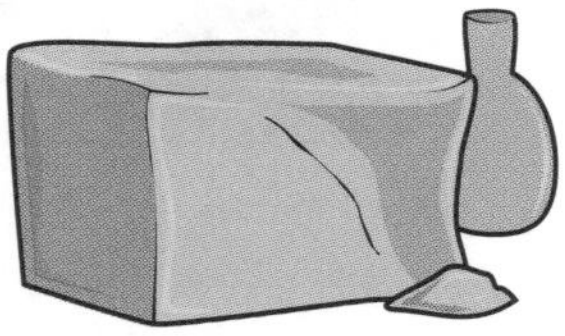	sail
	tray
	clay
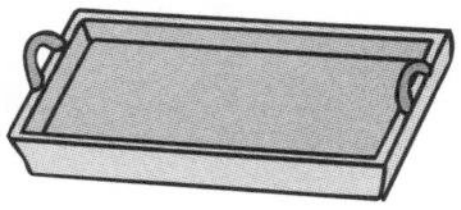	rain

Name ___________________________

Vowel Pairs: EE and EA

The vowel pairs **ee** and **ea** make the sound of long **e**.

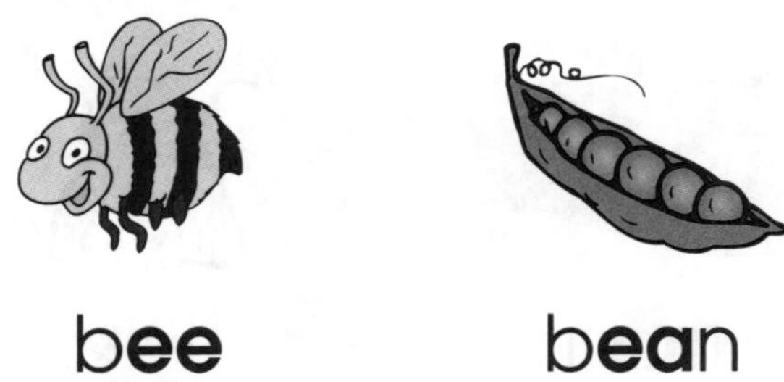

b**ee** b**ea**n

Directions: Say the name of each picture. Write a word from the Word Box that names each picture.

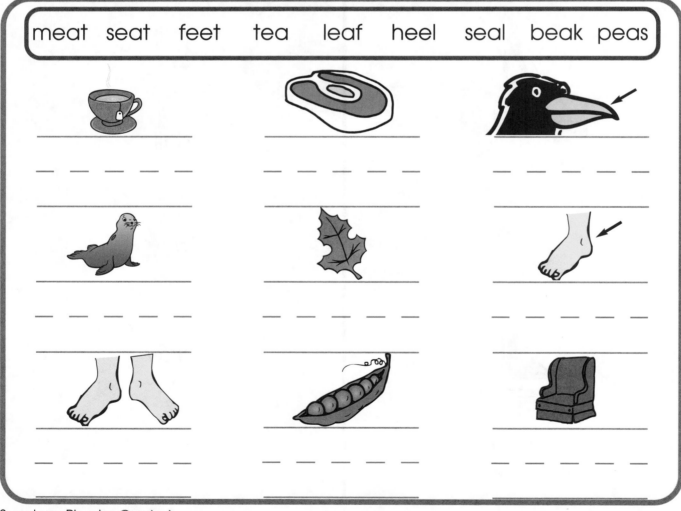

meat	seat	feet	tea	leaf	heel	seal	beak	peas

Name ______________________________

Review: Vowel Pairs With A and E

Directions: Say the name of each picture. Write a word that rhymes with each word on the left.

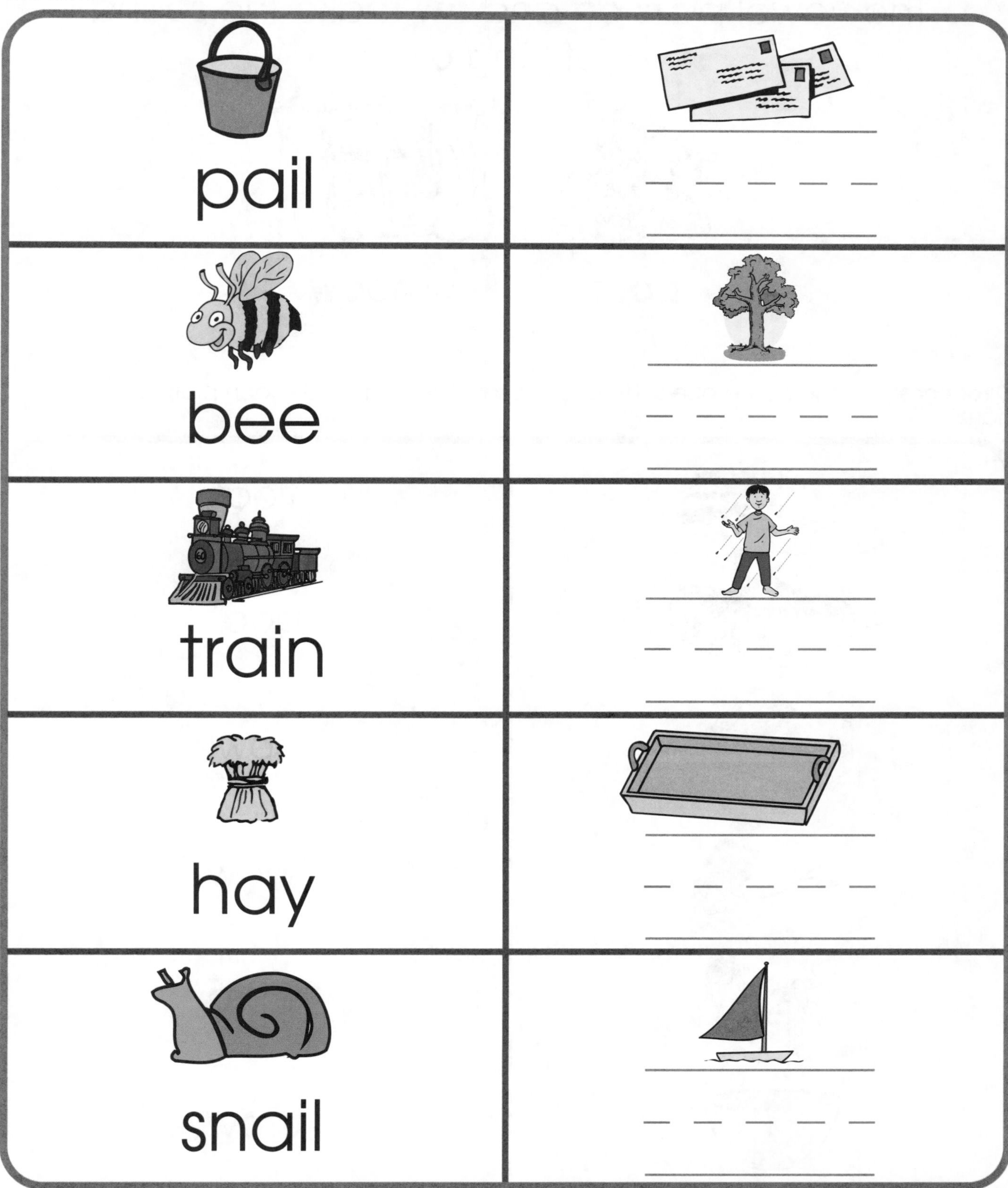

Name ___________________________

Vowel Pairs: OA and OW

The vowel pairs **oa** and **ow** make the sound of long **o**.

c**oa**t windo**w**

Directions: Say the name of each picture. Draw lines to match each picture with its name.

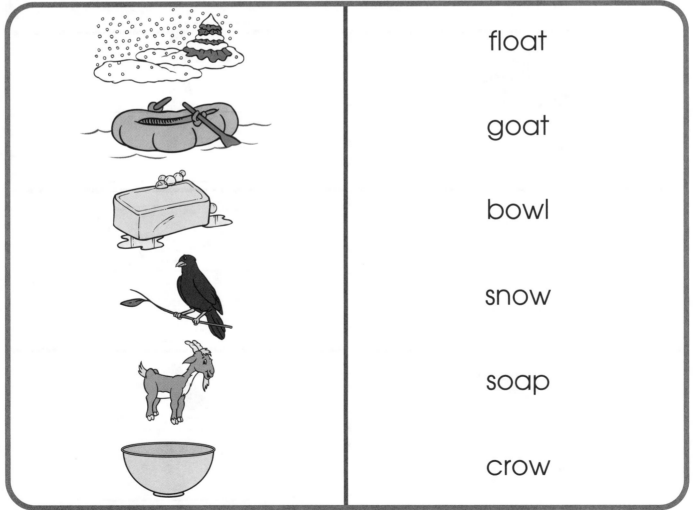

float

goat

bowl

snow

soap

crow

Name ______________________________

Vowel Pairs: OO

The vowel pair **oo** makes the sound you hear in the middle of the word **moon**.

m**oo**n

Directions: Write the missing letters **oo** for each word.

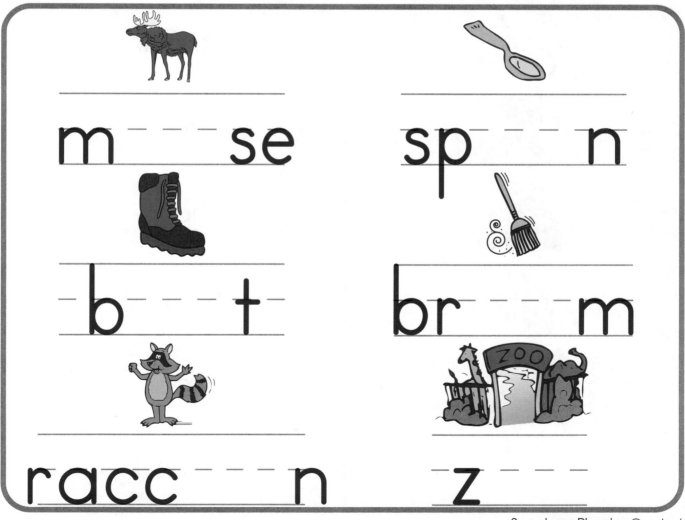

m ___ se

sp ___ n

b ___ t

br ___ m

racc ___ n

z ___

Name ______________________________

Vowel Pairs: OO

The vowel pair **oo** makes another sound. It is the sound you hear in the middle of the word **book**.

b**oo**k

Directions: Say the name of each picture. Draw lines to match each picture to its name.

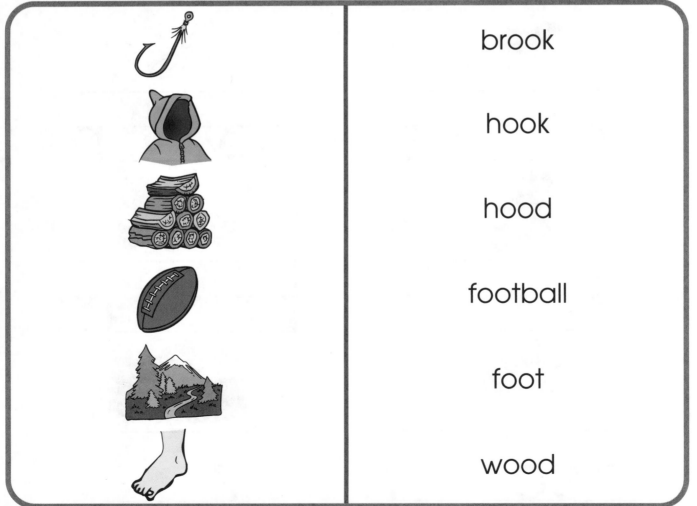

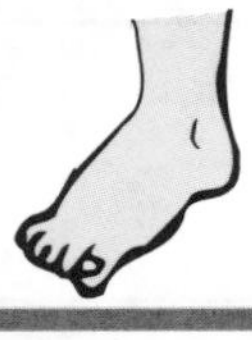

brook

hook

hood

football

foot

wood

Name ______________________________

Vowel Pairs: OO

Directions: Each of the words below have the vowel pair **oo**. Draw a picture of each word.

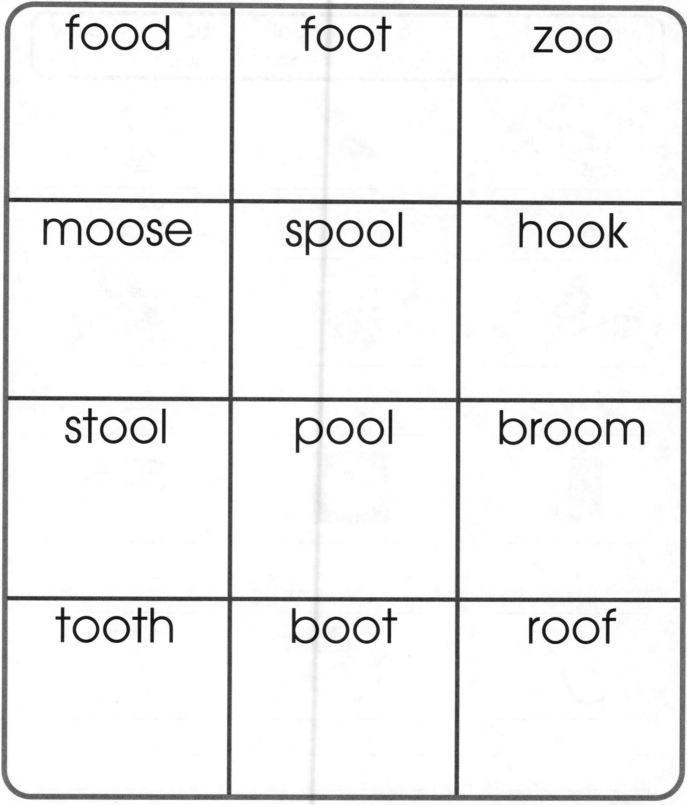

food	foot	zoo
moose	spool	hook
stool	pool	broom
tooth	boot	roof

Name ____

Review: Vowel Pairs With OA, OO, OW

Directions: Say the name of each picture. Write the word from the Word Box that names each picture.

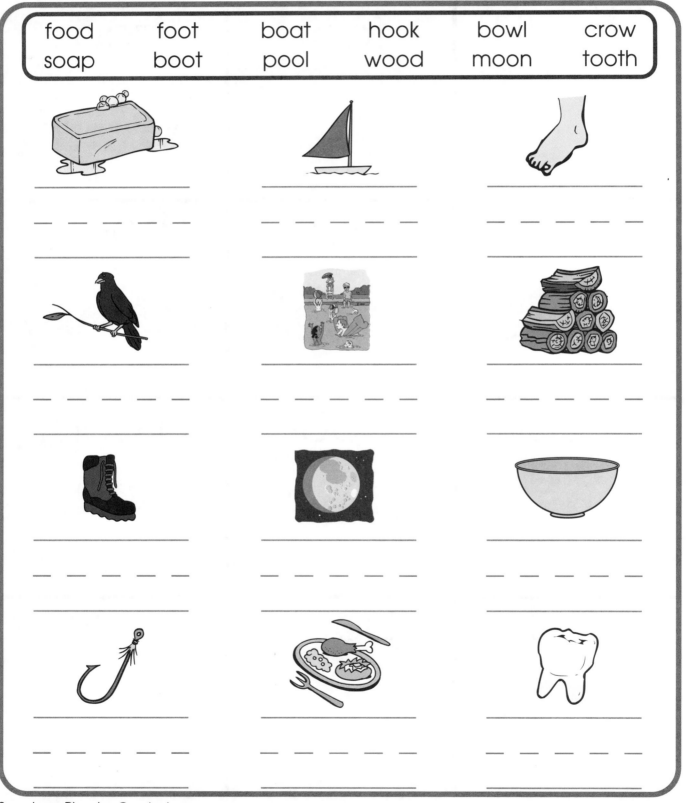

food	foot	boat	hook	bowl	crow
soap	boot	pool	wood	moon	tooth

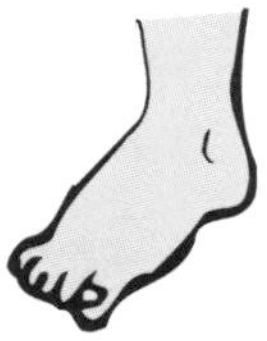

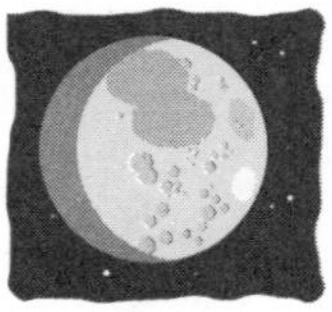

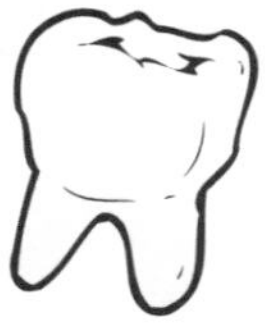

Name ____________________

Y as Long i

At the end of some words,
the letter **y** has the long **i** sound.

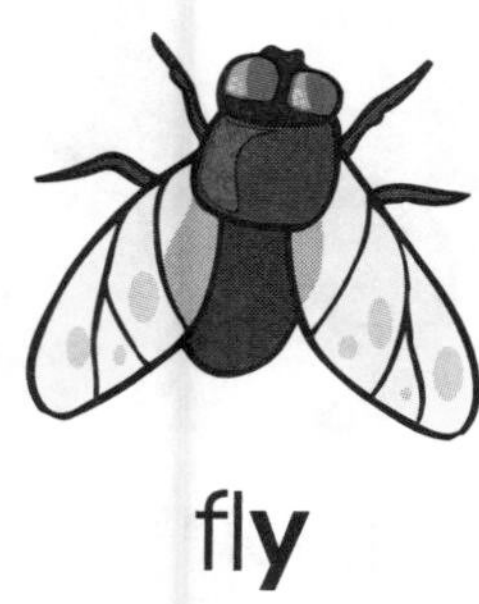

fl**y**

Directions: Name each picture and write the word from the Word Box. Then, write two sentences. Use one word from the Word Box in each sentence.

cry	fry	fly	sky

____

____

____

____

1. ____________________

2. ____________________

Name ______________________________

Y as Long e

At the end of some words, the letter **y** has the long **e** sound.

pon**y**

Directions: Say the name of each picture. Write the word from the Word Box that names each picture.

puppy	baby	lady	city

1. ______________________________

2. ______________________________

Name ___________________________

Review: The Sounds of Y

Directions: Each of the words below have one of the two sounds of **y**. Draw a picture of each word.

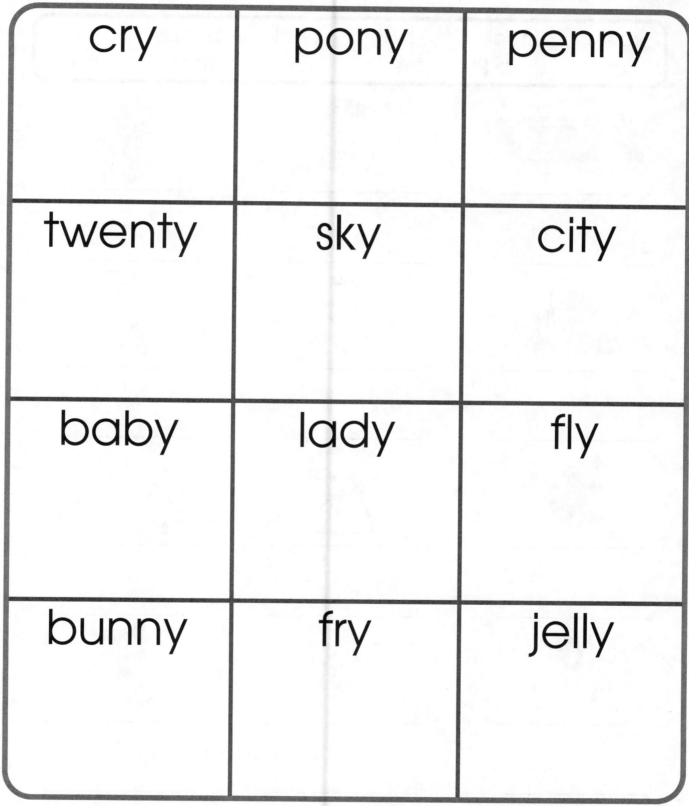

cry	pony	penny
twenty	sky	city
baby	lady	fly
bunny	fry	jelly

Name ___________________________

Review: Vowel Pairs and Sounds of Y

Directions: Say the name of each picture. Write the word from the Word Box that names each picture.

rain	stool	fly	book	puppy	leaf
tray	hood	feet	city	tooth	hay

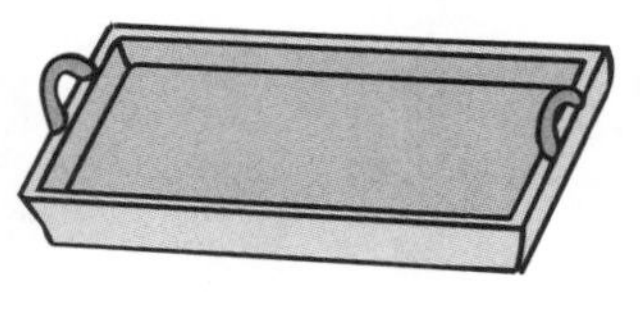

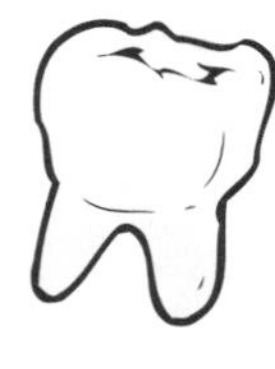

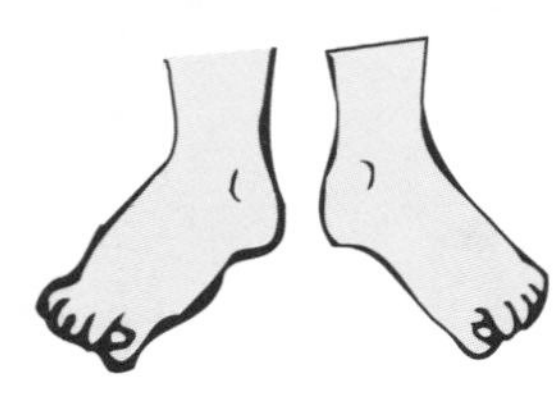

Name ______________________________

Consonant Pairs: CH and SH

chair

shoe

Directions: Say the name of each picture. Circle the pictures in each row that have the same beginning sound.

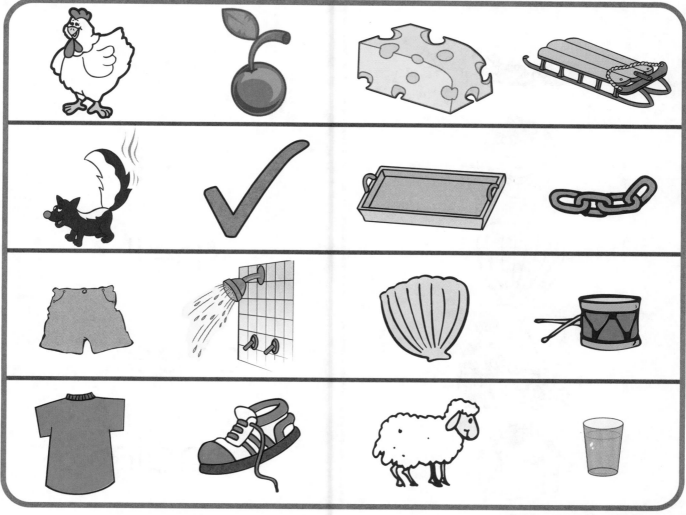

Name ____________________

Consonant Pairs: CH and SH

Directions: Say the name of each picture. Draw lines to match each picture with its name.

	sheep
	shed
	chin
	ship
	chop
	shell
	cheek
	chain

Name ______________________

Consonant Pairs: TH and WH

thin **wh**eel

Directions: Say the name of each picture. Write the letters **th** or **wh** to complete each word.

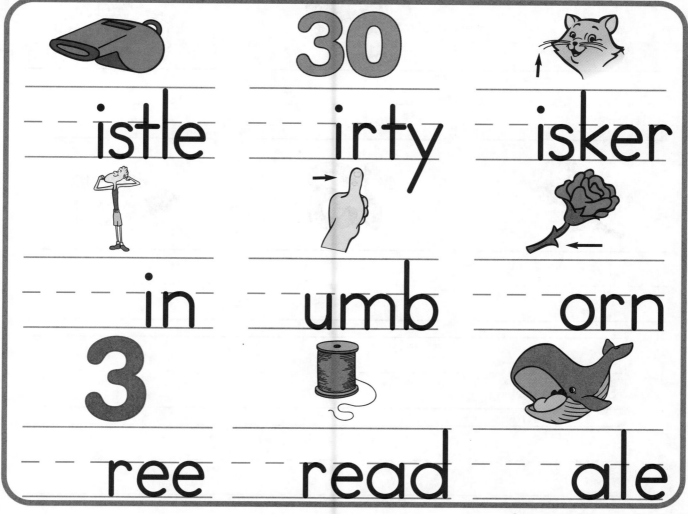

__istle	30 __irty	__isker
__in	__umb	__orn
3 __ree	__read	__ale

Name

Consonant Pairs: TH and WH

Directions: Name each picture. Write the word for each name from the Word Box. Then, write two sentences. Use one word from the Word Box in each sentence.

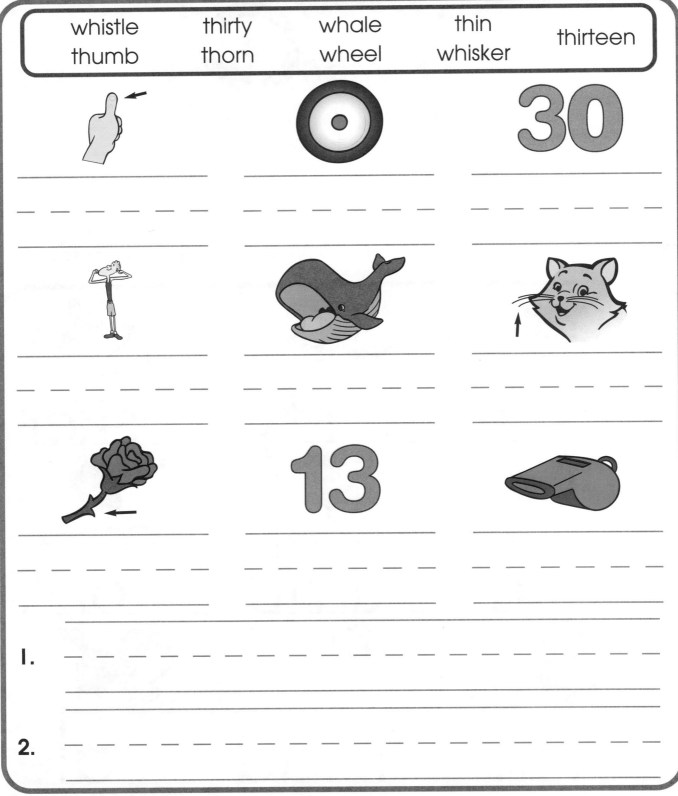

whistle	thirty	whale	thin	thirteen
thumb	thorn	wheel	whisker	

30

13

1.

2.

Name ______________________________

Consonant Pairs Endings: CH, SH, TH

ea**ch**

wi**sh**

wi**th**

Directions: Say the name of each picture. Circle the pictures that have the same consonant pair ending sounds.

Name ______________________________

Consonant Pairs Endings: CH, SH, TH

ea**ch**

wi**sh**

wi**th**

Directions: Name each picture and circle the consonant pair that shows the ending sound. Then, write two sentences. Use one word from above in each sentence.

ch sh th	ch sh th	ch sh th
ch sh th	ch sh th	ch sh th
ch sh th	ch sh th	ch sh th

1. ______________________________

2. ______________________________

Name

Consonant Pair: NG

ri**ng**

Directions: Write the consonant pair **ng** below each picture whose name ends with the sound of **ng**.

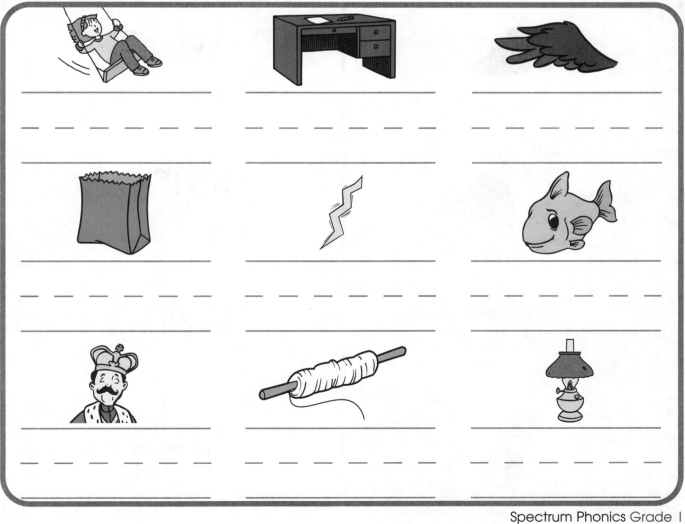

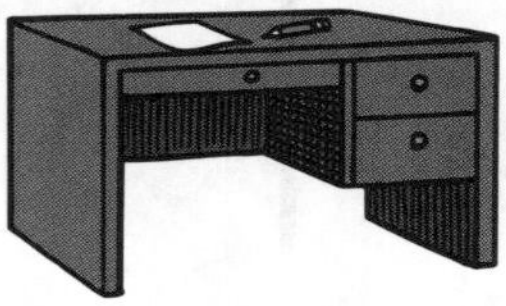

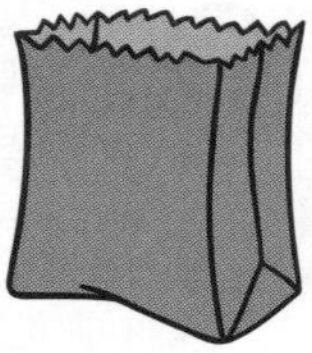

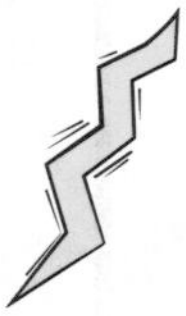

Name ____________________

Consonant Pair: NG

Directions: Say the name of each picture. Draw lines to match each picture with its name.

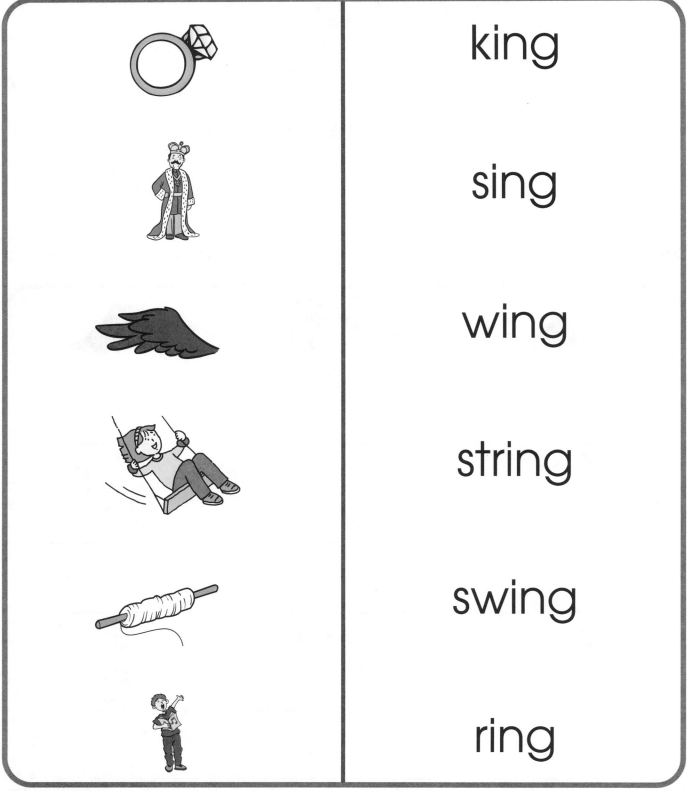

	king
	sing
	wing
	string
	swing
	ring

Name ______________________________

Review: Consonant Pairs

Directions: Say each word. Draw a picture of each word.

chain	thorn	swing
sheep	fish	bath
wheel	bench	chest

Name ______________________________

Review: Consonant Pairs

Directions: Say the name of each picture. Write a word from the Word Box that names each picture.

wing	thirteen	swing	tooth	bench
wheel	brush	king	wash	

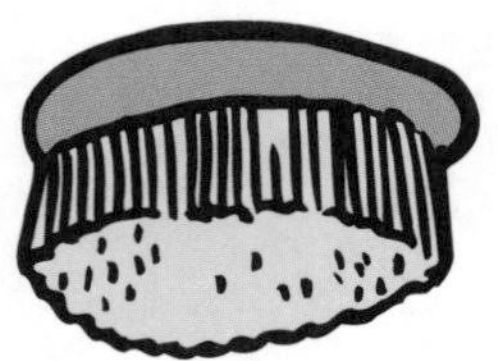

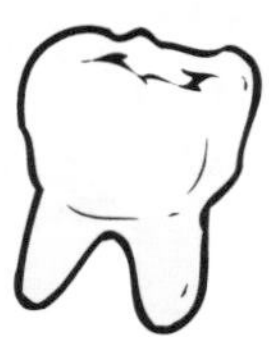

13

Name ________________________________

Letters and Their Sounds

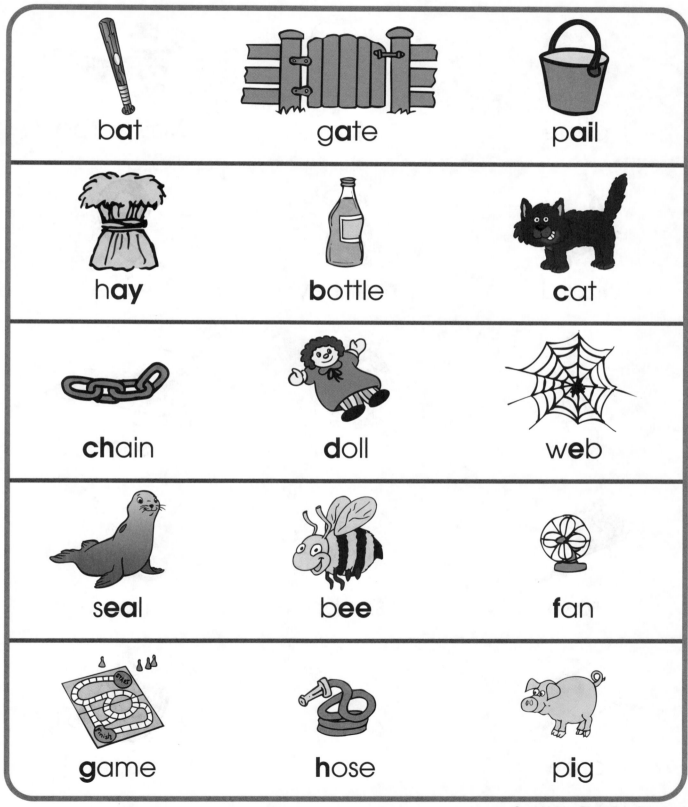

 b**a**t	 g**a**te	 p**ai**l
 h**ay**	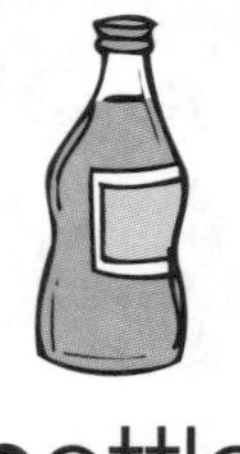 **b**ottle	 **c**at
 **ch**ain	 **d**oll	 w**e**b
 s**ea**l	 b**ee**	 **f**an
 **g**ame	 **h**ose	 p**i**g

Name ______________________________

Letters and Their Sounds

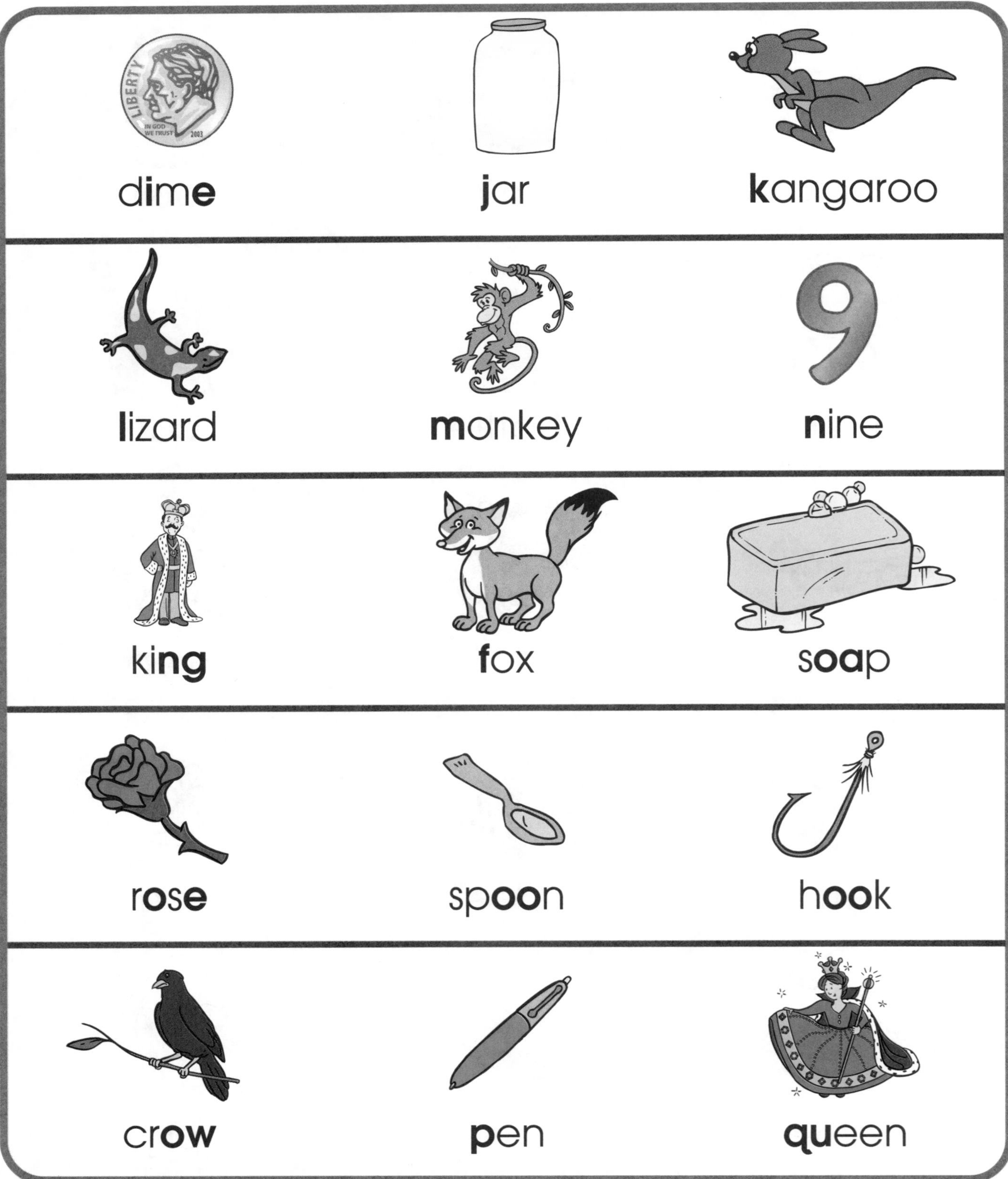

Name ___________________________________

Letters and Their Sounds

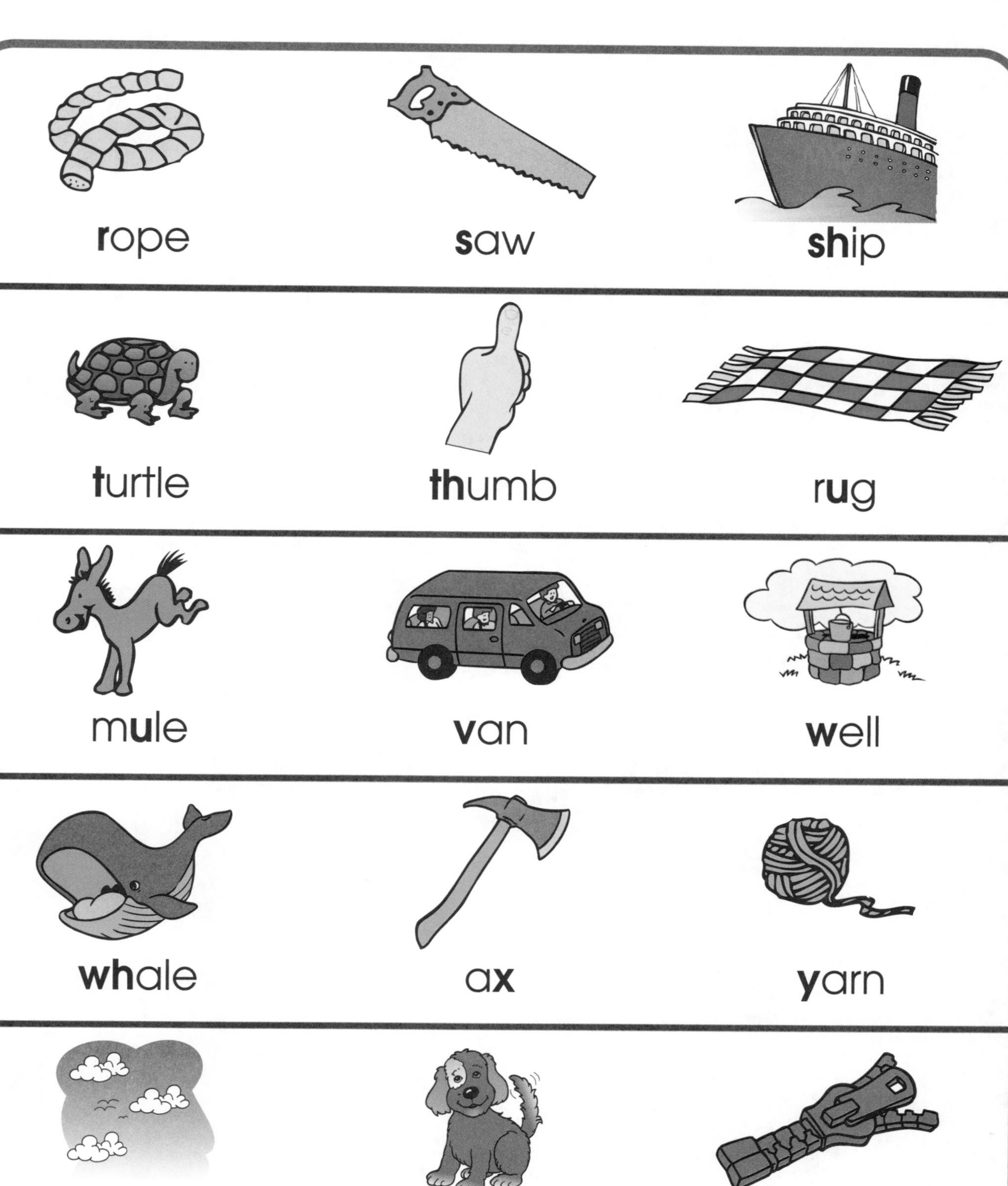

Name

Practice Page

Name ______________________

Practice Page

Name ____________________

Practice Page

Name ______________________________

Practice Page

Answer Key

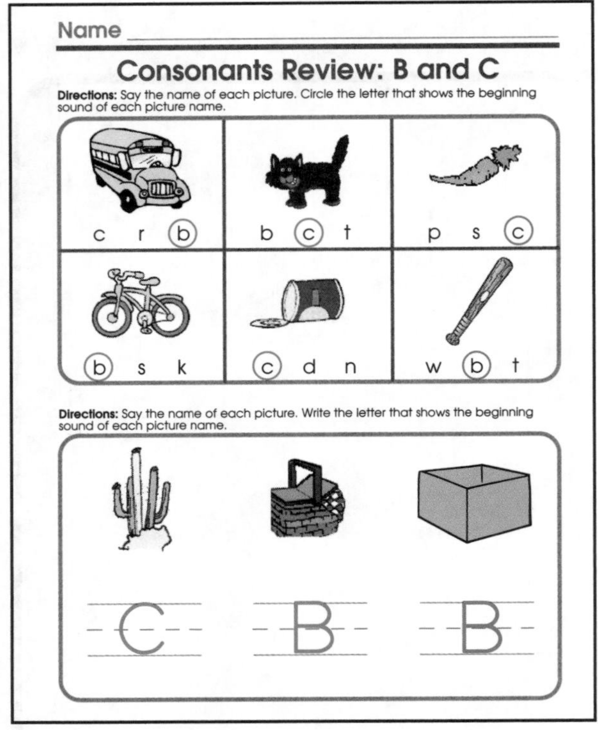

Name ______________________

Consonants Review: B and C

Directions: Say the name of each picture. Circle the letter that shows the beginning sound of each picture name.

c r (b) | b (c) t | p s (c)

(b) s k | (c) d n | w (b) t

Directions: Say the name of each picture. Write the letter that shows the beginning sound of each picture name.

C B B

5

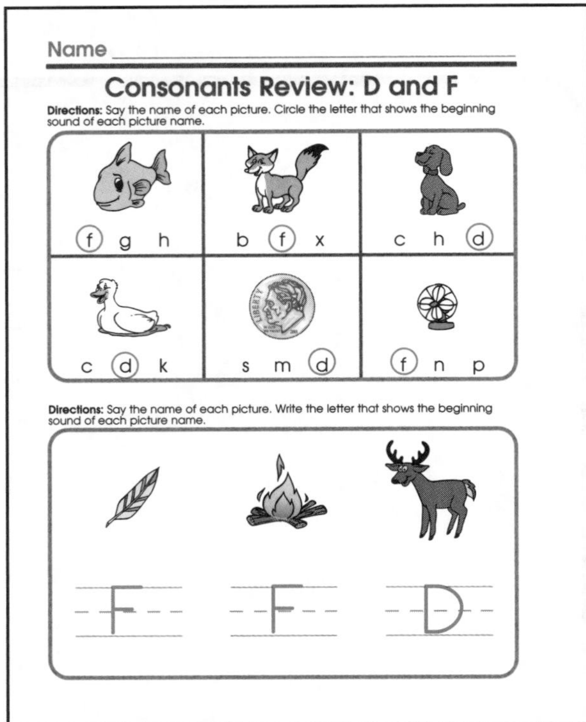

Name ______________________

Consonants Review: D and F

Directions: Say the name of each picture. Circle the letter that shows the beginning sound of each picture name.

(f) g h | b (f) x | c h (d)

c (d) k | s m (d) | (f) n p

Directions: Say the name of each picture. Write the letter that shows the beginning sound of each picture name.

F F D

6

Name ______________________

Consonants Review: G and H

Directions: Say the name of each picture. Circle the letter that shows the beginning sound of each picture name.

(h) j m | g (h) k | (g) h m

f (g) r | f g (h) | (g) k t

Directions: Say the name of each picture. Write the letter that shows the beginning sound of each picture name.

H H G

7

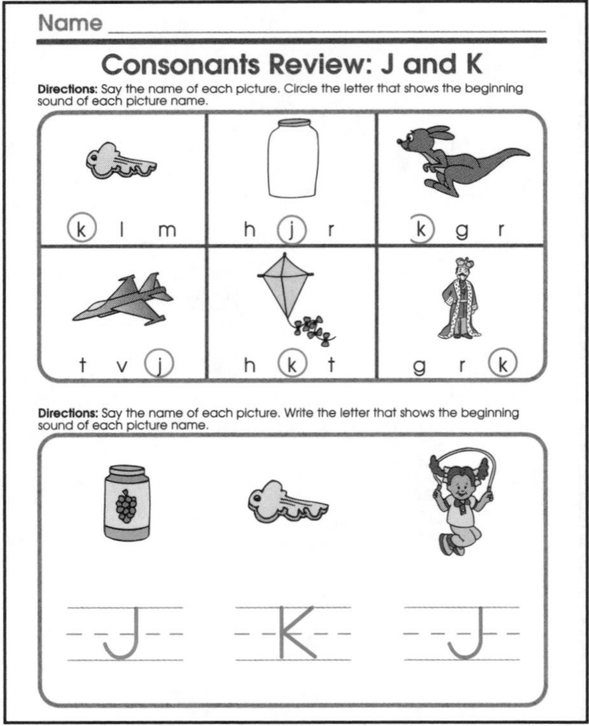

Name ______________________

Consonants Review: J and K

Directions: Say the name of each picture. Circle the letter that shows the beginning sound of each picture name.

(k) l m | h (j) r | (k) g r

t v (j) | h (k) t | g r (k)

Directions: Say the name of each picture. Write the letter that shows the beginning sound of each picture name.

J K J

8

Answer Key

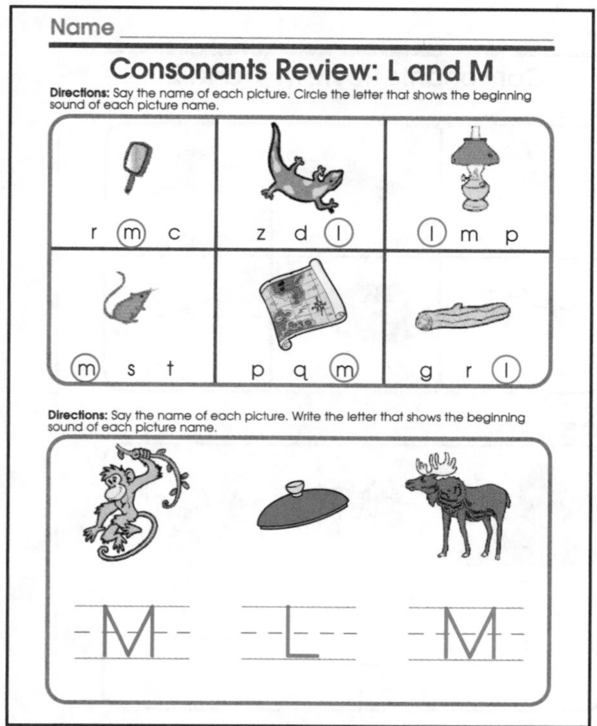
Name

Consonants Review: L and M

Directions: Say the name of each picture. Circle the letter that shows the beginning sound of each picture name.

r **(m)** c	z d **(l)**	**(l)** m p
(m) s t	p q **(m)**	g r **(l)**

Directions: Say the name of each picture. Write the letter that shows the beginning sound of each picture name.

M L M

9

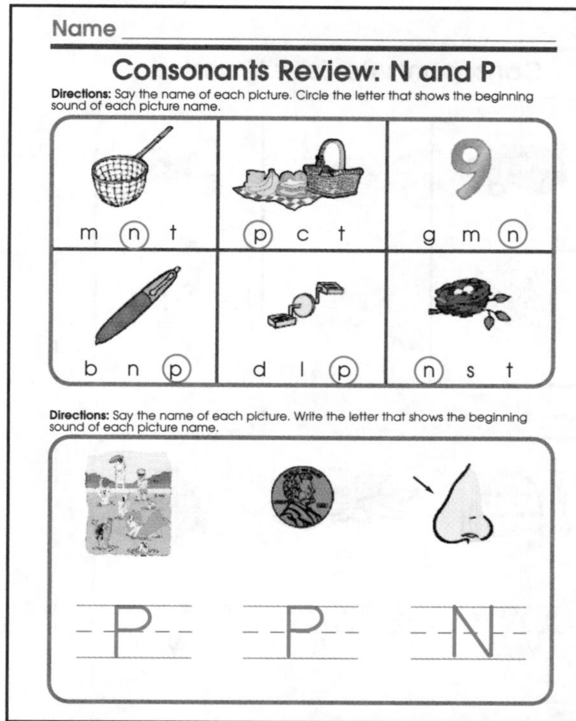
Name

Consonants Review: N and P

Directions: Say the name of each picture. Circle the letter that shows the beginning sound of each picture name.

m **(n)** t	**(p)** c t	g m **(n)**
b n **(p)**	d l **(p)**	**(n)** s t

Directions: Say the name of each picture. Write the letter that shows the beginning sound of each picture name.

P P N

10

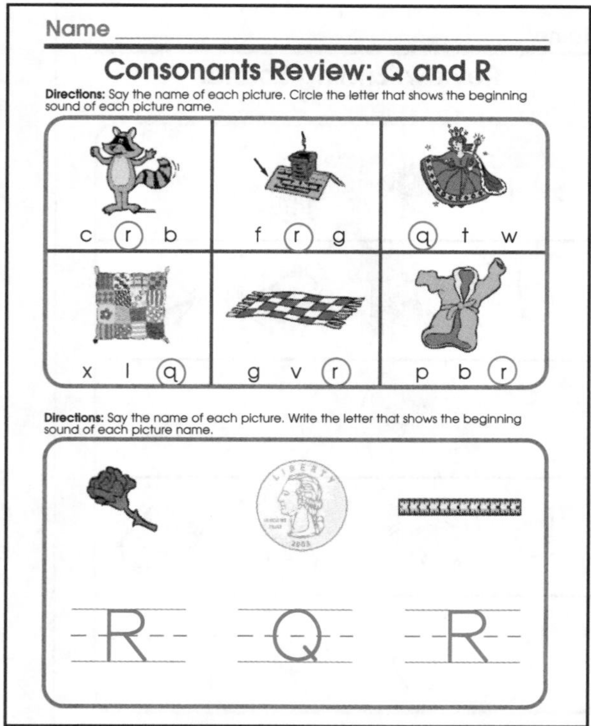
Name

Consonants Review: Q and R

Directions: Say the name of each picture. Circle the letter that shows the beginning sound of each picture name.

c **(r)** b	f **(r)** g	**(q)** t w
x l **(q)**	g v **(r)**	p b **(r)**

Directions: Say the name of each picture. Write the letter that shows the beginning sound of each picture name.

R Q R

11

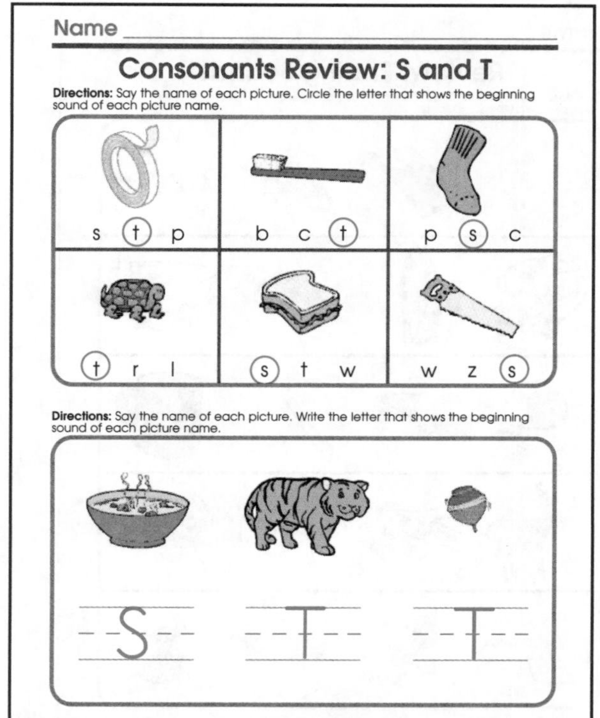
Name

Consonants Review: S and T

Directions: Say the name of each picture. Circle the letter that shows the beginning sound of each picture name.

s **(t)** p	b c **(t)**	p **(s)** c
(t) r l	**(s)** t w	w z **(s)**

Directions: Say the name of each picture. Write the letter that shows the beginning sound of each picture name.

S T T

12

Answer Key

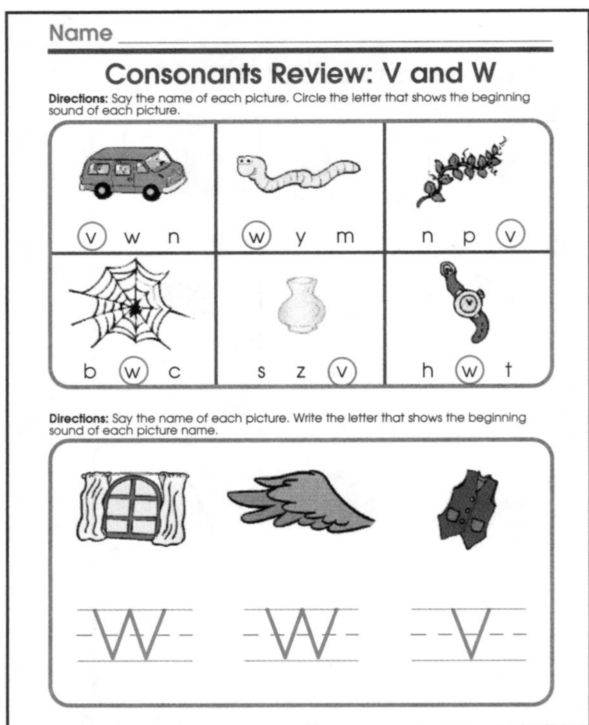

Name ______________________

Consonants Review: V and W

Directions: Say the name of each picture. Circle the letter that shows the beginning sound of each picture.

(v) w n	(w) y m	n p (v)
b (w) c	s z (v)	h (w) t

Directions: Say the name of each picture. Write the letter that shows the beginning sound of each picture name.

W W V

13

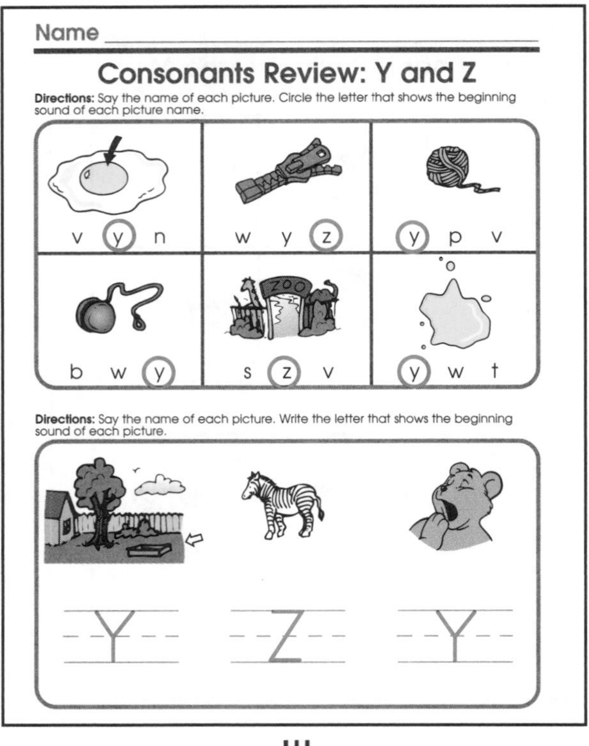

Name ______________________

Consonants Review: Y and Z

Directions: Say the name of each picture. Circle the letter that shows the beginning sound of each picture name.

v (y) n	w y (z)	(y) p v
b w (y)	s (z) v	(y) w t

Directions: Say the name of each picture. Write the letter that shows the beginning sound of each picture.

Y Z Y

14

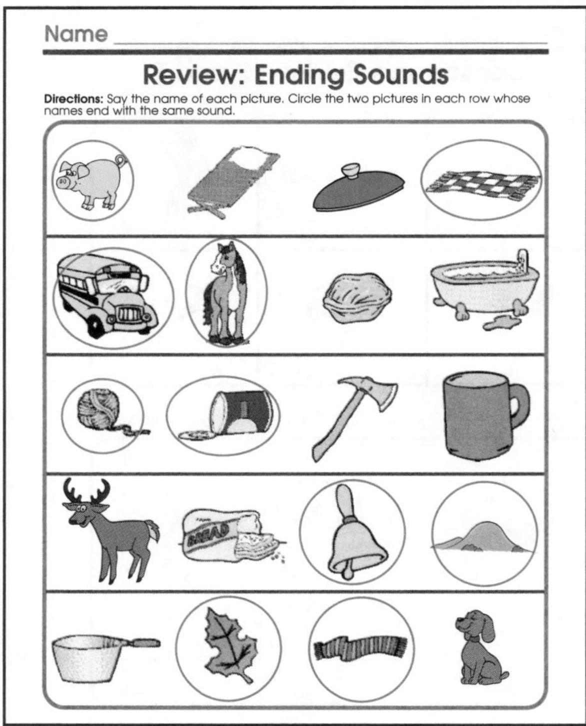

Name ______________________

Review: Ending Sounds

Directions: Say the name of each picture. Circle the two pictures in each row whose names end with the same sound.

15

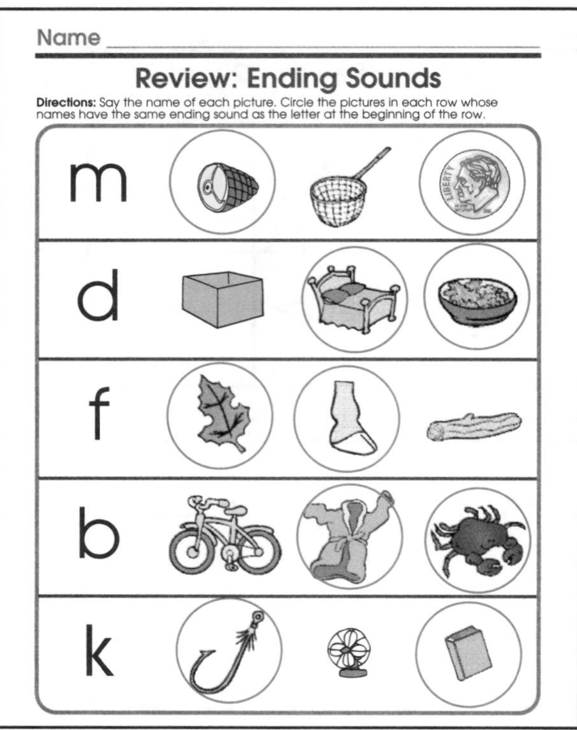

Name ______________________

Review: Ending Sounds

Directions: Say the name of each picture. Circle the pictures in each row whose names have the same ending sound as the letter at the beginning of the row.

m

d

f

b

k

16

Answer Key

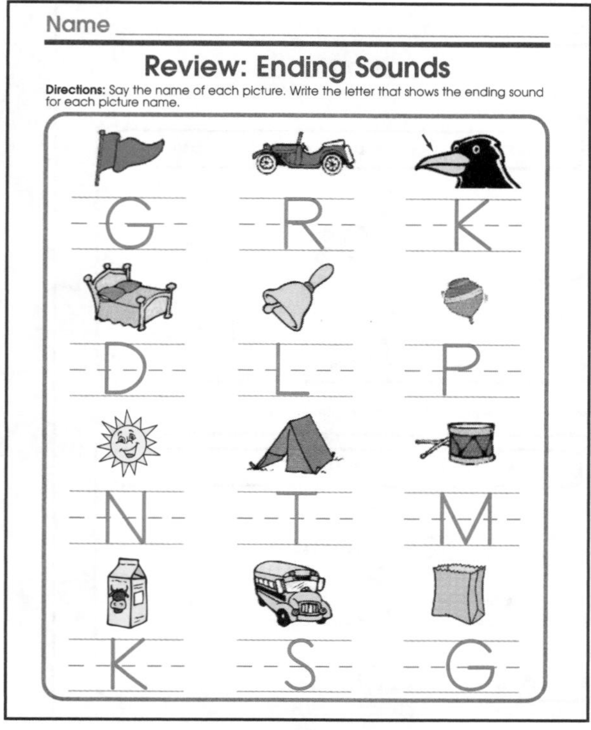
Name

Review: Ending Sounds

Directions: Say the name of each picture. Write the letter that shows the ending sound for each picture name.

G R K

D L P

N T M

K S G

17

Name

Consonant Review

Directions: Say the name of each picture. Write the missing letter for each picture name.

frog wig van

bed mug can

fan book web

18

Name

Short a

Directions: Say the name of each picture. Draw an **X** through each picture whose name does **not** have the short **a** sound.

19

Name

Short a

Directions: Say the name of each picture. Write the letter **a** below each picture whose name has the short **a** sound.

a

a a a

Directions: Say the name of each picture. Write the letter **a** to complete each word.

bag pan bat

20

Answer Key

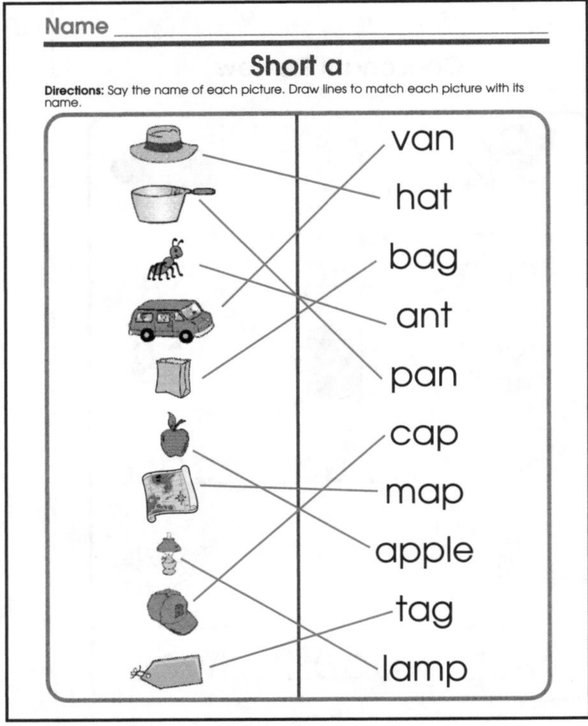
Name

Short a

Directions: Say the name of each picture. Draw lines to match each picture with its name.

van
hat
bag
ant
pan
cap
map
apple
tag
lamp

21

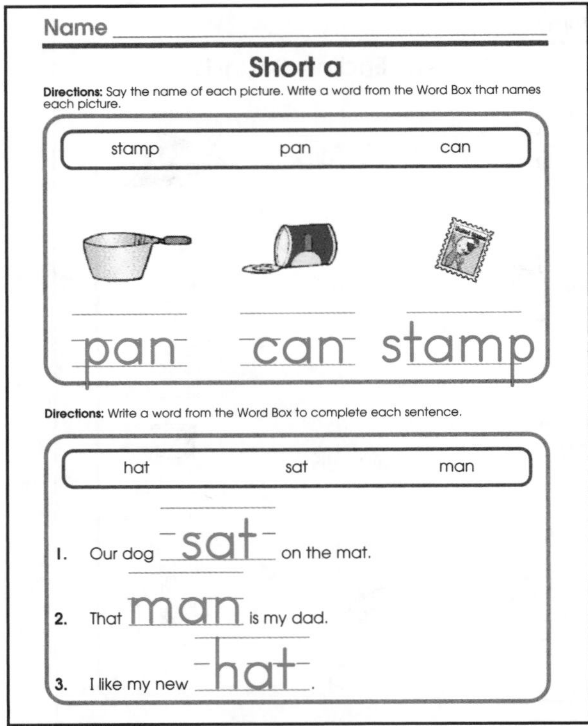
Name

Short a

Directions: Say the name of each picture. Write a word from the Word Box that names each picture.

stamp pan can

pan can stamp

Directions: Write a word from the Word Box to complete each sentence.

hat sat man

1. Our dog sat on the mat.
2. That man is my dad.
3. I like my new hat.

22

Name

Short e

Directions: Say the name of each picture. Draw an **X** through each picture that does **not** have the short **e** sound.

23

Name

Short e

Directions: Say the name of each picture. Write the letter **e** below each picture that has the short **e** sound.

e e

e e

Directions: Say the name of each picture. Write the letter **e** to complete each word.

vest bed belt

24

Answer Key

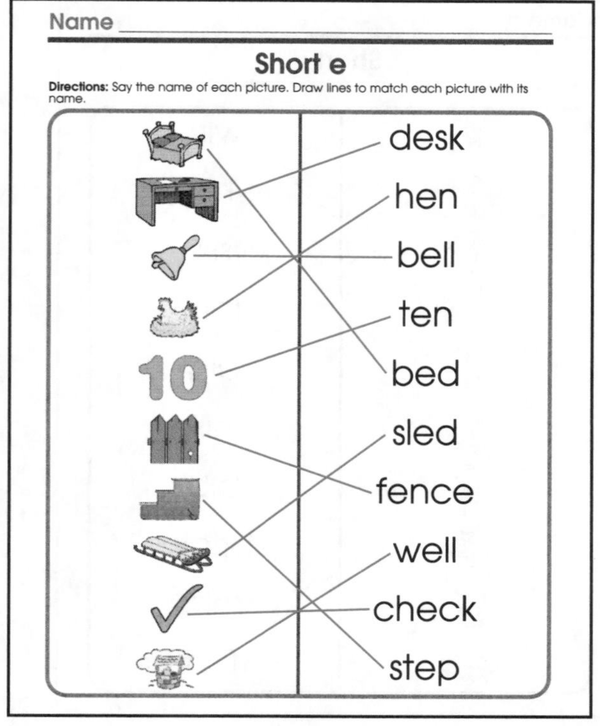
Name

Short e

Directions: Say the name of each picture. Draw lines to match each picture with its name.

desk
hen
bell
ten
bed
sled
fence
well
check
step

25

Name

Short e

Directions: Say the name of each picture. Write a word from the Word Box that names each picture.

egg net jet

net egg jet

Directions: Write a word from the Word Box to complete each sentence.

bed hen beg

1. The hen sat on an egg.
2. It is time for bed.
3. My dog can beg.

26

Name

Review: Short a and Short e

Directions: Write the letter that shows the short vowel sound for each picture name.

e a e
e a a
a a e
a e e

27

Name

Short i

Directions: Say the name of each picture. Draw an **X** through each picture that does **not** have the short **i** sound.

28

Answer Key

Name

Short i

Directions: Say the name of each picture. Write the letter **i** below each picture that has the short **i** sound.

i i

i i

Directions: Say the name of each picture. Write the letter **i** to complete each word.

pig lips lid

29

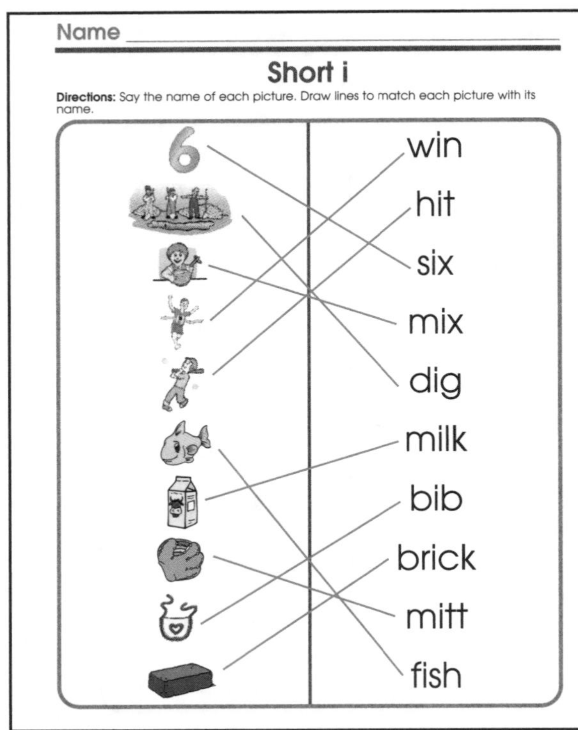

Name

Short i

Directions: Say the name of each picture. Draw lines to match each picture with its name.

win
hit
six
mix
dig
milk
bib
brick
mitt
fish

30

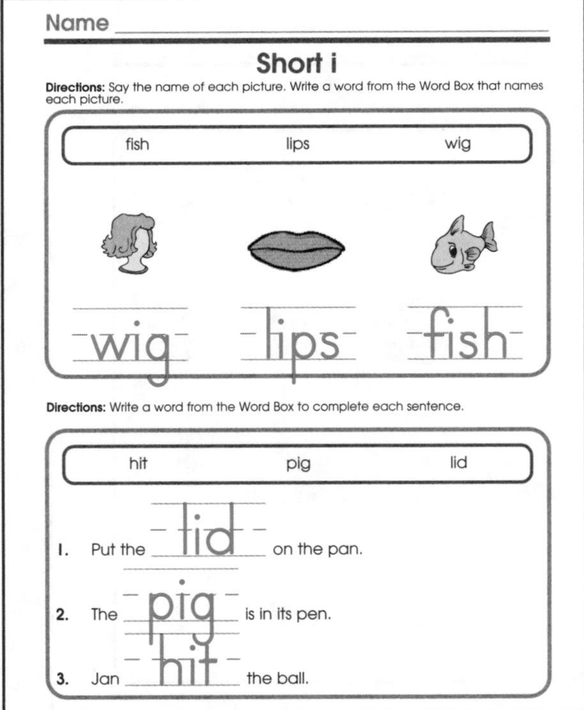

Name

Short i

Directions: Say the name of each picture. Write a word from the Word Box that names each picture.

fish	lips	wig

wig lips fish

Directions: Write a word from the Word Box to complete each sentence.

hit	pig	lid

1. Put the lid on the pan.
2. The pig is in its pen.
3. Jan hit the ball.

31

Name

Short o

Directions: Say the name of each picture. Draw an **X** through each picture that does **not** have the short **o** sound.

32

Answer Key

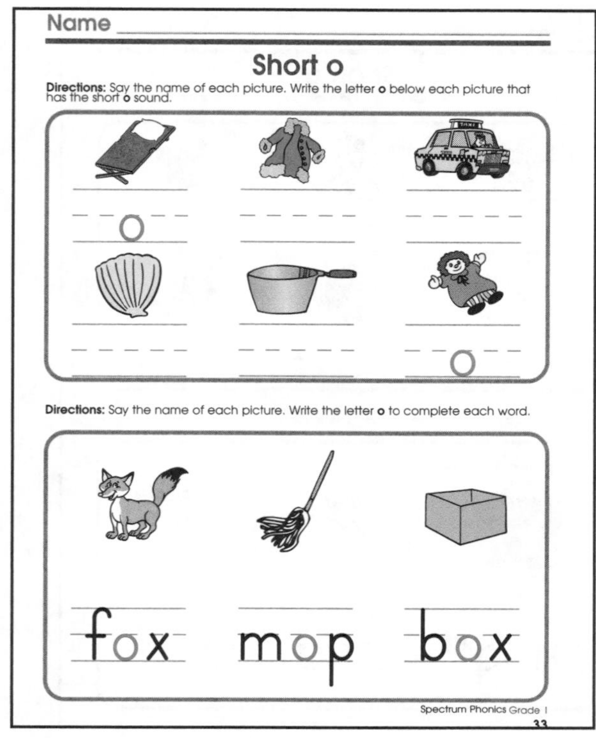
Name

Short o

Directions: Say the name of each picture. Write the letter **o** below each picture that has the short **o** sound.

o

o

Directions: Say the name of each picture. Write the letter **o** to complete each word.

fox mop box

Spectrum Phonics Grade 1
33

33

Name

Short o

Directions: Say the name of each picture. Draw lines to match each picture with its name.

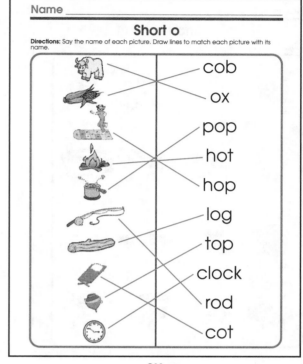

cob
ox
pop
hot
hop
log
top
clock
rod
cot

34

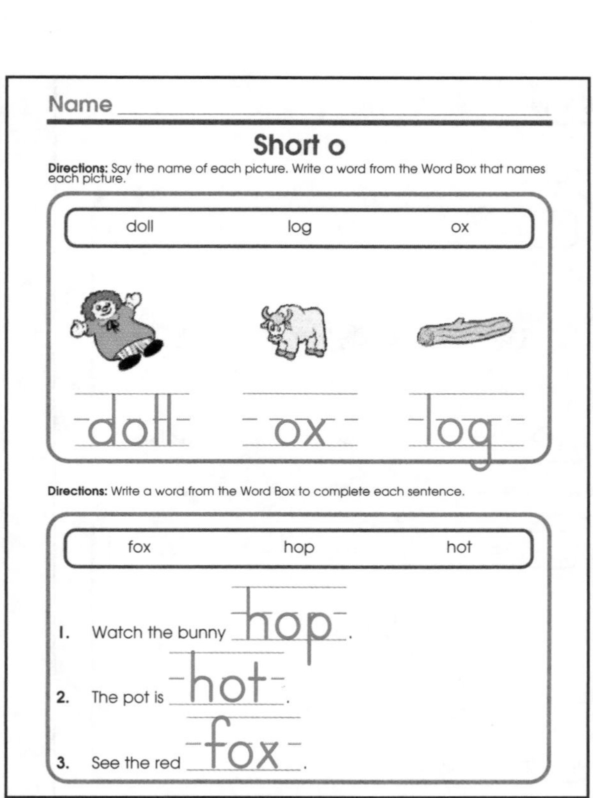
Name

Short o

Directions: Say the name of each picture. Write a word from the Word Box that names each picture.

doll	log	ox

doll ox log

Directions: Write a word from the Word Box to complete each sentence.

fox	hop	hot

1. Watch the bunny hop.
2. The pot is hot.
3. See the red fox.

35

Name

Review: Short i and Short o

Directions: Write the letter that shows the short vowel sound for each picture name.

i o o

i i o

o o i

i o o

36

Answer Key

Name

Short u

Directions: Say the name of each picture. Draw an **X** through each picture that does **not** have the short **u** sound.

37

Name

Short u

Directions: Say the name of each picture. Write the letter **u** below each picture that has the short **u** sound.

u

u

u

u

Directions: Say the name of each picture. Write the letter **u** to complete each word.

hug mud run

38

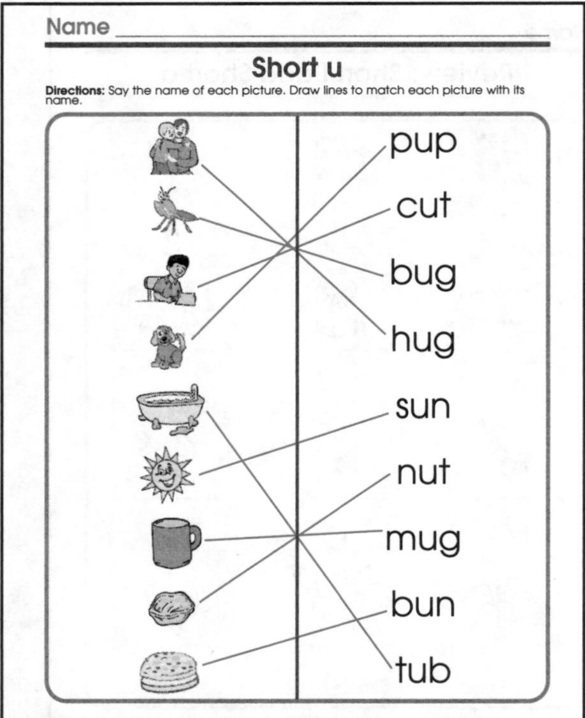
Name

Short u

Directions: Say the name of each picture. Draw lines to match each picture with its name.

pup
cut
bug
hug
sun
nut
mug
bun
tub

39

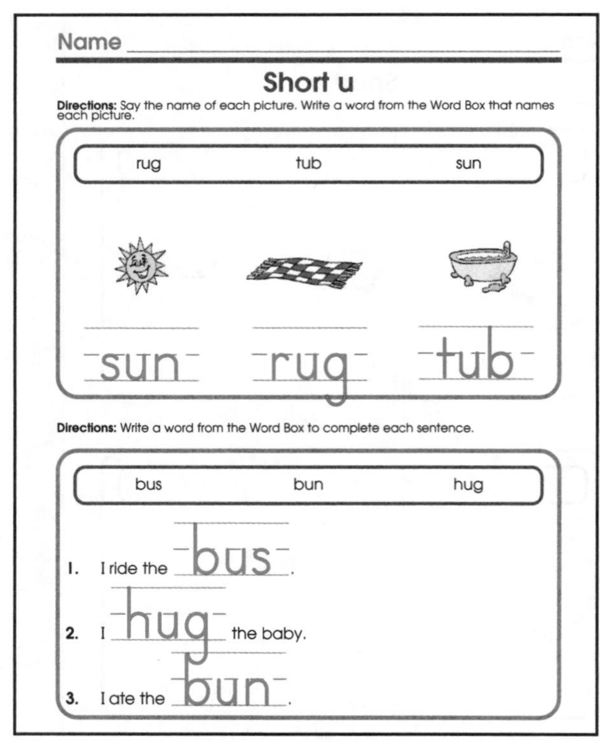
Name

Short u

Directions: Say the name of each picture. Write a word from the Word Box that names each picture.

rug tub sun

sun rug tub

Directions: Write a word from the Word Box to complete each sentence.

bus bun hug

1. I ride the bus.
2. I hug the baby.
3. I ate the bun.

40

Answer Key

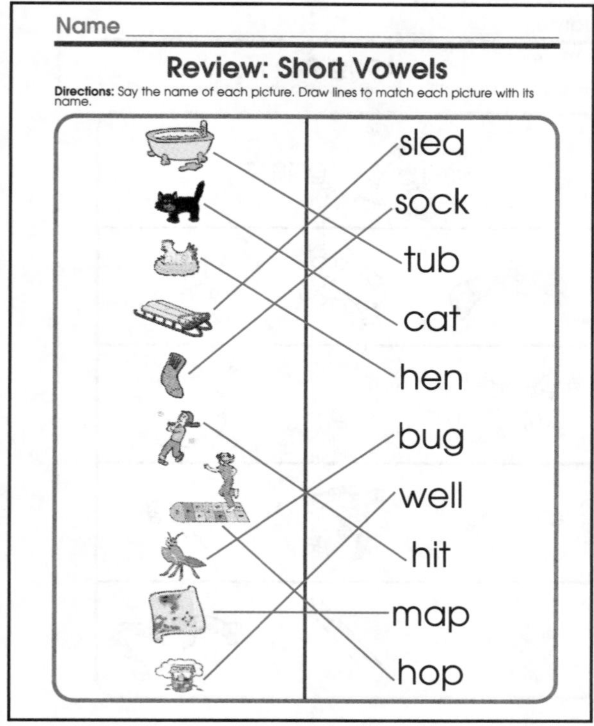

Name
Review: Short Vowels
Directions: Say the name of each picture. Draw lines to match each picture with its name.
sled
sock
tub
cat
hen
bug
well
hit
map
hop

41

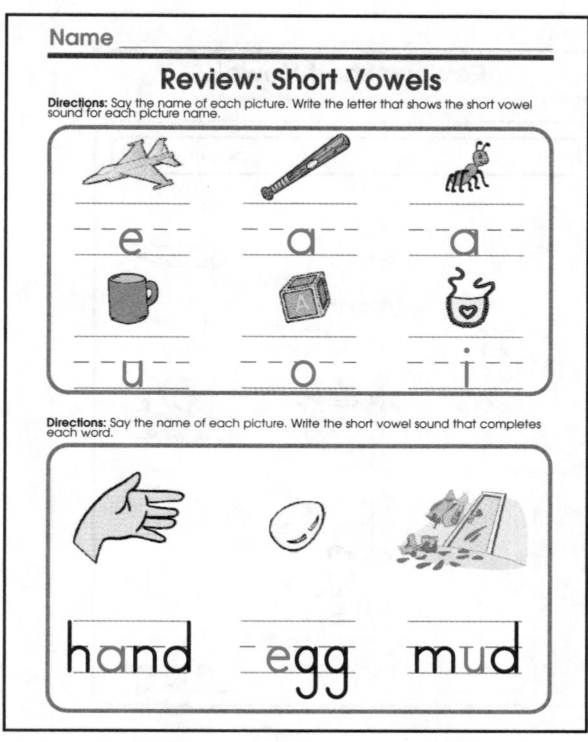

42

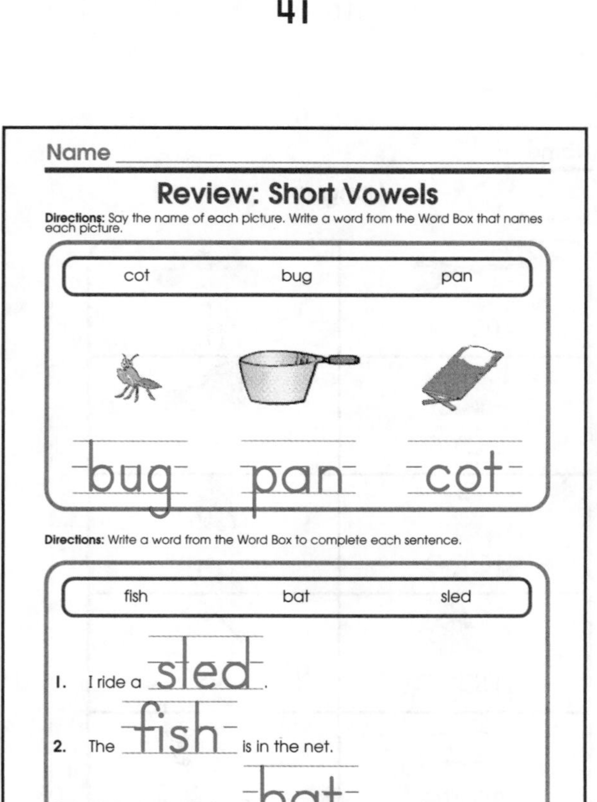

43

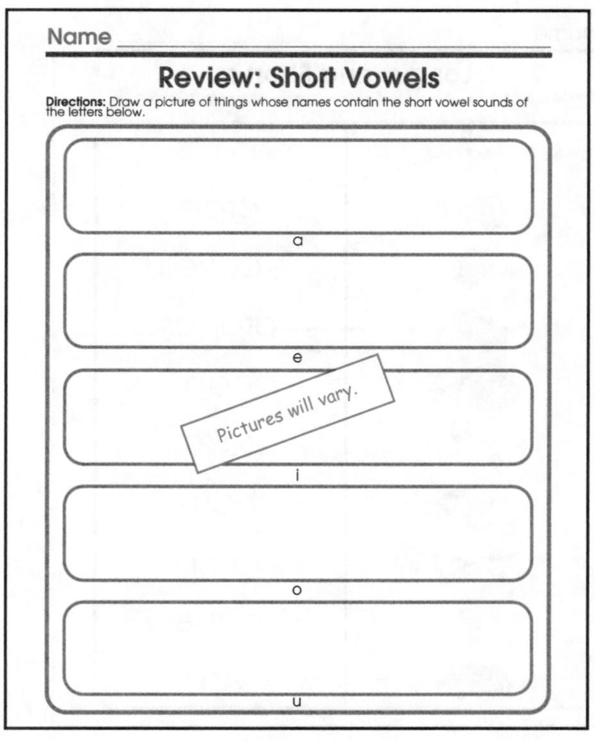

Name
Review: Short Vowels
Directions: Draw a picture of things whose names contain the short vowel sounds of the letters below.
a
e
Pictures will vary.
i
o
u

44

Answer Key

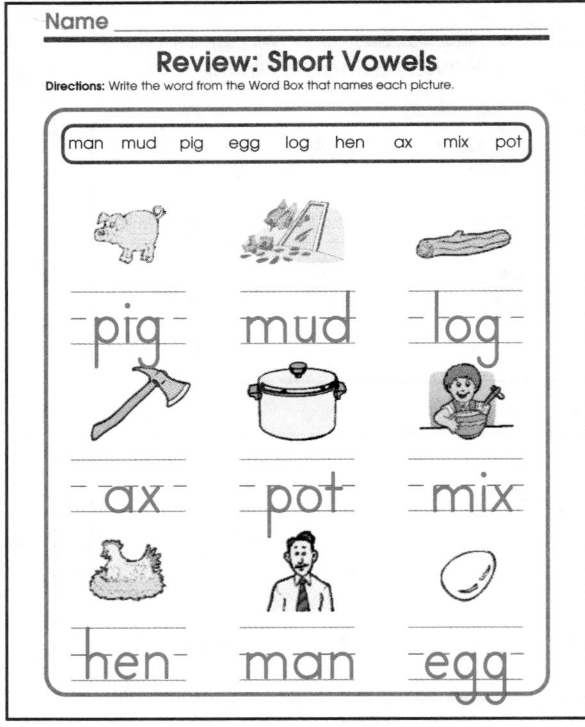

Name
Review: Short Vowels
Directions: Write the word from the Word Box that names each picture.
man mud pig egg log hen ax mix pot
pig
mud
log
ax
pot
mix
hen
man
egg

45

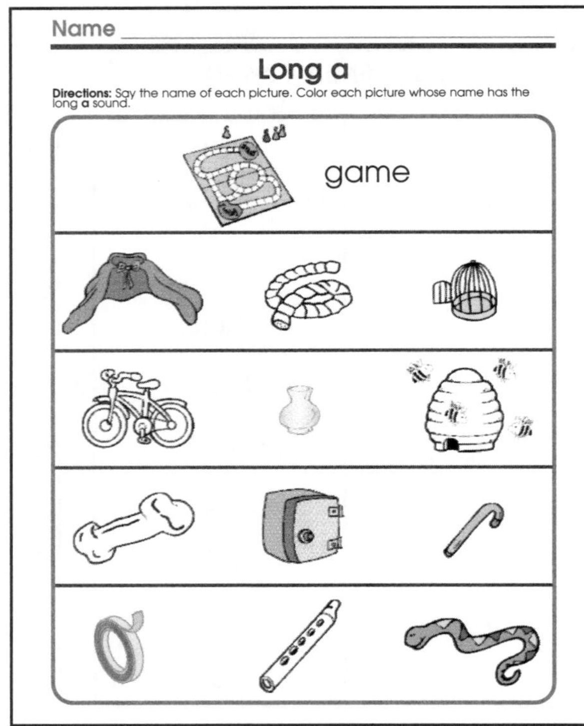

46

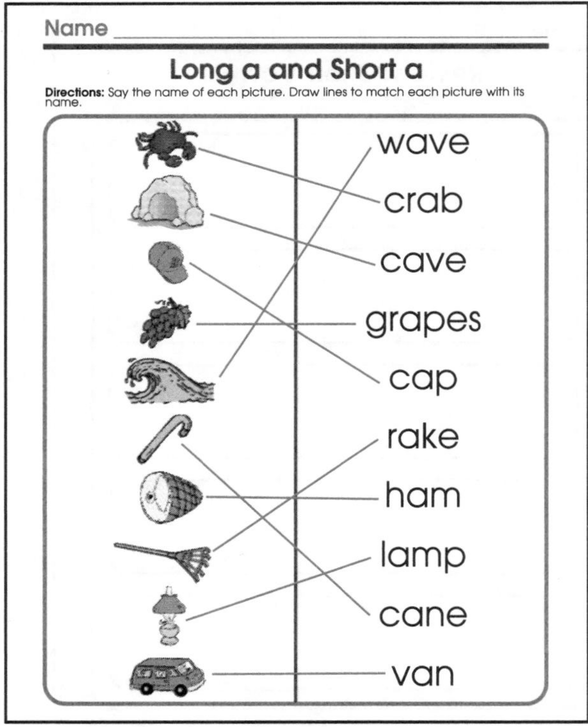

Name
Long a and Short a
Directions: Say the name of each picture. Draw lines to match each picture with its name.
wave
crab
cave
grapes
cap
rake
ham
lamp
cane
van

47

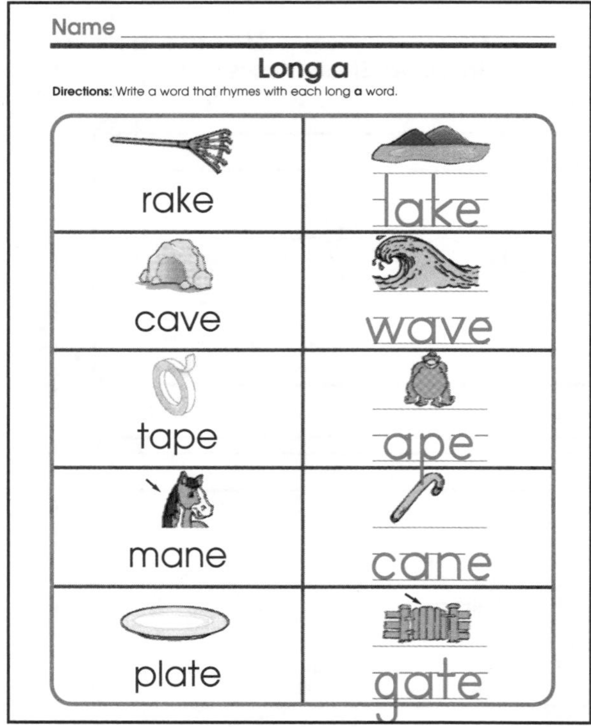

Name
Long a
Directions: Write a word that rhymes with each long a word.
rake
lake
cave
wave
tape
ape
mane
cane
plate
gate

48

Answer Key

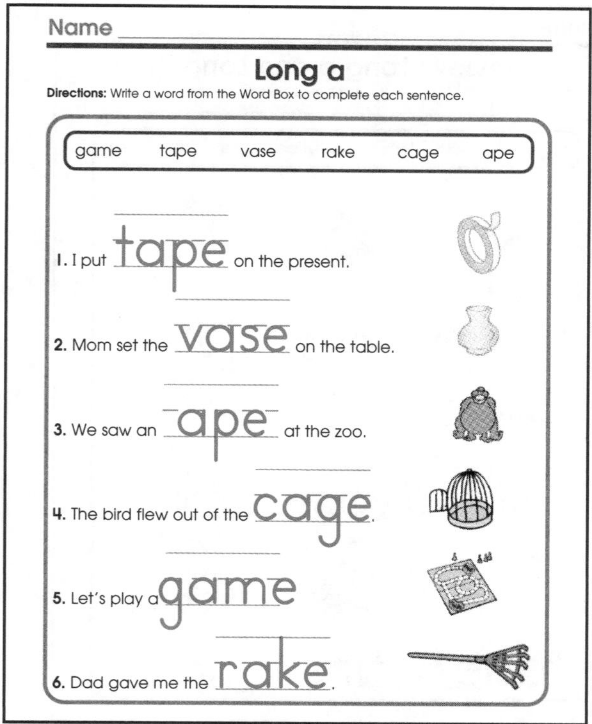
Name

Long a

Directions: Write a word from the Word Box to complete each sentence.

game tape vase rake cage ape

1. I put tape on the present.
2. Mom set the vase on the table.
3. We saw an ape at the zoo.
4. The bird flew out of the cage.
5. Let's play a game
6. Dad gave me the rake.

49

Name

Long i

Directions: Say the name of each picture. Color each picture whose name has the long i sound.

dime

50

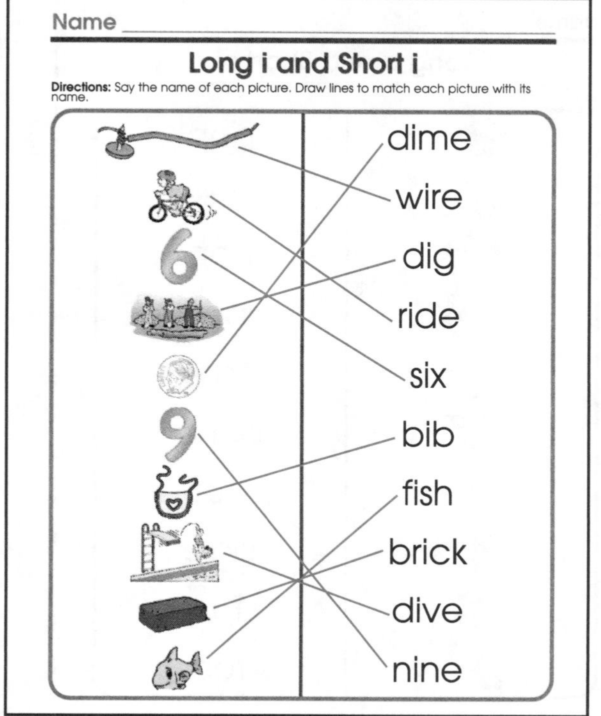
Name

Long i and Short i

Directions: Say the name of each picture. Draw lines to match each picture with its name.

dime
wire
dig
ride
six
bib
fish
brick
dive
nine

51

Name

Long i

Directions: Write a word that rhymes with each long **i** word.

hive	dive
tire	fire
bite	kite
pine	vine
slide	ride

52

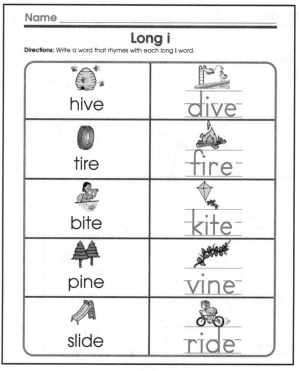

Answer Key

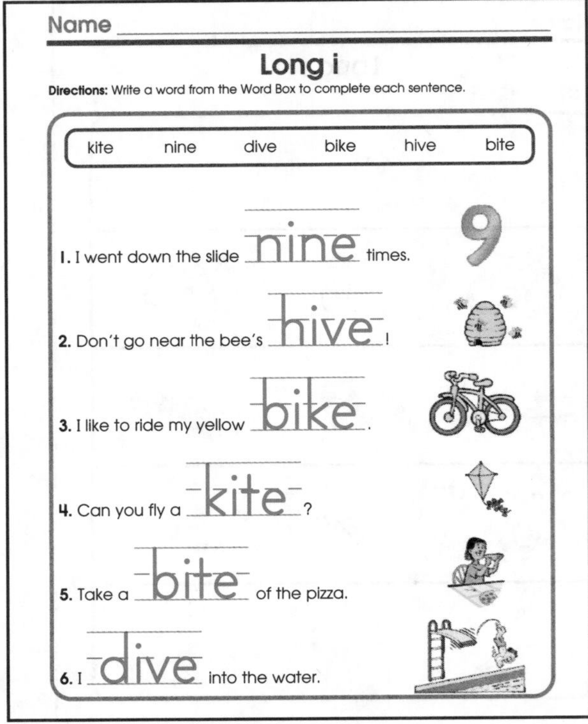

53

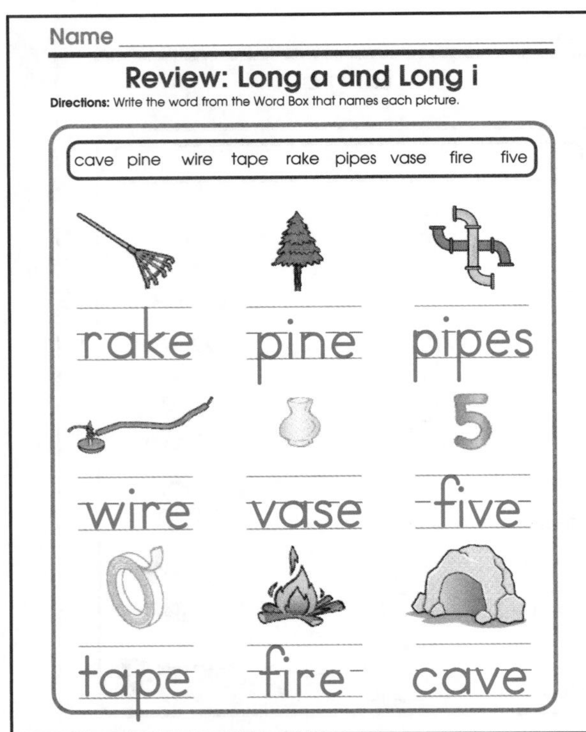

Name
Review: Long a and Long i
Directions: Write the word from the Word Box that names each picture.
cave pine wire tape rake pipes vase fire five
rake pine pipes
wire vase five
tape fire cave

54

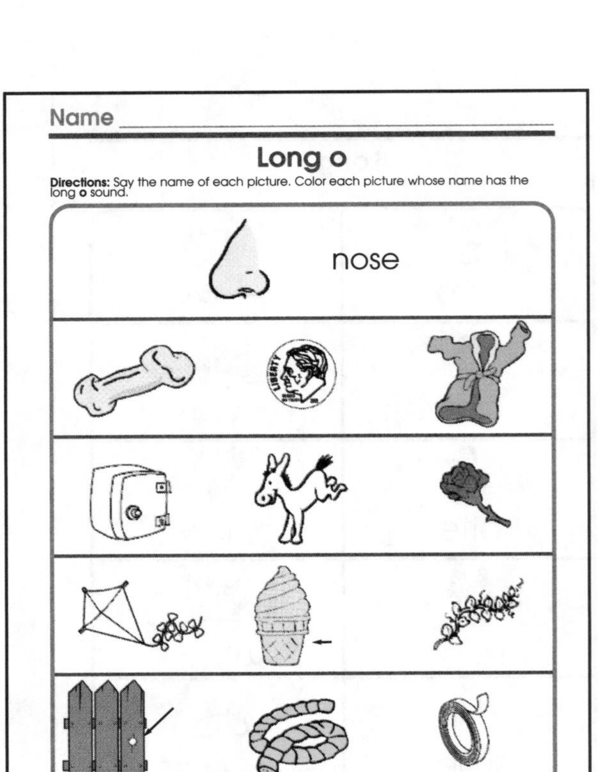

55

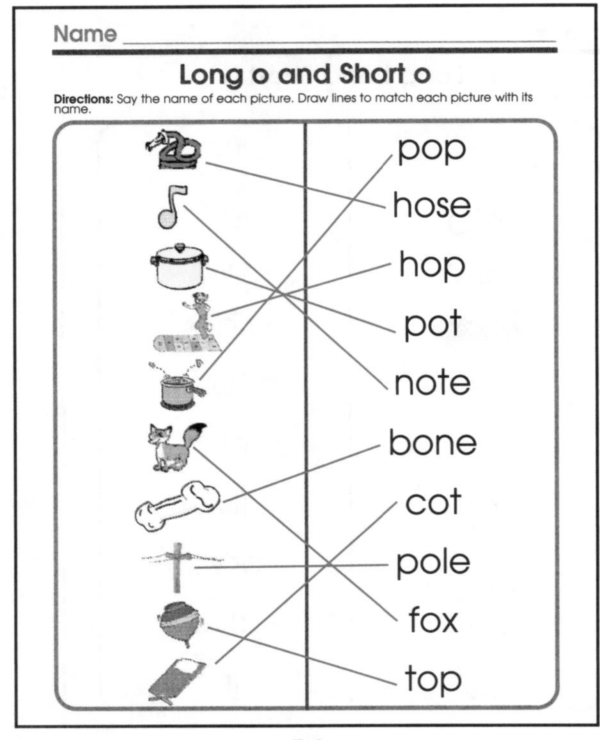

Name
Long o and Short o
Directions: Say the name of each picture. Draw lines to match each picture with its name.
pop
hose
hop
pot
note
bone
cot
pole
fox
top

56

Answer Key

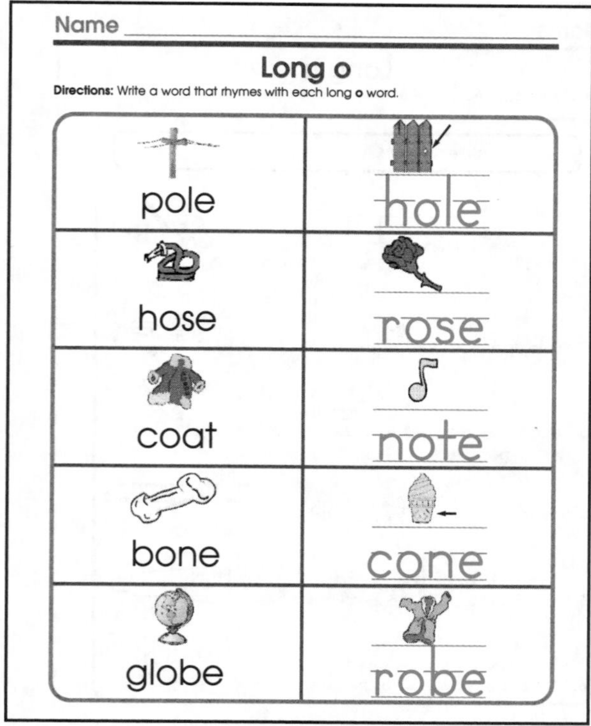

Name
Long o
Directions: Write a word that rhymes with each long o word.
pole
hole
hose
rose
coat
note
bone
cone
globe
robe

57

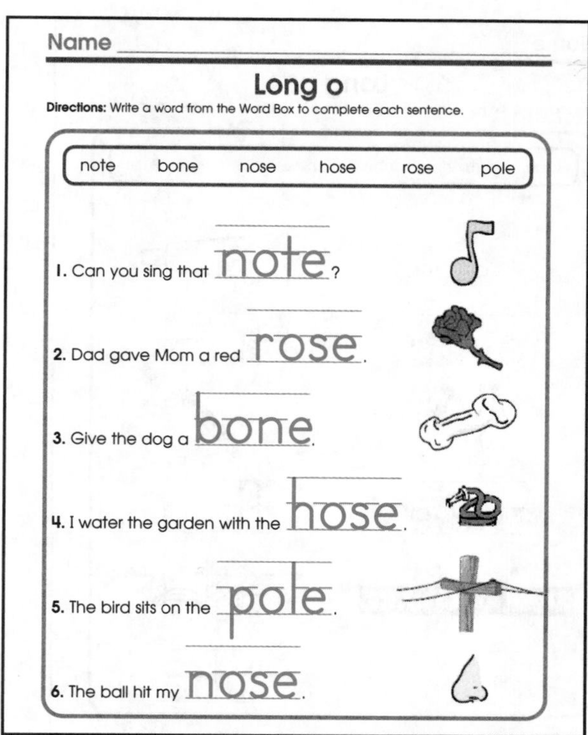

Name
Long o
Directions: Write a word from the Word Box to complete each sentence.
note bone nose hose rose pole
1. Can you sing that note?
2. Dad gave Mom a red rose.
3. Give the dog a bone.
4. I water the garden with the hose.
5. The bird sits on the pole.
6. The ball hit my nose.

58

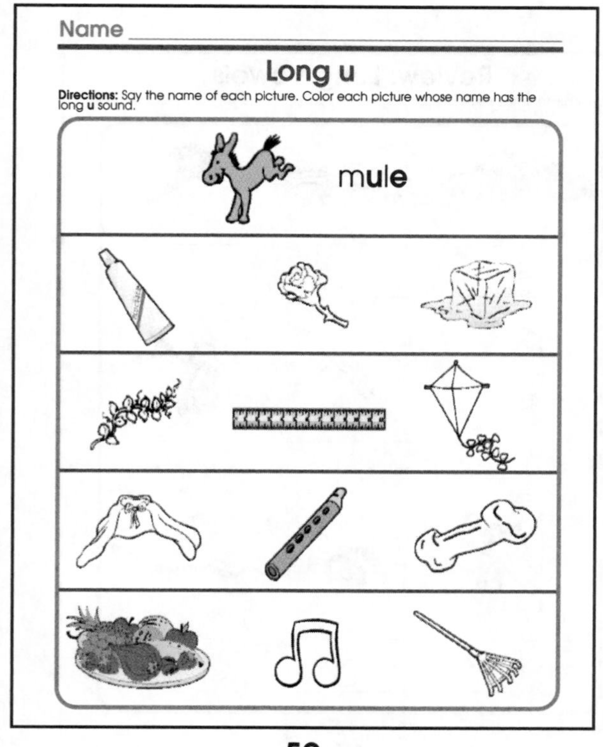

59

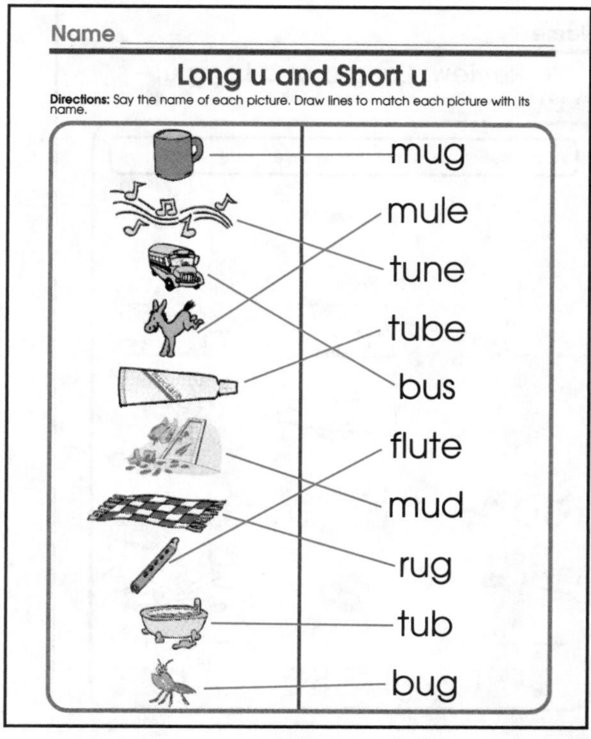

Name
Long u and Short u
Directions: Say the name of each picture. Draw lines to match each picture with its name.
mug
mule
tune
tube
bus
flute
mud
rug
tub
bug

60

Answer Key

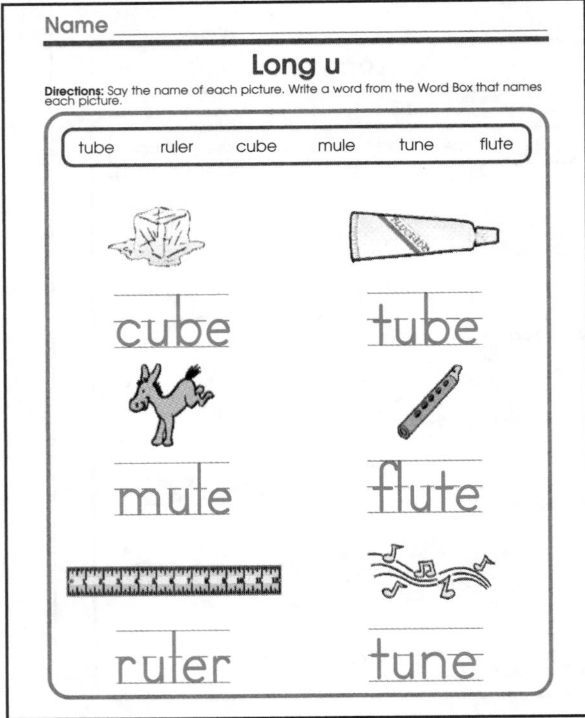

Name

Long u

Directions: Say the name of each picture. Write a word from the Word Box that names each picture.

tube ruler cube mule tune flute

cube tube

mule flute

ruler tune

61

Name

Long u

Directions: Write a word from the Word Box to complete each sentence.

ruler mule tube cube tune flute

1. Tanya saw a mule at the farm.
2. Steve sings a tune.
3. Becca plays the flute.
4. Where is my ruler?
5. I found my tube of toothpaste.
6. I put a cube of ice in my cup.

62

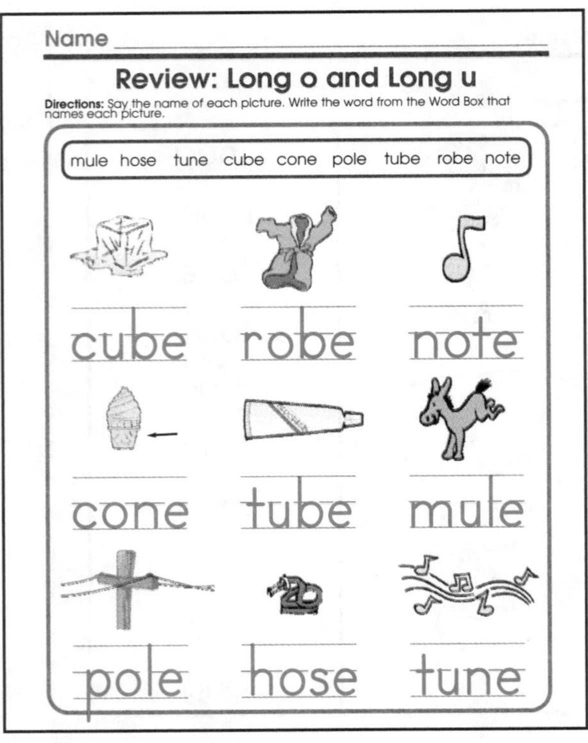

Name

Review: Long o and Long u

Directions: Say the name of each picture. Write the word from the Word Box that names each picture.

mule hose tune cube cone pole tube robe note

cube robe note

cone tube mule

pole hose tune

63

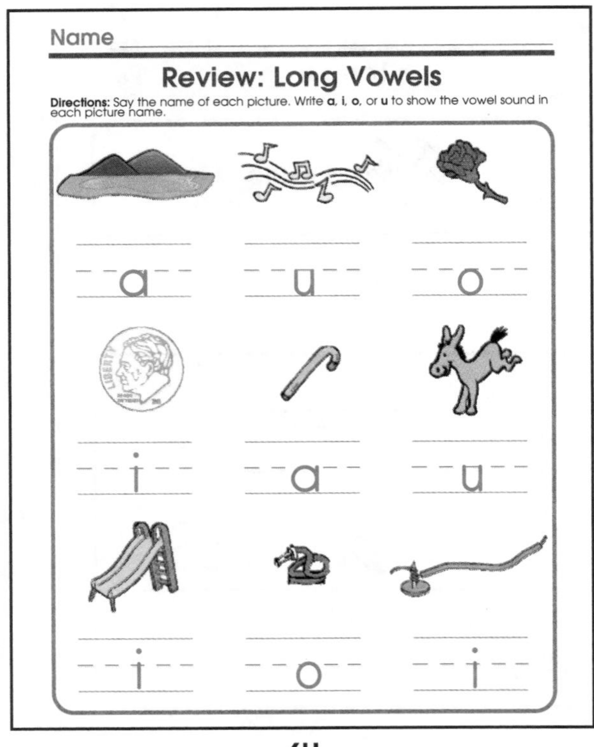

Name

Review: Long Vowels

Directions: Say the name of each picture. Write **a**, **i**, **o**, or **u** to show the vowel sound in each picture name.

a u o

i a u

i o i

64

Answer Key

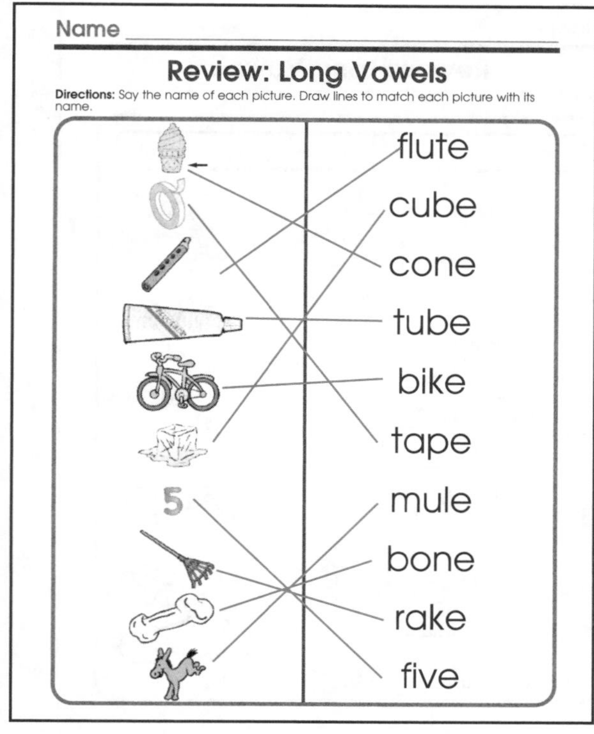
Name

Review: Long Vowels

Directions: Say the name of each picture. Draw lines to match each picture with its name.

flute
cube
cone
tube
bike
tape
mule
bone
rake
five

65

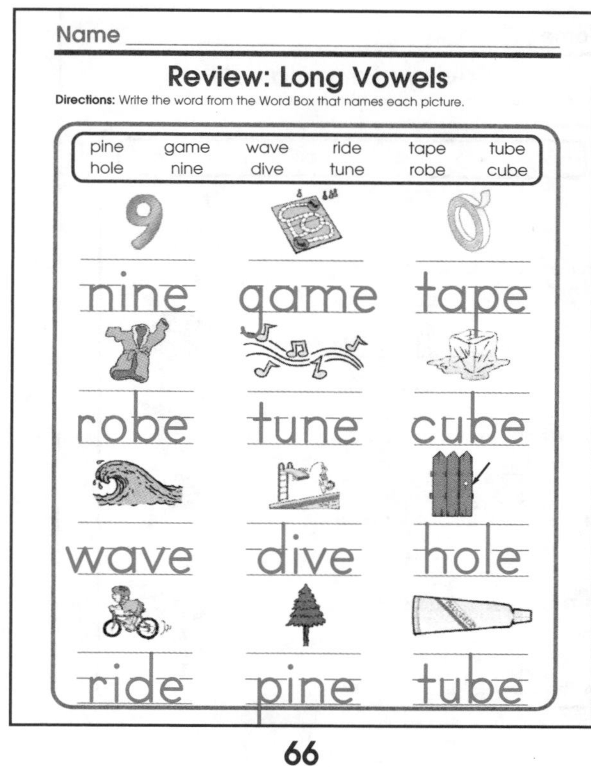
Name

Review: Long Vowels

Directions: Write the word from the Word Box that names each picture.

pine	game	wave	ride	tape	tube
hole	nine	dive	tune	robe	cube

nine	game	tape
robe	tune	cube
wave	dive	hole
ride	pine	tube

66

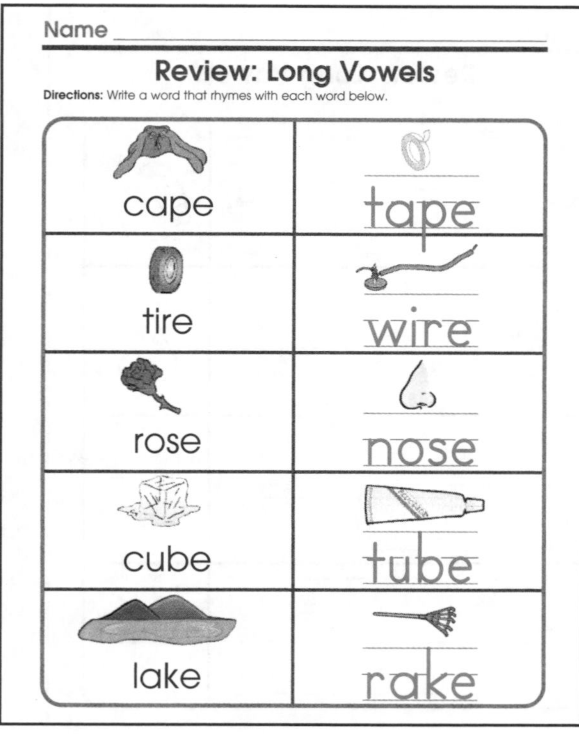
Name

Review: Long Vowels

Directions: Write a word that rhymes with each word below.

cape	tape
tire	wire
rose	nose
cube	tube
lake	rake

67

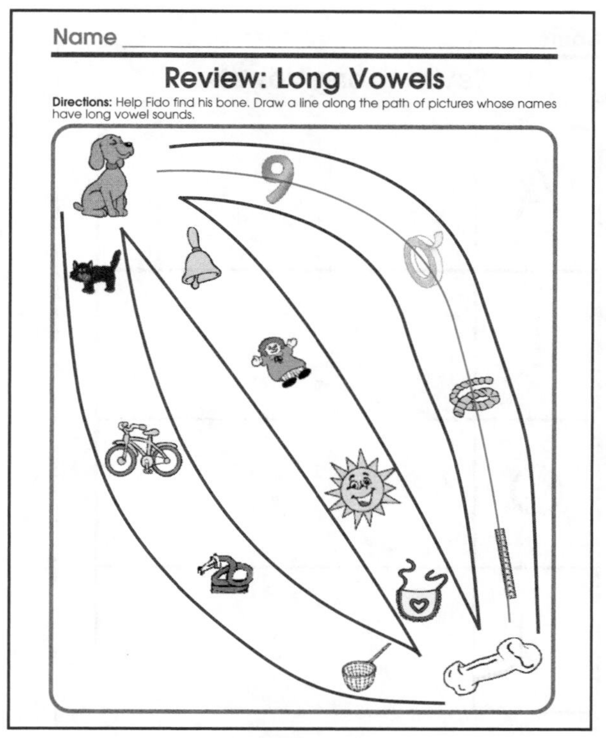
Name

Review: Long Vowels

Directions: Help Fido find his bone. Draw a line along the path of pictures whose names have long vowel sounds.

68

Answer Key

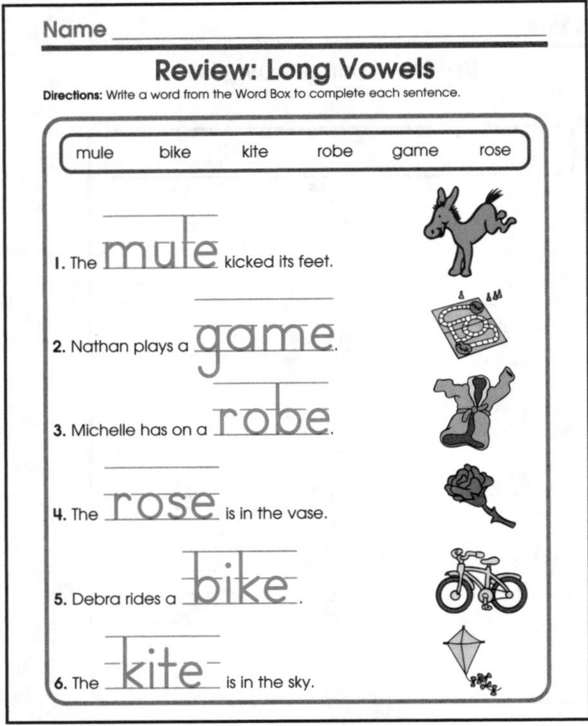

Name
Review: Long Vowels
Directions: Write a word from the Word Box to complete each sentence.
mule bike kite robe game rose
1. The mule kicked its feet.
2. Nathan plays a game.
3. Michelle has on a robe.
4. The rose is in the vase.
5. Debra rides a bike.
6. The kite is in the sky.

69

Name

Review: Long Vowels

Directions: Write a word from the Word Box to complete each sentence.

cape bone vine tune rope mule

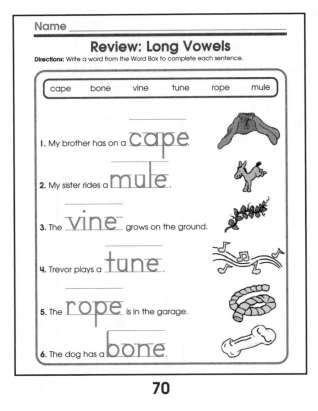

1. My brother has on a cape.
2. My sister rides a mule.
3. The vine grows on the ground.
4. Trevor plays a tune.
5. The rope is in the garage.
6. The dog has a bone.

70

Name

Review: Long Vowels

Directions: Draw a picture of things whose names contain the long vowel sounds of the letters below.

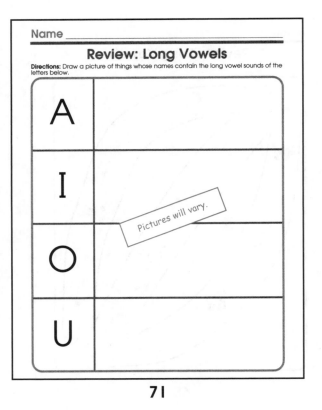

A	
I	Pictures will vary.
O	
U	

71

Name

Review: Long Vowels

Directions: Write a sentence using each word that is pictured below.

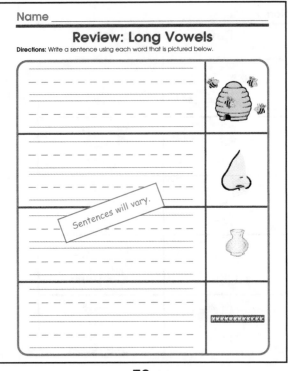

Sentences will vary.

72

Answer Key

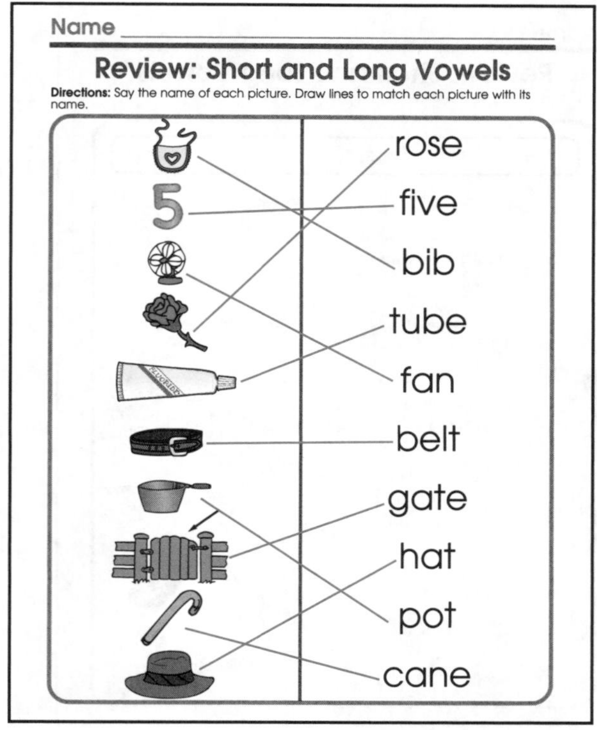

Name

Review: Short and Long Vowels

Directions: Say the name of each picture. Draw lines to match each picture with its name.

rose
five
bib
tube
fan
belt
gate
hat
pot
cane

73

Name

Review: Short and Long Vowels

Directions: Say the name of each picture. Write the word from the Word Box that names each picture below.

bun	cube	milk	man	desk	fox
ten	dive	cave	pine	hose	cob

cave dive desk

bun cube fox

cob man pine

milk hose ten

74

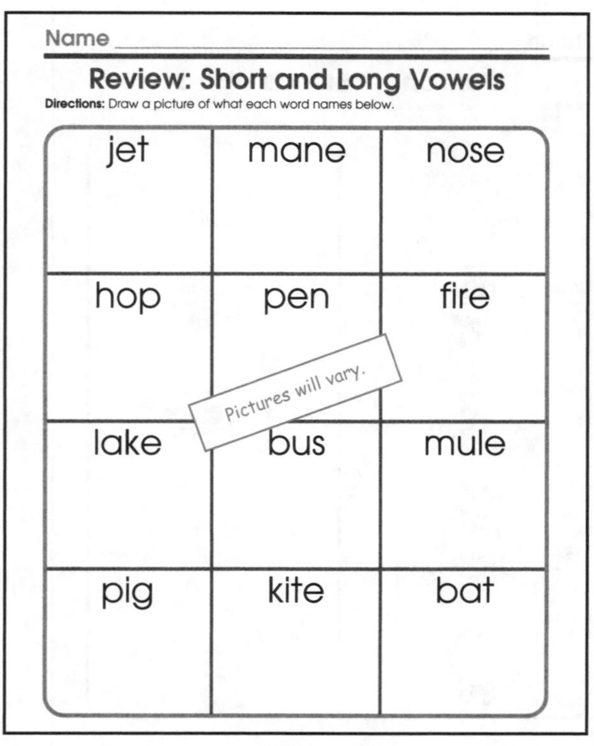

Name

Review: Short and Long Vowels

Directions: Draw a picture of what each word names below.

jet	mane	nose
hop	pen	fire
lake	bus	mule
pig	kite	bat

Pictures will vary.

75

Name

Review: Short and Long Vowels

Directions: Write a word from the Word Box to complete each sentence.

cub cave can bike box hive

1. The cub is a baby bear.
2. The bear sleeps in a cave.
3. Soup comes in a can.
4. I ride my bike.
5. We put our toys away in the box.
6. The bee is in the hive.

76

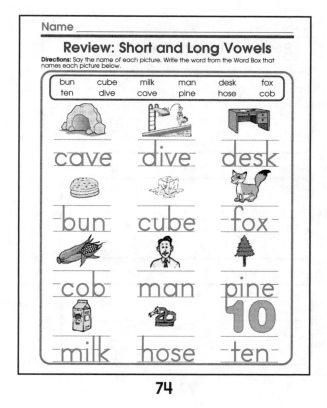

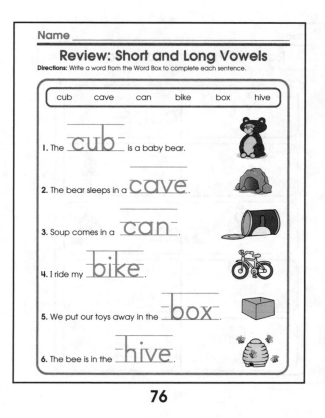

Answer Key

Name

Review: Short and Long Vowels

Directions: Write 6 words that have a **short** vowel sound.

Directions: Write 6 words that have a **long** vowel sound.

Answers will vary.

Directions: Write a sentence using two words from your lists above. Choose one word that has a **short** vowel sound and one word that has a **long** vowel sound.

77

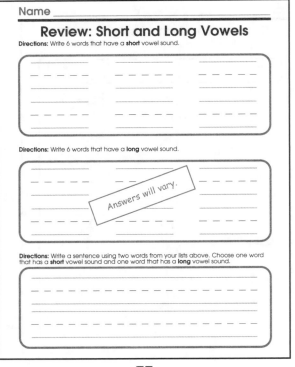

Name

Review: Short and Long Vowels

Directions: Write a word or words from the Word Box to complete each sentence.

cane kite tape tub rug cap

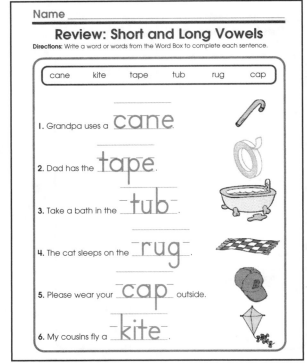

1. Grandpa uses a cane.
2. Dad has the tape.
3. Take a bath in the tub.
4. The cat sleeps on the rug.
5. Please wear your cap outside.
6. My cousins fly a kite.

78

Name

Review: Short and Long Vowels

Directions: Make a new word by adding the letter **e** to each word below.

cub	cube
pin	pine
man	mane
cut	cute
can	cane

79

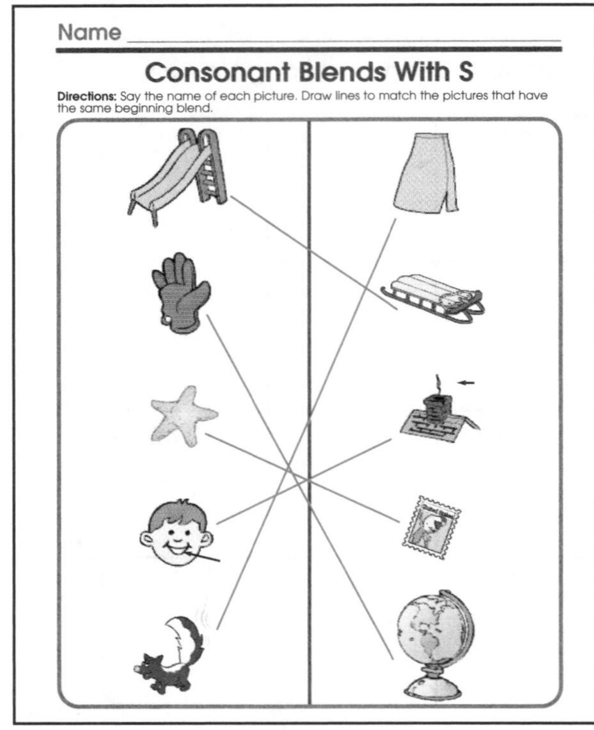

80

Answer Key

Name
Consonant Blends With S
Directions: Say the name of each picture. Circle the pictures in each row that have the same beginning blend.

81

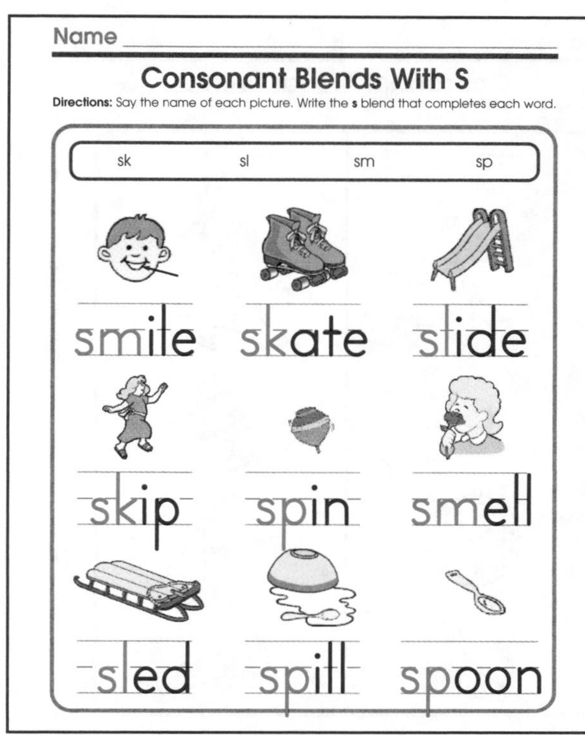

82

83

84

Answer Key

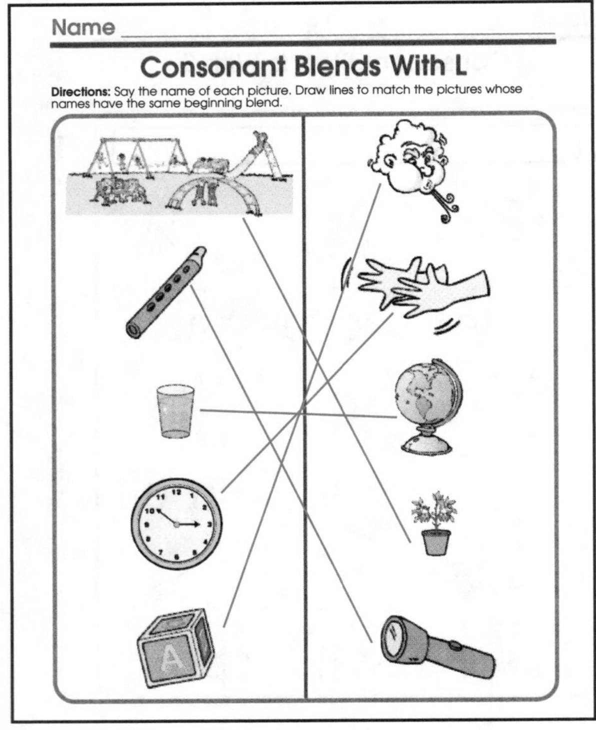

85

86

87

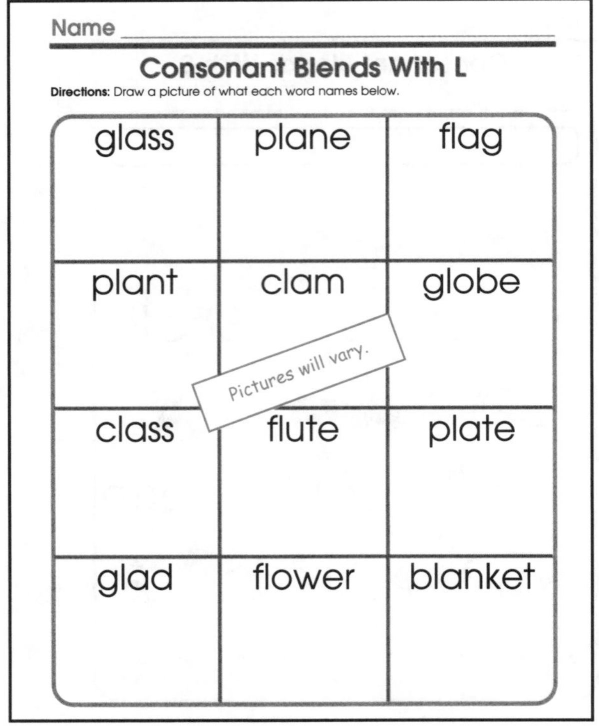

88

Answer Key

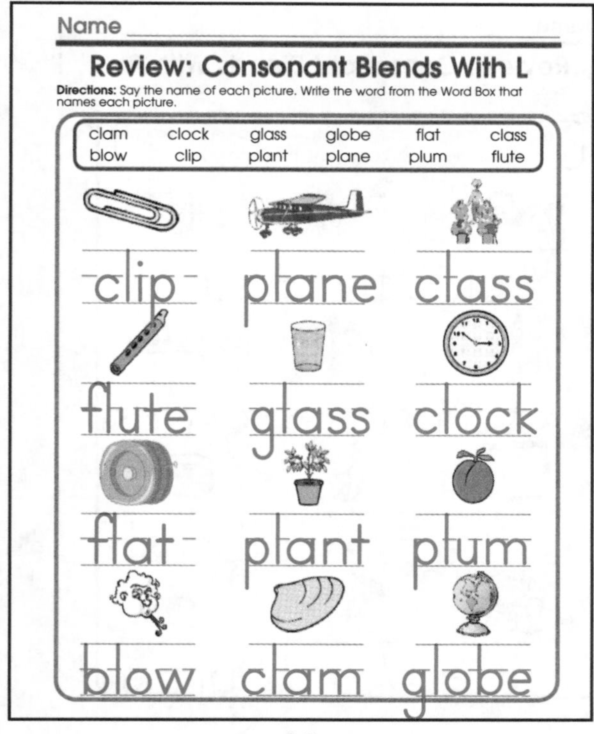
Name

Review: Consonant Blends With L

Directions: Say the name of each picture. Write the word from the Word Box that names each picture.

clam	clock	glass	globe	flat	class
blow	clip	plant	plane	plum	flute

clip plane class
flute glass clock
flat plant plum
blow clam globe

89

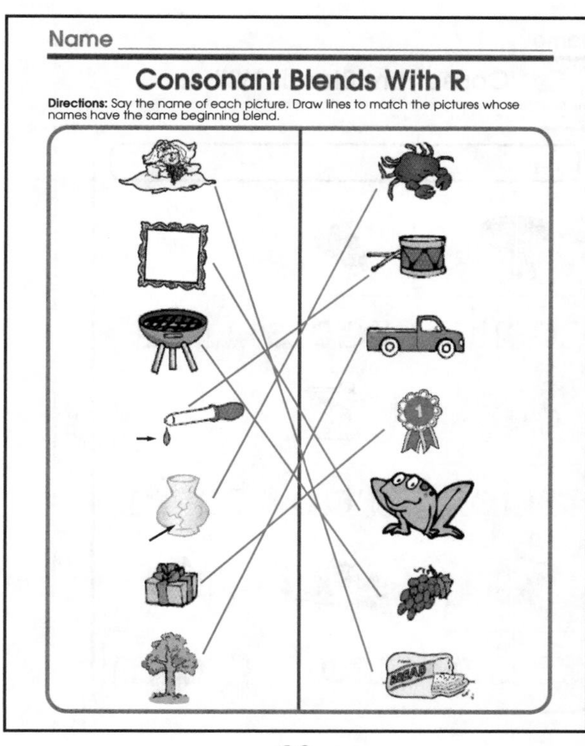
Name

Consonant Blends With R

Directions: Say the name of each picture. Draw lines to match the pictures whose names have the same beginning blend.

90

Name

Consonant Blends With R

Directions: Say the name of each picture. Circle the pictures in each row whose names have the same beginning blend.

91

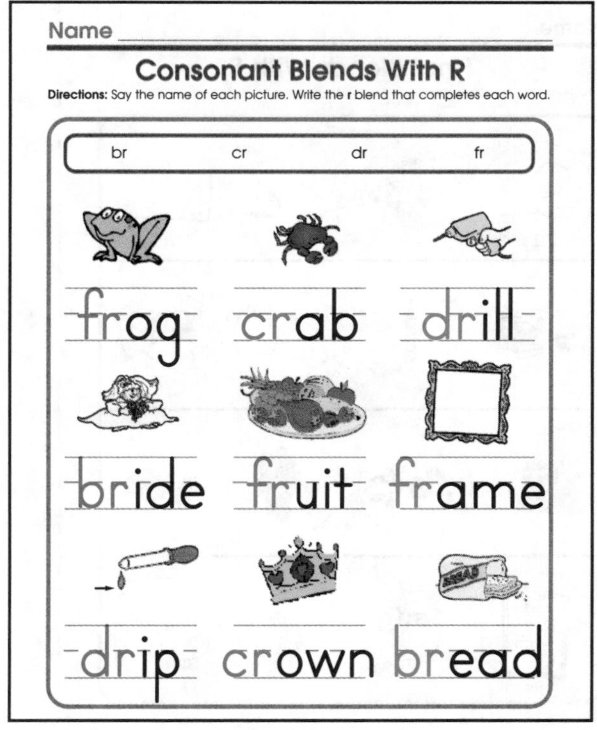
Name

Consonant Blends With R

Directions: Say the name of each picture. Write the **r** blend that completes each word.

br	cr	dr	fr

frog crab drill
bride fruit frame
drip crown bread

92

Answer Key

Name

Consonant Blends With R

Directions: Say the name of each picture. Write the **r** blend that completes each word.

gr pr tr

grill grapes prize

trip trap grin

graze train present

93

Name

Review: Consonant Blends With R

Directions: Say the name of each picture. Write the word from the Word Box that names each picture.

crayon	braid	brush	dress	grass	broom
trip	frame	prize	drum	bride	truck

truck trip drum

crayon dress grass

frame sweep brush

bride braid prize

94

Name

Final Blends With S

Directions: Say the name of each picture. Circle the pictures in each row whose names have the same ending blend.

95

Name

Final Blends With S

Directions: Say the name of each picture. Write the final **s** blend that completes each word.

sk st

crust vest cast

desk list tusk

mask fist chest

96

Answer Key

97

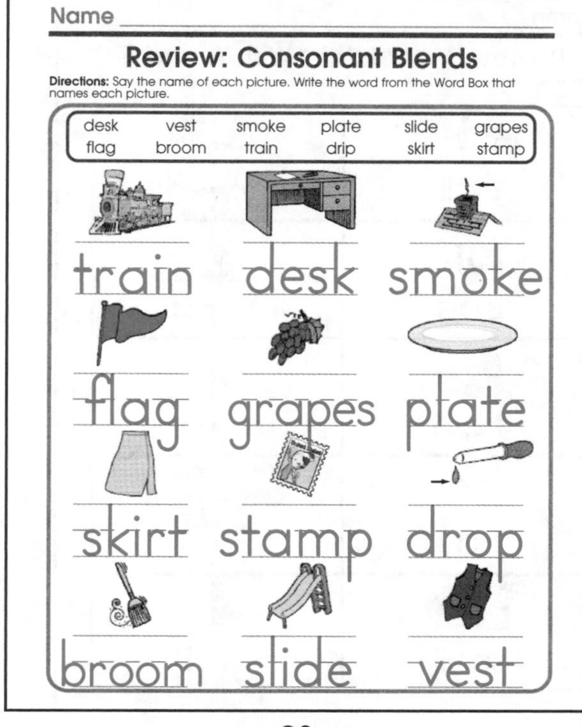

98

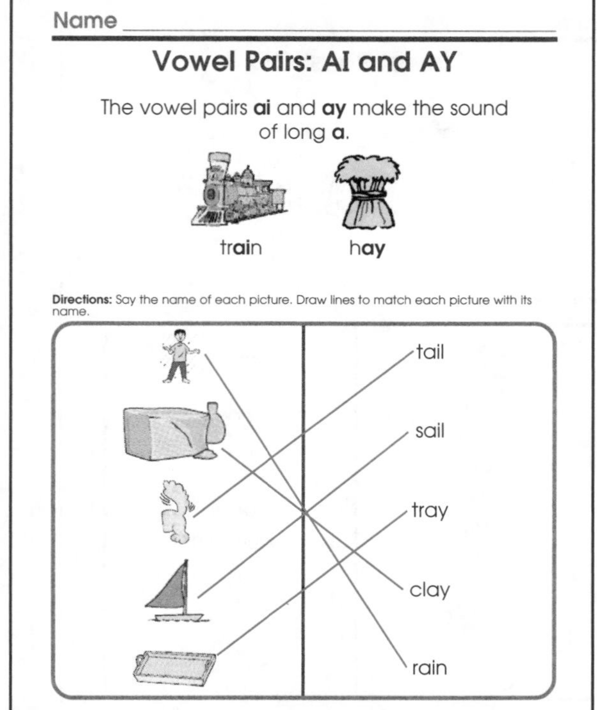

Name
Vowel Pairs: AI and AY
The vowel pairs ai and ay make the sound of long a.
train hay
Directions: Say the name of each picture. Draw lines to match each picture with its name.
tail
sail
tray
clay
rain

99

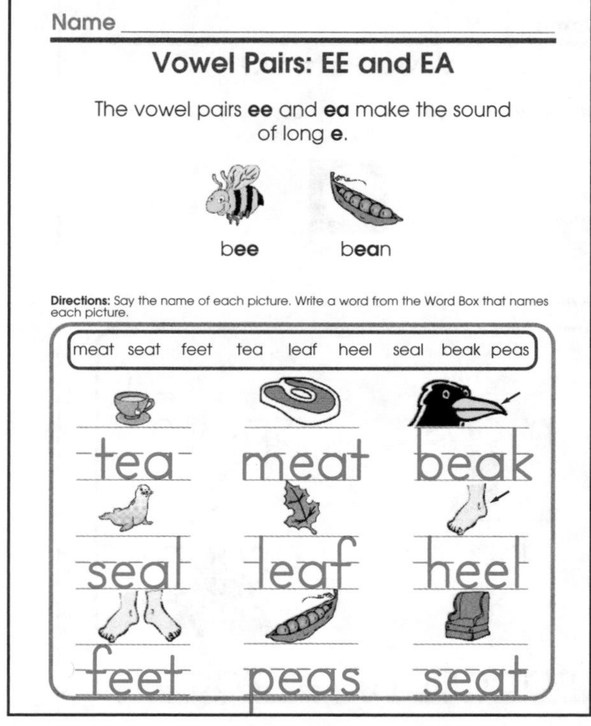

100

Answer Key

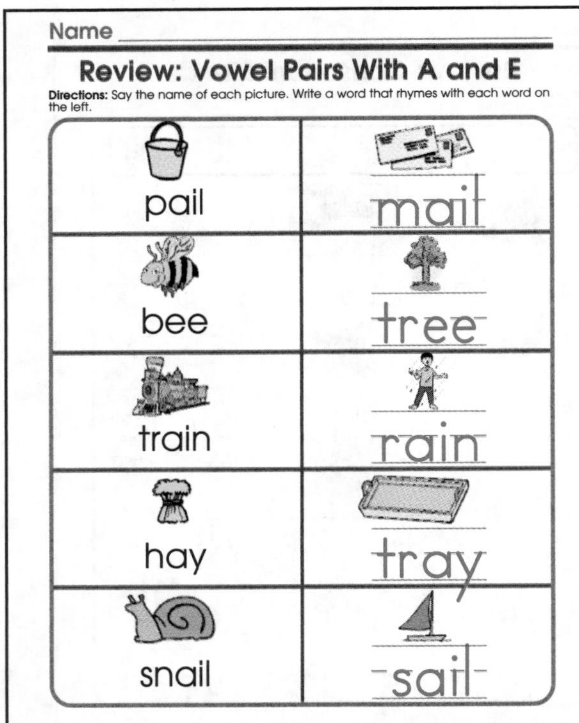
Name

Review: Vowel Pairs With A and E

Directions: Say the name of each picture. Write a word that rhymes with each word on the left.

pail	mail
bee	tree
train	rain
hay	tray
snail	sail

101

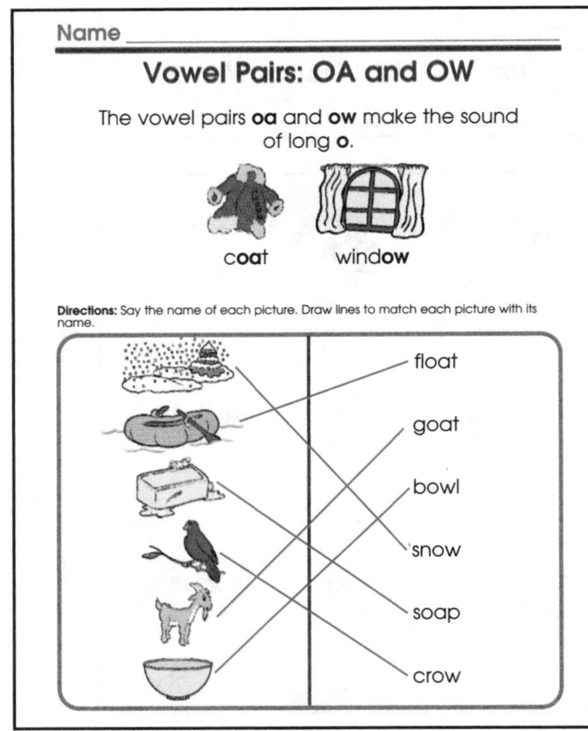
Name

Vowel Pairs: OA and OW

The vowel pairs **oa** and **ow** make the sound of long **o**.

c**oa**t　wind**ow**

Directions: Say the name of each picture. Draw lines to match each picture with its name.

float
goat
bowl
snow
soap
crow

102

Name

Vowel Pairs: OO

The vowel pair **oo** makes the sound you hear in the middle of the word **moon**.

m**oo**n

Directions: Write the missing letters**oo** for each word.

moose	spoon
boot	broom
raccoon	zoo

103

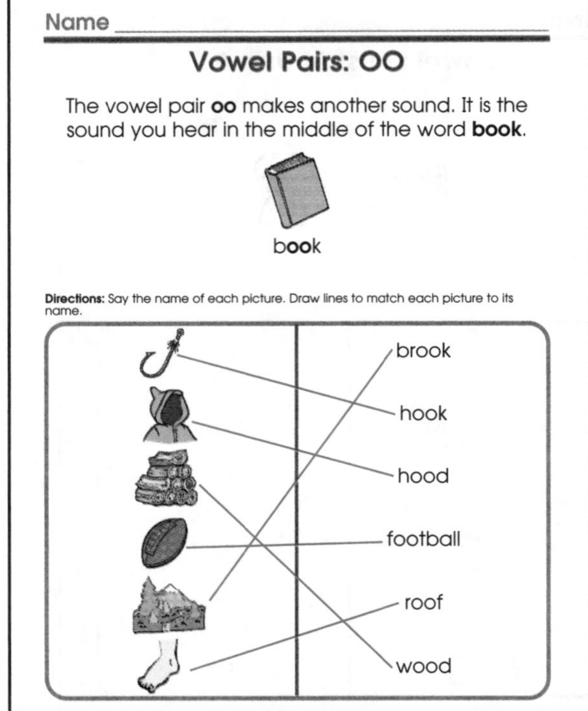
Name

Vowel Pairs: OO

The vowel pair **oo** makes another sound. It is the sound you hear in the middle of the word **book**.

b**oo**k

Directions: Say the name of each picture. Draw lines to match each picture to its name.

brook
hook
hood
football
roof
wood

104

Answer Key

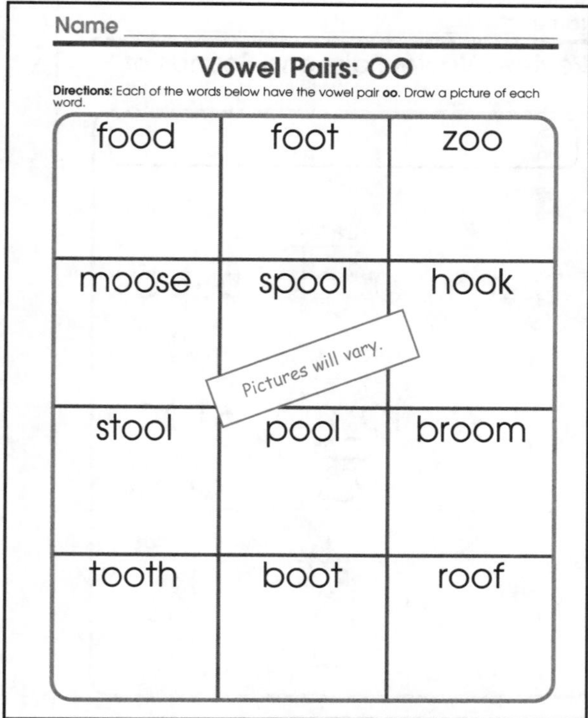

Name
Vowel Pairs: OO
Directions: Each of the words below have the vowel pair oo. Draw a picture of each word.
food
foot
zoo
moose
spool
hook
Pictures will vary.
stool
pool
broom
tooth
boot
roof

105

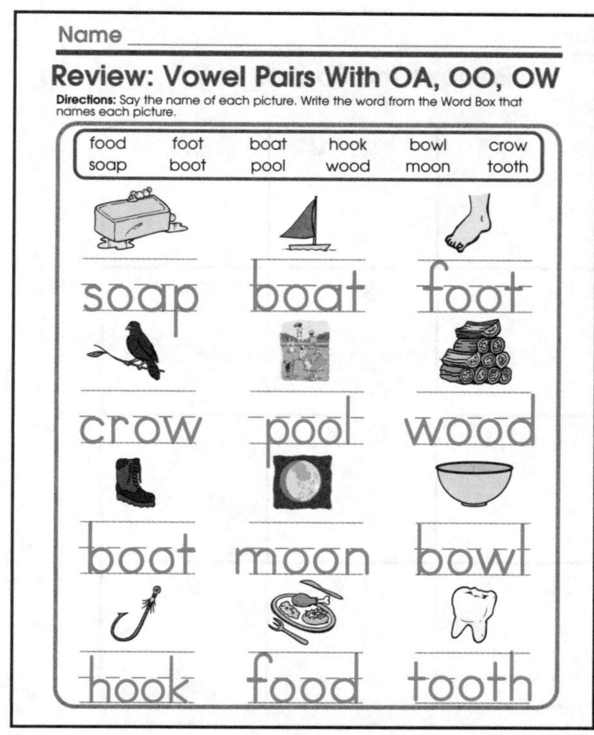

106

107

108

Answer Key

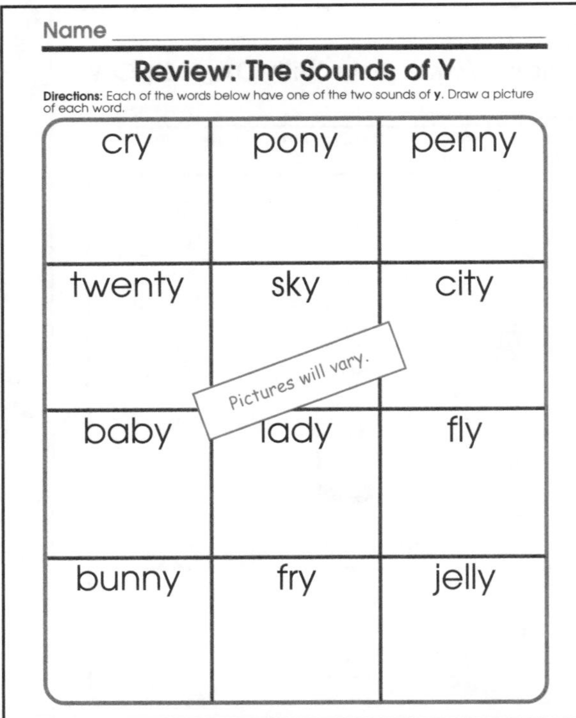
Name

Review: The Sounds of Y

Directions: Each of the words below have one of the two sounds of **y**. Draw a picture of each word.

cry	pony	penny
twenty	sky	city
baby	lady	fly
bunny	fry	jelly

Pictures will vary.

109

Name

Review: Vowel Pairs and Sounds of Y

Directions: Say the name of each picture. Write the word from the Word Box that names each picture.

rain	stool	fly	book	puppy	leaf
tray	hood	feet	city	tooth	hay

tray book puppy

city tooth stool

leaf hay feet

fly rain hood

110

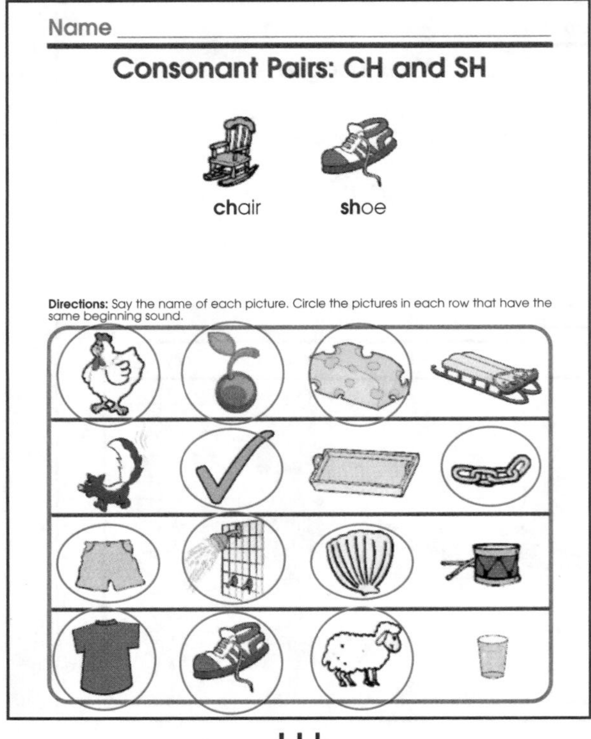
Name

Consonant Pairs: CH and SH

chair **sh**oe

Directions: Say the name of each picture. Circle the pictures in each row that have the same beginning sound.

111

Name

Consonant Pairs: CH and SH

Directions: Say the name of each picture. Draw lines to match each picture with its name.

sheep

shed

chin

ship

chop

shell

cheek

chain

112

Answer Key

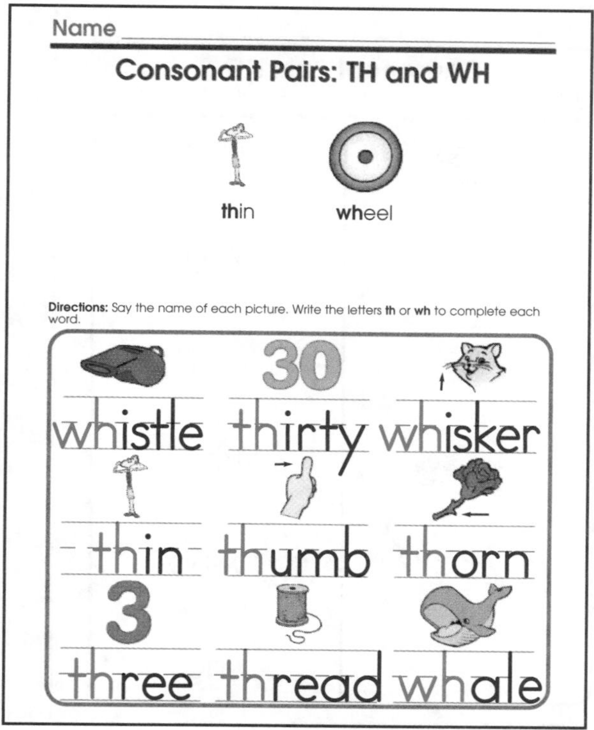
Name

Consonant Pairs: TH and WH

thin wheel

Directions: Say the name of each picture. Write the letters **th** or **wh** to complete each word.

whistle thirty whisker
thin thumb thorn
three thread whale

113

Name

Consonant Pairs: TH and WH

Directions: Name each picture, and write the word from the Word Box. Then, write two sentences. Use one word from the Word Box in each sentence.

whistle	thirty	whale	thin	thirteen
thumb	thorn	wheel	whisker	

thumb wheel thirty
thin whale whisker
thorn thirteen whistle

1.
2.

Sentences will vary.

114

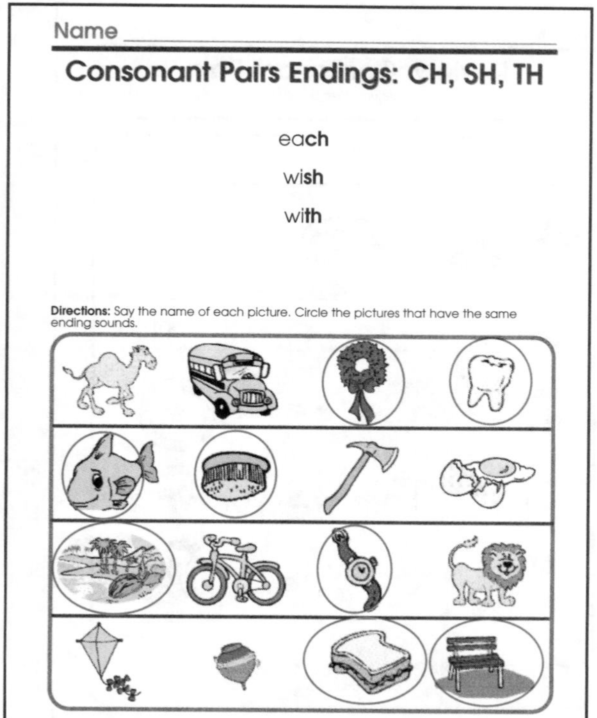
Name

Consonant Pairs Endings: CH, SH, TH

each
wish
with

Directions: Say the name of each picture. Circle the pictures that have the same ending sounds.

115

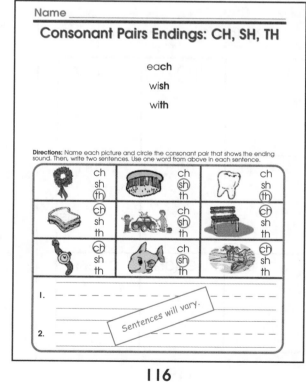

Name

Consonant Pairs Endings: CH, SH, TH

each
wish
with

Directions: Name each picture and circle the consonant pair that shows the ending sound. Then, write two sentences. Use one word from above in each sentence.

ch sh (th)	ch (sh) th	ch sh (th)
(ch) sh th	ch (sh) th	(ch) sh th
(ch) sh th	ch (sh) th	(ch) sh th

1.
2.

Sentences will vary.

116

Answer Key

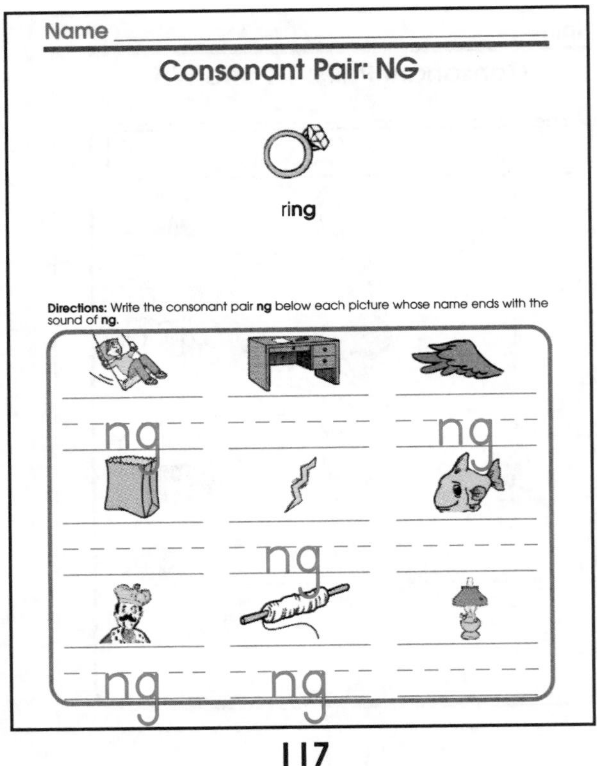

117

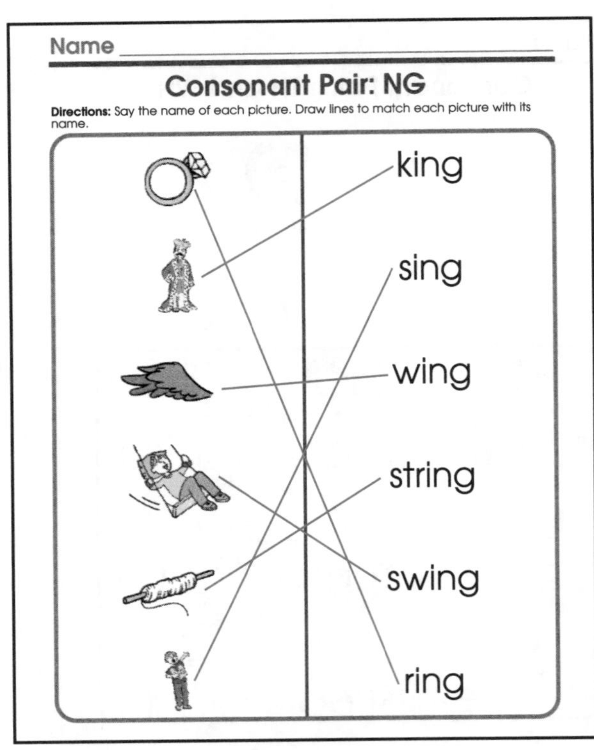

118

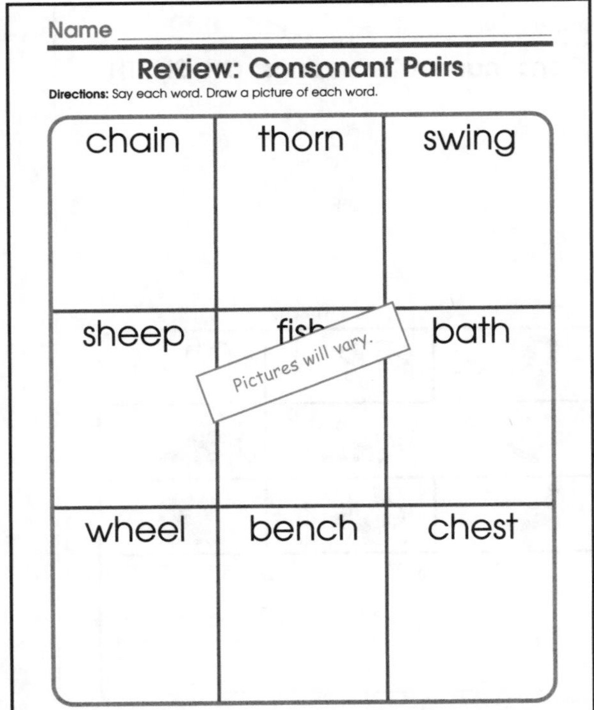

119

120

Notes

Notes